Using Chef with Microsoft Azure

Stuart Preston

Apress®

Using Chef with Microsoft Azure

Stuart Preston
London, United Kingdom

ISBN-13 (pbk): 978-1-4842-1477-0   ISBN-13 (electronic): 978-1-4842-1476-3
DOI 10.1007/978-1-4842-1476-3

Library of Congress Control Number: 2016941179

Managing Director: Welmoed Spahr
Lead Editor: Gwenan Spearing
Technical Reviewer: John Fitzpatrick
Editorial Board: Steve Anglin, Pramila Balen, Louise Corrigan, Jim DeWolf, Jonathan Gennick,
   Robert Hutchinson, Celestin Suresh John, Nikhil Karkal, James Markham, Susan McDermott,
   Matthew Moodie, Douglas Pundick, Ben Renow-Clarke, Gwenan Spearing
Coordinating Editor: Melissa Maldonado
Copy Editor: Karen Jameson
Compositor: SPi Global
Indexer: SPi Global
Artist: SPi Global

Distributed to the book trade worldwide by Springer Science+Business Media New York, 233 Spring Street, 6th Floor, New York, NY 10013. Phone 1-800-SPRINGER, fax (201) 348-4505, e-mail orders-ny@springer-sbm.com, or visit www.springer.com. Apress Media, LLC is a California LLC and the sole member (owner) is Springer Science + Business Media Finance Inc (SSBM Finance Inc). SSBM Finance Inc is a Delaware corporation.

For information on translations, please e-mail rights@apress.com, or visit www.apress.com.

Apress and friends of ED books may be purchased in bulk for academic, corporate, or promotional use. eBook versions and licenses are also available for most titles. For more information, reference our Special Bulk Sales–eBook Licensing web page at www.apress.com/bulk-sales.

Any source code or other supplementary material referenced by the author in this text is available to readers at www.apress.com. For detailed information about how to locate your book's source code, go to www.apress.com/source-code/.

Printed on acid-free paper

Contents at a Glance

Contents at a Glance

Contents

About the Author

Stuart Preston. The story begins in the early 1980s when Mum and Dad bought me an Acorn Electron computer for my sixth birthday. It was love at first sight and the rest is history.

While technology continues to evolve and change at pace, the curiosity that was present in the six-year-old Stuart is still as strong today. Throughout a varied career I have had the privilege of working with a vast range of technologies and some incredible people. The greatest sense of achievement comes from tackling new and complex problems, drawing on those experiences to provide simple technical solutions to real-world problems spanning the business and technical domains.

It was early 2015 when a tempting new challenge presented itself - how to automate Microsoft's Azure Cloud Platform. While many vendors and tools had delivered part of the solution, the ecosystem was only just beginning to mature. Over the next 12 months I set about collaborating with Chef and Microsoft, solving problems as they presented themselves and at times running to keep up with the pace of innovation in both companies.

As a firm believer in open source and the strength of community, the tools I have built (many of which are used in this book) are available on GitHub at https://github.com/pendrica, and contributors are very welcome!

When I'm not attempting to "Code the Impossible", my curiosity will generally lead me to a good pub or an airport. A keen traveler, I enjoy nothing more than getting my bearings in a new city, sampling the local food, and of course the local beers too.

About the Technical Reviewer

John Fitzpatrick is a Technical Trainer for Chef and also works on coaching companies in EMEA as Official Chef Training Partners within the region. John has worked for Chef since September 2013; however, he has been using the Chef platform since May 2010 from when he worked at RightScale. He is active in the community and is an organizer of both the 'DevOps Belfast' and the 'Chef Users London' meetup groups. John lives and works from Belfast in Northern Ireland. He is married to Colette, has one daughter Jane, and a dog.

Introduction

One of the challenges of working in technology today is the relentless pace of change. As practices evolve and new tools are introduced, documentation either does not exist or becomes rapidly out of date, which is part of the reason there were very few resources available to me when I started my journey of using Chef with the Microsoft Azure platform. I struggled to find the information I needed in one place but instead gathered nuggets of knowledge that were scattered far and wide, eventually learning the hard way how to accomplish the results I wanted. This book aims to bring the most important points into one place - and be the book I wish I had on my desk when I started out.

Automating your infrastructure in the cloud has many benefits. Clicking around in an online portal certainly feels easy from a usability point of view but you may be missing out on some of the great advantages of the cloud that can be realized when you adopt an Infrastructure-as-Code approach. Using Chef, you can version your infrastructure configuration, introduce quality tooling into your infrastructure pipeline, and integrate the provisioning of new environments into your continuous delivery process. Leveraging the flexibility of the cloud to pay for only what you need can reduce infrastructure spend considerably and maintaining your platform as code allows for testing that protects the system against human error, reducing failures and unforeseen issues.

If you are new to Chef, Microsoft Azure, or both this book should give you an overview of the best practices for managing your platform alongside some detailed examples that help to step you through the process. I've tried to keep things simple, while ensuring real-world considerations are not omitted.

A small word of warning. Releases to both Chef and Microsoft Azure happen at an alarming pace (thanks, Continuous Delivery!) and so I expect aspects of this book will soon become out of date, or superseded by the new thinking. To ensure the book remains a useful resource as both Chef and Azure evolve I will try and keep track of any significant changes via the book's home page at `http://bit.ly/chefazure`.

My aim for this book is to give you the raw materials and guidance required to get started using Chef with the Microsoft Azure toolset - first of all, setting out the tools you can use individually and then in the later chapters using continuous provisioning approaches. I look forward to hearing about the solutions you create using the tools.

CHAPTER 1

■ ■ ■

Configuration Management using Chef

The automation of configuration management is not a particularly new practice in the world of software delivery. However, scripted approaches of the past suffered from a lack of common standards, documentation, and understanding. A team member would select a preferred scripting language, adopt their own patterns, and implement it in their own unique way. This approach required an in-depth knowledge of the dependencies for all the software to be installed and configured on a machine and often made assumptions about the initial state of the machine before applying changes. Upgrades to software were rarely considered, and because the knowledge was invested in a single person it was difficult to support and maintain. Not everything would or could be automated, and so there would also generally be an amount of manual tweaking required to achieve the desired state, so it wasn't entirely automated and left scope for human error.

Modern configuration management tools such as Chef aim to solve these problems by abstracting away the actions to be taken on a target resource from their actual implementation. We utilize a common domain-specific language (DSL) across all resources to describe the desired state of the system, and behind the scenes Chef takes care of the rest.

Chef has enjoyed enormous success and adoption since its creation in 2008, with companies such as Facebook and Microsoft using the product to manage their infrastructure. At the heart of this success is the global community it has built. By open sourcing the core product and working hard on the cross-platform story, Chef has enlisted thousands of potential contributors to help drive innovation and to support each other with the challenges of automating infrastructure at scale. The culture and community permeate through all aspects of the Chef offering and draws yet more contributions into the ecosystem, making it a powerful force in the world of automation.

In this chapter we will discuss the principles and purpose of automated provisioning and configuration management, walk through an overview of Chef, and go through the steps required to set up a Chef workstation environment that can be used to automate configuration management in the cloud.

Electronic supplementary material The online version of this chapter (doi:10.1007/978-1-4842-1476-3_1) contains supplementary material, which is available to authorized users.

S. Preston, *Using Chef with Microsoft Azure*, DOI 10.1007/978-1-4842-1476-3_1

The Purpose and Principles of Automated Provisioning and Configuration Management

It would be remiss of me not to mention the DevOps movement early on in this book. While there are many definitions, I tend to go along with the definition of DevOps being a cultural and technical movement that focuses on building organizations that are able to operate with stability at high velocity. The term itself targets the silos that these groups have traditionally found themselves in.

Automation is one of the pillars of the DevOps movement because it can provide quality assurance, consistency, and repeatability across the realms of both development and operations. This is especially true in the case of infrastructure automation where manually building individual servers, configuring their base applications, applying their updates, and patching them was not only a time-consuming task but also complex and prone to human error. Minor deviations would occur between resources that should be configured identically, causing unforeseen issues and brittle setups that were hard to reproduce. The term **snowflake server** is often used to reflect the uniqueness of those systems.

Many large enterprises have met with challenges scaling their on-premises infrastructure, teams, and processes to meet the demands of the high-velocity, agile development teams they now service. Organizational structures would introduce multiple hand-offs into the process with a set of project requirements being agreed upon up front (generally by a designated architect before the development team is even assembled). The environments would be designed and scheduled into the pipeline of work across a large team of disparate skillsets to complete their relevant tasks and then hand over to the development team on the scheduled date, sometimes weeks and months after the initial requirements were agreed upon.

In the initial days and weeks of using the environment the development team, struggling to run their application on the delivered environment, would identify new requirements or issues in configuration. After an indisputable root cause had been established the correcting actions would be scheduled again through the same waterfall process, elongating the feedback loop, preventing QA activities in the environments, and often delaying the project launch.

A more incremental, automated approach to provisioning can drastically reduce the feedback loop on configuration changes and allow development teams to operate at velocity without environment impediments. By describing your infrastructure platform as code it can be updated frequently as the requirements of the application evolve over time and because Chef recipes are **idempotent,** once the desired state is achieved, future executions of the recipe will result in a no-op (i.e., no changes will be made). Automation also removes the opportunity for human error to introduce unwanted deviations between environments and "configuration drift" over time into an unknown state.

Many organizations are moving away from on-premises infrastructure into a cloud environment; and as they do so, the opportunities to leverage Infrastructure as Code practices greatly increase. Using a cross-platform provisioning and configuration management tool such as Chef you can now provision an application architecture consisting of IaaS, PaaS, and SaaS services across a global distribution of data centers using a common language and framework. Although many examples in this book will focus on IaaS scenarios, I encourage you not to overlook the many PaaS and SaaS options available in Azure, some of which may prevent you from reinventing the wheel.

Figure 1-1 shows the separation of Provisioning from Configuration Management from Release Management. Often in the cloud sense, these terms are used interchangeably whereas I prefer to draw out the separation of each area as a separate concern. This is because different tooling and artifacts are involved for each layer of the architecture:

- **Provisioning** is concerned with the specification of the guest and operating system on top of a host. The host could be a virtualization layer such as a hypervisor or a cloud platform such as Microsoft Azure. The point is that in this layer we know nothing about the application that is going to run on top of it.

- **Configuration Management** is concerned with the configuration of the Operating System after it has been provisioned, as well as any applications and their configuration that sit on top of that Operating System.

- **Release Management** is concerned with the releasing of an application payload on top of the application that has been deployed.

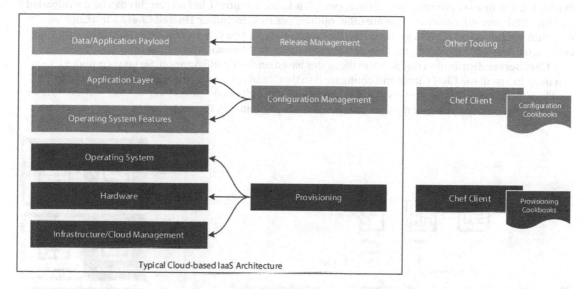

Figure 1-1. Provisioning vs. Configuration Management vs. Release Management

One other huge advantage of using Infrastructure as Code practices in a cloud environment is the ability to provide ephemeral environments in a fast, repeatable, and consistent way. With the right automation in place you could potentially spin up a new environment for a day, or even for a few minutes, at a minimal cost and with a negligible lead time. Compare this to the increased complexity and overhead you would experience if trying to achieve the same in an on-premises, manual setup, and it becomes clear that the cloud was made for automation.

Chef Architecture

Let's quickly cover some of the core terminology of Chef as (hopefully) a refresher for you.

■ **Note** If this isn't a refresher for you, I highly recommend you spend a couple of days going through the excellent resources and hands-on labs available at `http://learn.chef.io` to familiarize yourself with the Chef platform and terminology.

Chef is built around the concepts of converging toward desired state and modeling Infrastructure as Code via resources that are building blocks. Simply put, a **cookbook** is made up from a collection of **recipes**, which in turn are an ordered set of instructions you would like to perform on a **node** (a node being defined as any server or device capable of running a Chef client). Recipes themselves are written in the Chef domain-specific language (DSL) built on top of the Ruby language. Cookbooks can also contain Resources, which do the work behind the scenes to take the code specified in the recipe, detect the current state of the system, and make the necessary changes to converge the system toward the correct target state.

Along with recipes and resources, a cookbook contains all the files and configuration templates required, as well as supporting artifacts such as any data that is used by the component being deployed. It also contains unit tests that can be used to ensure we have written our recipes correctly.

Nodes communicate with a **Chef Server**, which is the repository for all the cookbooks that need deploying. The most common deployment approach is to use a central Chef server; this can be downloaded and installed yourself, however there are other options available including **Hosted Chef** - a full Chef environment hosted on servers managed by Chef themselves, or you can even boot up an image from your cloud provider's Marketplace in the case of Microsoft Azure and Amazon Web Services.

Chef Server distributes cookbooks to the nodes based on their configuration. So on your nodes, you need to install the **Chef Client** and configure it so that it can connect to the server and retrieve the cookbooks. This installation process is commonly referred to as 'bootstrapping'.

The relationships between the Chef components are presented in Figure 1-2.

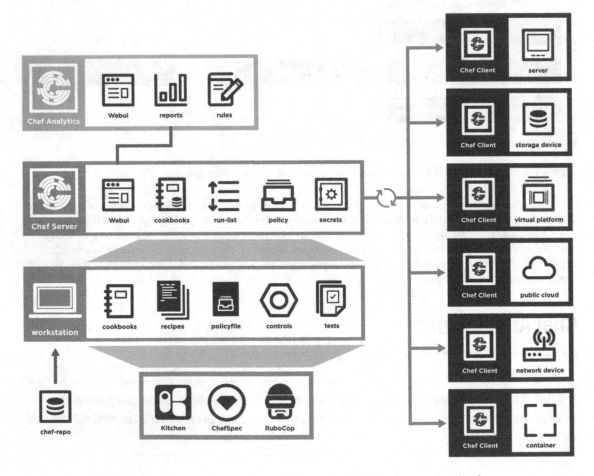

Figure 1-2. *Chef components overview - see* `https://docs.chef.io/chef_overview.html`

> ■ **Note** Chef Analytics is a premium feature of Chef and while it has a role to play in an enterprise Chef deployment, we won't cover it in detail in this book.

Chef Client and Chef Server-supported Platforms

One of the greatest advantages of using Chef is that it provides a consistent approach to configuration management in a cross-platform environment. Chef can be installed on a huge variety of platforms, which makes it easier to build and manage hybrid platforms utilizing multiple technologies in a single deployment architecture. This allows teams to select the best technology for the job from an ever-increasing number of available options, without diverging on the administration tools and practices used to manage those applications.

Table 1-1 lists the operating platforms the Chef Client is aimed at and an indication whether or not that platform is supported in Azure.

Table 1-1. *Chef Client-supported platforms*

Platform	Azure Support	Version
AIX	N	6.1, 7.1
CentOS	Y	5, 6, 7
FreeBSD	Y	9, 10
Debian	Y	7 (Wheezy), 8 (Jessie)
Mac OS X	N	10.8, 10.9, 10.10
Oracle Linux	Y	5, 6, 7
Red Hat Enterprise Linux	Y	5, 6, 7
Solaris	N	10, 11
Ubuntu	Y	12.04, 14.04
Microsoft Windows	Y (servers)	2008, 2008r2, 2012, 2012r2, 2016, 7, 8, 8.1, 10

> ■ **Note** Chef has a categorization of platforms into support tiers. The definitions of Tier 1 support, Tier 2 support, and Not supported can be found in the Chef RFC021 – see https://github.com/chef/chef-rfc/blob/master/rfc021-platform-support-policy.md

For the Chef Server, the platforms listed in Table 1-2 are supported:

Table 1-2. *Chef Server-supported platforms*

Platform	Azure Support?	Version
CentOS	Y	5, 6, 7
Oracle Linux	Y	5, 6
Red Hat Enterprise Linux	Y	5, 6, 7
Ubuntu	Y	12.04 LTS, 14.04 LTS

With the announcement in November 2015 that Microsoft and Red Hat are partnering to provide access to Red Hat Enterprise on Azure, you are now able to run a completely supported environment with Chef Server running in Azure on the Red Hat Enterprise Linux platform if you wanted to. This demonstrates Microsoft's commitment to providing a fully supported, industry-leading cloud platform, whether you are running Windows or not.

Getting Ready for Chef Development

Now that we've had a brief refresher of Chef architecture, let's look at what it takes to set up a workstation for use with Chef and to execute a very basic recipe locally. Many of these setup tasks are prerequisites for exercises later in the book, so even if you are already using Chef I suggest using this section as a helpful checklist to run through and ensure you have everything you need to get started.

■ **Note**   In chapter 2 we'll look at the tools needed to work with the Microsoft Azure platform; for now let's focus on getting our Chef environment set up correctly.

Installing the Chef Development Kit (ChefDK)

The Chef Development Kit (hereafter known as **ChefDK**) includes everything you need to develop and test for the Chef platform. There are a number of components included, and I'll just pull out the key ones:

- Chef Client (including Chef-Zero, a way of simulating a Chef server without a deployment footprint)

- Chef Provisioning (a set of tools and drivers that let you provision machines and compute resources for both on-premises deployment and cloud providers such as Microsoft Azure)

- Berkshelf and Policyfiles (dependency management solutions)

- Cookbook generators

- Tools such as Knife for working against the Chef Server

- Test-Kitchen (tooling that lets you test your Chef cookbooks and recipes across a matrix of operating system platforms and client versions)

ChefDK runs on Microsoft Windows, Mac OSX, and Linux (Debian, Ubuntu, Red Hat Enterprise Linux and CentOS) and thanks to the hard work of the maintainers it works in mostly the same way on all of them. We'll take a look at how to install on Windows, OSX, and Ubuntu in this chapter.

Installing ChefDK on Windows

To download the ChefDK for a Windows machine, we need to visit http://downloads.chef.io in a browser, navigate to **Chef Development Kit,** and press the button marked **Get It** (as shown in Figure 1-3).

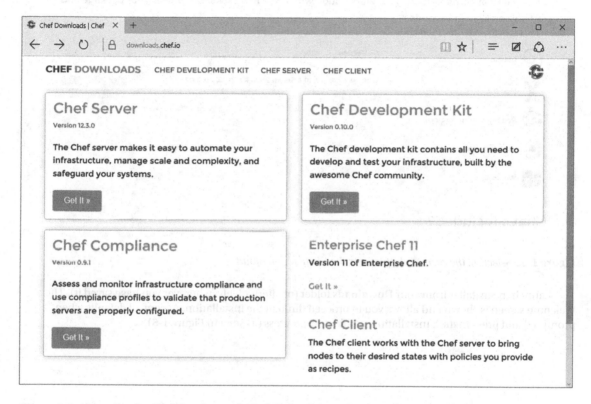

Figure 1-3. *Accessing the Chef Development Kit (ChefDK) downloads area at* http://downloads.chef.io

After selecting the correct version of the installer for your platform (as shown in Figure 1-4) and downloading it, we can progress to running the installer.

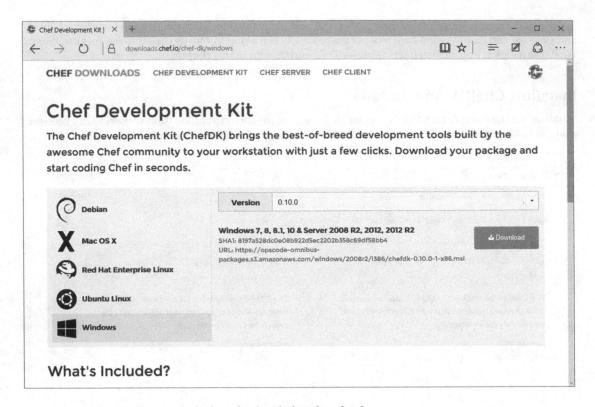

Figure 1-4. *Selecting the correct platform for the ChefDK download*

Launch the installer from your **Downloads** folder (or alternatively, wherever you have saved it). The Welcome screen is shown and allows you to proceed through the installation. Accept all defaults when prompted and press **Install**. Installation should now progress (as seen in Figure 1-5).

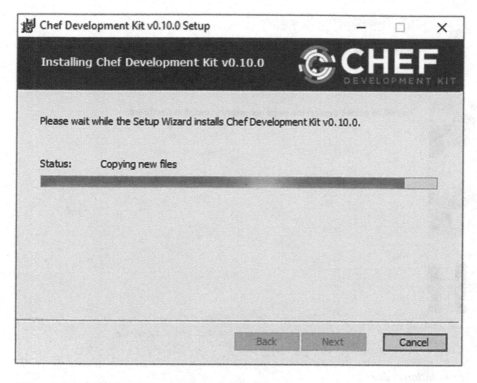

Figure 1-5. *ChefDK installer on Microsoft Windows*

Once installation has completed, you may wish to reboot or log off and back on to your machine, to ensure that the path variables are correctly set up and ready to use.

Installing ChefDK on Mac OS X

The installation process on OS X is similar to the Windows package in that there's a package to download and execute as part of the setup. The installer is a standard package that can be launched after mounting the downloaded image file. Figure 1-6 shows the Welcome screen of the package installer.

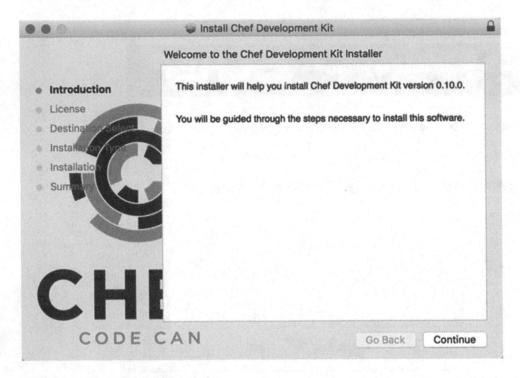

Figure 1-6. *ChefDK installation dialog*

Launch the package and accept all the defaults, inputting your local credentials at the correct time, of course.

Once the installation has completed as shown in Figure 1-7, exit the installer and then unmount/eject the image file.

Figure 1-7. *Installation completed on Mac OS X*

Once the installation completes, proceed to the verification steps.

Installing ChefDK on Linux

On Ubuntu and Debian, you need to download the correct .deb file for your platform and then at a Terminal prompt, locate your .deb file and type:

```
$ sudo dkpg -i chefdk_0.10.0.1_amd64.deb
```

Installation will take a few moments and complete as shown in Figure 1-8.

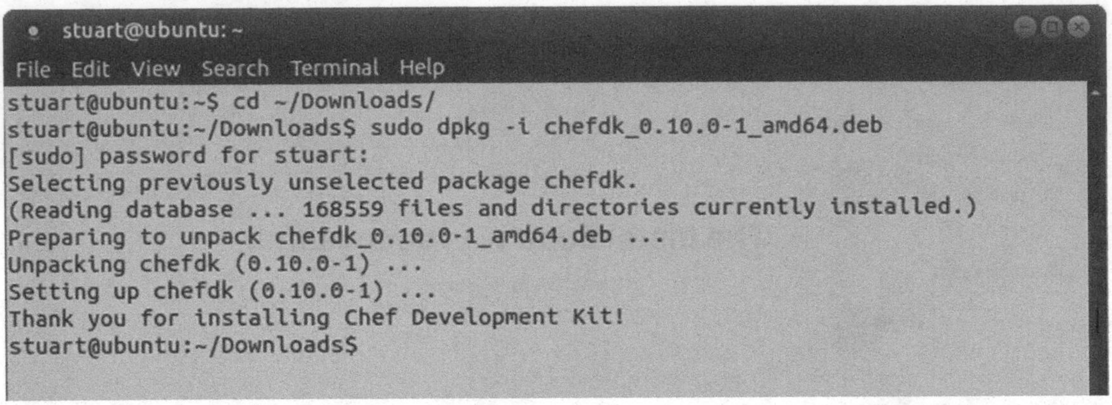

```
stuart@ubuntu: ~

File  Edit  View  Search  Terminal  Help
stuart@ubuntu:~$ cd ~/Downloads/
stuart@ubuntu:~/Downloads$ sudo dpkg -i chefdk_0.10.0-1_amd64.deb
[sudo] password for stuart:
Selecting previously unselected package chefdk.
(Reading database ... 168559 files and directories currently installed.)
Preparing to unpack chefdk_0.10.0-1_amd64.deb ...
Unpacking chefdk (0.10.0-1) ...
Setting up chefdk (0.10.0-1) ...
Thank you for installing Chef Development Kit!
stuart@ubuntu:~/Downloads$
```

Figure 1-8. *Installing the .deb on Ubuntu Linux*

On the RedHat and CentOS platforms, ChefDK is provided in the RPM format and you will need to download the correct .rpm file for your platform (noting there are different versions for RedHat 6 and RedHat 7, for example). Once you have the correct file, from the same directory type:

```
$ sudo rpm -Uvh chefdk-0.10.0-1.el7.x86_64.rpm
```

```
[sudo] password for stuart:
warning: chefdk-0.10.0-1.el7.x86_64.rpm: Header V4 DSA/SHA1 Signature, key ID 83ef826a: NOKEY
Preparing...                          ################################# [100%]
Updating / installing...
   1:chefdk-0.10.0-1.el7               ################################# [100%]
Thank you for installing Chef Development Kit!
```

Installation will take a few moments. Once the installation completes, proceed to the verification steps.

Verifying the ChefDK Installation

To verify the installation, we can use the chef -v command. This will let us know which versions of all the tools are installed.

```
PS C:\Users\StuartPreston> chef -v
```

You should see the following output or similar:

```
Chef Development Kit Version: 0.10.0
chef-client version: 12.5.1
berks version: 4.0.1
kitchen version: 1.4.2
```

If the ChefDK was successfully installed on your system, you have all the files required on your system that support you in the Chef development cycle. However, before we can start developing our recipes, we need to initialize our environment. Put simply this means ensuring that Chef and Ruby paths and environment variables are correctly pointing at the location ChefDK installed them to. The command `chef shell-init` lets you achieve this by generating the correct initialization script for your environment, and so all we need to do is run this command whenever we start a new session by placing a call to this command in the shell's start up (i.e., in the file located at $PROFILE on Windows and in ~/.bash_profile or ~/.zshrc on Mac OS X and Linux).

Initializing the environment (Windows)

To initialize our environment on Windows, we use the `chef shell-init powershell` command to our $PROFILE file (this is usually a file named C:\Users\<username>\Documents\WindowsPowerShell\Microsoft.PowerShell_profile.ps1). When any PowerShell commands are added to this file, they are loaded at the start of each PowerShell session. So to configure things correctly, we need to create a $PROFILE file if one doesn't exist already:

```
PS C:\Users\StuartPreston> if(!(Test-Path $PROFILE)) { New-Item -Force -ItemType File
$PROFILE }
```

We can then add the output of `chef shell-init powershell` to it as follows:

```
PS C:\Users\StuartPreston> chef shell-init powershell | Add-Content $PROFILE
```

Now, every time you open a new PowerShell session, your paths and environment variables will be set up correctly.

■ **Warning**   On new Windows installations, Windows PowerShell scripts will not work until an administrator sets the local execution policy for PowerShell scripts using the following command:

```
PS C:\Users\StuartPreston> Set-ExecutionPolicy RemoteSigned -Force
```

Initializing the environment (Bash/Zsh)

To use the ChefDK version of Ruby as the default Ruby on a system with **bash** as your shell, edit the $PATH and GEM environment variables to include paths to the ChefDK. To accomplish this, run:

```
$ echo 'eval "$(chef shell-init bash)"' >> ~/.bash_profile
```

If you use **zsh** as your shell, then you can use the following line to set up your environment:

```
$ echo 'eval "$(chef shell-init zsh)"' >> ~/.zshrc
```

Installing Git

The Chef toolset uses Git and its related tools extensively, so we need to ensure we have a working Git client on the machine in our path. On Windows the installation procedure has a few options so I've covered the installation process in detail.

Installing Git on Windows

To install Git on Windows, navigate to `https://git-scm.com/downloads` as shown in Figure 1-9 and download the Windows installer.

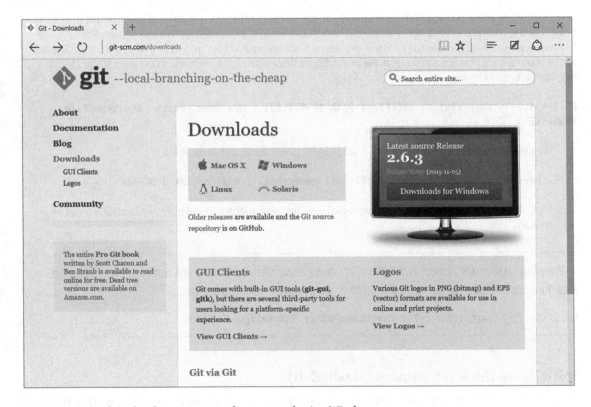

Figure 1-9. *Git download page as seen when accessed using Windows*

After downloading the installer, the Git Setup Wizard will launch. You will be prompted to accept the general public license, select a directory, identify the components you wish to install, select a start menu folder, adjust your PATH environment, configure your terminal emulator to use with Git Bash, and configure performance tweaks. It is tempting to select the default option for all of these but I recommend you adjust a few of these options to ensure you get the optimal set up for Chef development.

When given the option to adjust your PATH environment you should select the option to **Use Git from the Windows Command Prompt** to ensure Git is available to all processes on the system, as shown in Figure 1-10:

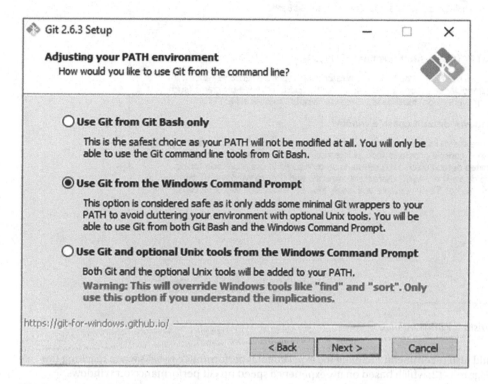

Figure 1-10. *Git installer on Windows*

When asked to configure the terminal emulator to use with Git Bash, select **Use Windows' default console window** as shown in Figure 1-11 as this is most compatible with the command-line tools used in Chef development.

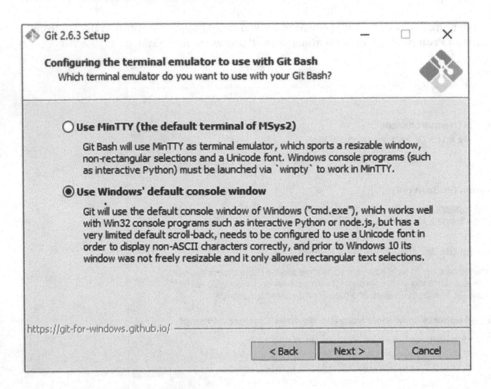

Figure 1-11. *Git installer on Windows*

Finally, I would also recommend enabling the experimental performance tweaks when reaching the screen shown in Figure 1-12, which based on my experience speed up Git performance on Windows.

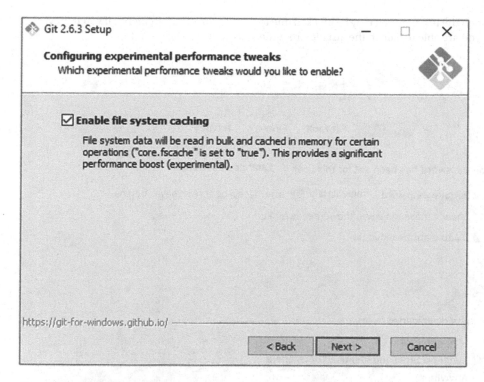

Figure 1-12. *Git installer on Windows*

After pressing **Next**, the installation will proceed. When it is complete you will need to either reboot or log out and back in to your desktop for the settings to apply correctly.

Git on Mac OS X

The OS X platform already has a few ways of distributing Git. If you have XCode installed already you may already have the Git client installed. To find out, open a new Terminal window and type git --version. If you get a version number in response then you don't need to install anything to work with source control and Git/GitHub repositories.

If you need to install Git you can download the installer from https://git-scm.com/downloads and follow the onscreen instructions, providing your password at the appropriate stage. I had no problems with the default options provided in the installer so I recommend you stick with those settings unless you have a specific reason not to.

When you launch the installer, you may be blocked due to OS X security requirements, if you then visit Security & Privacy you are able to launch the installer from there, as shown in Figure 1-13:

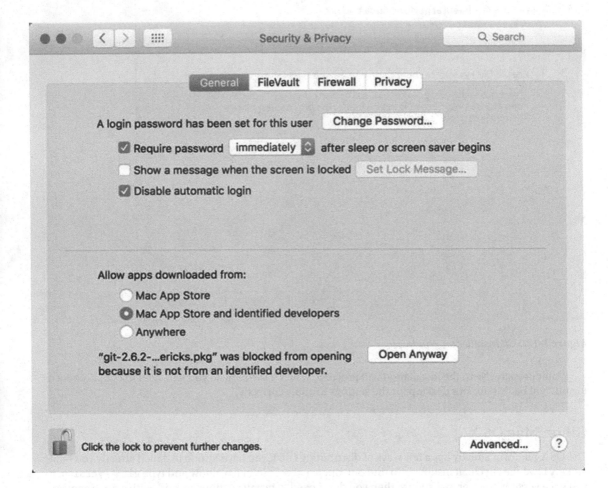

Figure 1-13. *Security dialog on Mac OS X, allowing launch of a "blocked" package*

Once you have installed the Git package, you can proceed to the next section.

Git on Linux

To configure Git on Linux, simply use your package manager (e.g., apt-get or yum) to install the git-all package. The following commands will automatically install and configure Git on the respective Linux builds:

Ubuntu/Debian

```
$ sudo apt-get install git-all
```

```
Output not shown
```

RedHat/CentOS

```
$ sudo yum install git-all
```

Output not shown

Developing Your First Recipe Using Chef

In this section, we're going to generate a blank repository and add a simple recipe to it. This is a basic example to ensure local setup is working how it should be and to demonstrate how Chef recipes can be used to bring your machine to a desired state and keep it in that state.

Code Editors

Before you start to develop your first recipe I recommend you review the code editor you are using. A good visual code editor is not a requirement, but it can be very helpful for working with Chef and selecting the right one can save you time. Selecting one is very much a matter of personal taste, and I encourage you to make sure you have one that supports some basic features.

When selecting a code editor, make sure it supports the following: Themes and Plugins, Snippets, Syntax coloring/highlighting for the Ruby language, Multiple cursors, a tree view of the entire folder/repository you are working with, and ideally Git integration.

Here's a list of three editors I've tried recently and had success with:

- Sublime Text - ($70 USD) - http://sublimetext.com

- GitHub Atom - (free/open source) - http://atom.io

- Visual Studio Code (free/open source) - http://code.visualstudio.com

Of course, if you have many years' experience of systems administration, you've probably grown used to an editor by now, but I would still encourage you to take the opportunity to download and try out some of the newer editors on the scene. You spend a lot of time in the editor and the longer you leave it, the harder it is to change.

I recommend using **Visual Studio Code** - it's a lightweight code editor based on the GitHub Electron framework, supports all the features I've listed above, runs on Windows, OS X and Linux, and it's open source. Figure 1-14 shows the main window of Visual Studio Code. There is also a Chef Extension for Visual Studio code available on the Visual Studio Code Marketplace (https://marketplace.visualstudio.com/items/Pendrica.Chef), which enables many of the features listed above.

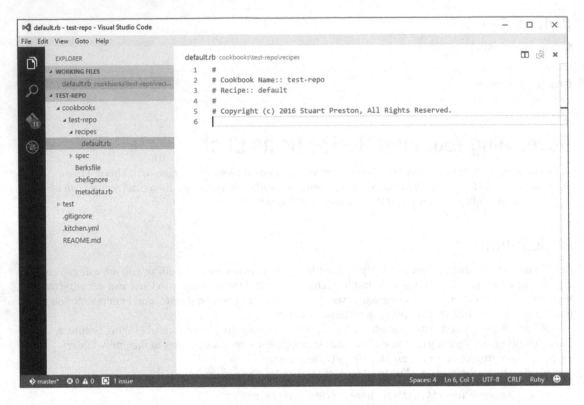

Figure 1-14. *Visual Studio Code main window on the Windows platform*

Initializing a Chef Repository

Let's get started by using one of the ChefDK features, a Chef generator, to generate us a complete application using the chef generate app command, specifying our name and e-mail address (these values can obviously be substituted with your own):

```
PS C:\Users\StuartPreston> chef generate app chefazure-ch01 --copyright "Stuart Preston"
--email "stuart@pendrica.com"
```

After a few seconds, you should see output similar to the following (note I have truncated the output).

```
Compiling Cookbooks...
Recipe: code_generator::app
  * directory[C:/Users/StuartPreston/chefazure-ch01] action create
    - create new directory C:/Users/StuartPreston/chefazure-ch01

[...]

  * directory[C:/Users/StuartPreston/chefazure-ch01/cookbooks] action create
    - create new directory C:/Users/StuartPreston/chefazure-ch01/cookbooks
  * directory[C:/Users/StuartPreston/chefazure-ch01/cookbooks/chefazure-ch01] action create
    - create new directory C:/Users/StuartPreston/chefazure-ch01/cookbooks/chefazure-ch01

[...]
```

```
    * directory[C:/Users/StuartPreston/chefazure-ch01/cookbooks/chefazure-ch01/recipes]
      action create
      - create new directory C:/Users/StuartPreston/chefazure-ch01/cookbooks/chefazure-ch01/
        recipes
    * template[C:/Users/StuartPreston/chefazure-ch01/cookbooks/chefazure-ch01/recipes/
      default.rb] action create
      - create new file C:/Users/StuartPreston/chefazure-ch01/cookbooks/chefazure-ch01/
        recipes/default.rb
      - update content in file C:/Users/StuartPreston/chefazure-ch01/cookbooks/chefazure-ch01/
        recipes/default.rb from none to 7358b0
        (diff output suppressed by config)
    * directory[C:/Users/StuartPreston/chefazure-ch01/cookbooks/chefazure-ch01/spec/unit/
      recipes] action create
      - create new directory C:/Users/StuartPreston/chefazure-ch01/cookbooks/chefazure-ch01/
        spec/unit/recipes

[...]

    * execute[initialize-git] action run
      - execute git init .
    * cookbook_file[C:/Users/StuartPreston/chefazure-ch01/.gitignore] action create
      - create new file C:/Users/StuartPreston/chefazure-ch01/.gitignore
      - update content in file C:/Users/StuartPreston/chefazure-ch01/.gitignore from none to
        33d469
        (diff output suppressed by config)
```

We can see from the output that we created a new directory **chefazure-ch01** and generated some files there. We can also see that git init . was executed in that directory, which means it is ready for use with Git commands executed locally.

■ **Tip** If you would like to learn more about Git basics, there's a great reference available online at http://git-scm.com/book/en/v2/Git-Basics-Getting-a-Git-Repository

---

Modifying and Running the Default Recipe

If we open up the directory **chefazure-ch01** within our code editor and navigate to **cookbooks/chefazure-ch01/recipes/default.rb** we are now looking at our default recipe for the cookbook **chefazure-ch01**.

Let's add a file resource that writes a file to our home directory. Edit the file so that it looks similar to the below. On OS X and Linux platforms change the file name (chefazure.txt) to a writable location (e.g., /tmp/chefazure.txt)

```
#
# Cookbook Name:: chefazure-ch01
# Recipe:: default
#
# Copyright (c) 2015 Stuart Preston, All Rights Reserved.
```

```
file 'chefazure.txt' do
  action :create
  content 'Using Chef with Azure'
end
```

■ **Tip**   The Ruby language style guide encourages the use of two spaces per indentation level. Many editors have 4 spaces or a Tab as the default setting. This can usually be changed in your code editor's settings. For further discussion see https://github.com/bbatsov/ruby-style-guide#source-code-layout

---

This recipe should create a file with the specified contents. We can run the recipe on our local machine and manually inspect the file to ensure this recipe is working as expected. When we installed the ChefDK on our machine, a Chef Client was also installed and we can use this in 'local mode', which allows us to execute recipes without the use of a Chef server.

Ensuring you are running PowerShell "as Administrator" on Windows or via sudo on OS X and Linux we can run chef-client --local-mode from the root of the chef repository:

PS C:\Users\StuartPreston\chefazure-ch01> **chef-client --local-mode .\cookbooks\chefazure-ch01\recipes\default.rb**

```
[2015-11-14T13:45:29+00:00] WARN: No config file found or specified on command line, using
command line options.
Starting Chef Client, version 12.5.1
resolving cookbooks for run list: []
Synchronizing Cookbooks:
Compiling Cookbooks...
[2015-11-14T13:45:48+00:00] WARN: Node DESKTOP-TIDJ3S8 has an empty run list.
Converging 1 resources
Recipe: @recipe_files::C:/users/stuartpreston/chefazure-ch01/cookbooks/chefazure-ch01/
recipes/default.rb
  * file[chefazure.txt] action create
    - create new file chefazure.txt
    - update content in file chefazure.txt from none to 7ba0df
    --- chefazure.txt   2015-11-14 13:45:48.000000000 +0000
    +++ ./chefazure.txt20151114-6260-1z0avyn    2015-11-14 13:45:48.000000000 +0000
    @@ -1 +1,2 @@
    +Using Chef with Azure

Running handlers:
Running handlers complete
Chef Client finished, 1/1 resources updated in 19 seconds
```

Let's find this file (it will have been created at the root of the first drive on your system) and modify it using a text editor (remembering to run this text editor as Administrator or via sudo). Change the text in the file to read 'Using Chef with **Microsoft** Azure'

Now let's run the chef-client again to see what happens:

```
PS C:\Users\StuartPreston\chefazure-ch01> chef-client --local-mode .\cookbooks\chefazure-
ch01\recipes\default.rb
```

```
Converging 1 resources
Recipe: @recipe_files::C:/users/stuartpreston/chefazure-ch01/cookbooks/chefazure-ch01/
recipes/default.rb
  * file[chefazure.txt] action create
    - update content in file chefazure.txt from 2331dd to 7ba0df
    --- chefazure.txt    2015-11-14 13:51:43.000000000 +0000
    +++ ./chefazure.txt20151114-6776-fy5dz7      2015-11-14 13:52:10.000000000 +0000
    @@ -1,2 +1,2 @@
    -Using Chef with Microsoft Azure
    +Using Chef with Azure

Running handlers:
Running handlers complete
Chef Client finished, 1/1 resources updated in 20 seconds
```

We can see that the Chef client restored our file back to the desired state as described in our recipe. The corrective action taken was based on the state of the machine at the time of recipe execution. This was a simple example, but it demonstrates that being able to describe configuration in terms of a desired state is very powerful as we will see throughout the book.

We have seen how we can execute recipes in local mode but what if we want to run that recipe on a target machine, or across tens, hundreds or thousands of machines? We need to upload our recipes so others can consume them. We need an account on a Chef Server.

Getting Started with Hosted Chef

As we mentioned earlier in the chapter Chef Server can be hosted locally, in a cloud provider or we can use an account on servers that are hosted by Chef themselves. For the purpose of this this section we're going to sign up for a Hosted Chef account and connect our local Chef Client to it; that way we can upload our cookbooks to it and execute them using our local machine as a node, exactly how we would in a production scenario.

First of all we need to visit `https://manage.chef.io/signup` in a browser as shown in Figure 1-15.

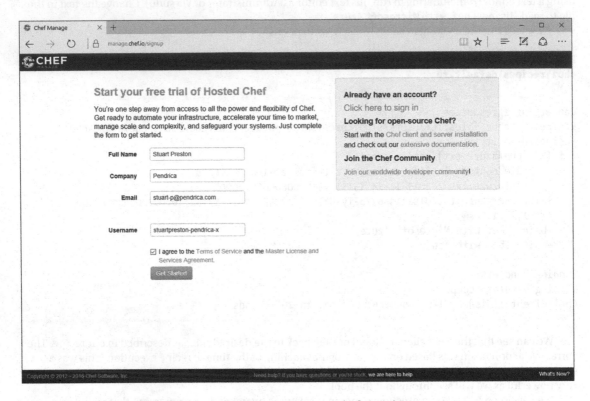

Figure 1-15. *Signing up for Hosted Chef via* `https://manage.chef.io/signup`

You'll be asked to provide some details such as your name and e-mail address. After pressing the **Get Started** button you will immediately be sent an e-mail as shown in Figure 1-16.

Figure 1-16. *Validation e-mail that is received when you sign up to Hosted Chef*

After clicking the link in the e-mail you are taken to a page as shown in Figure 1-17 where you can associate a password with your account.

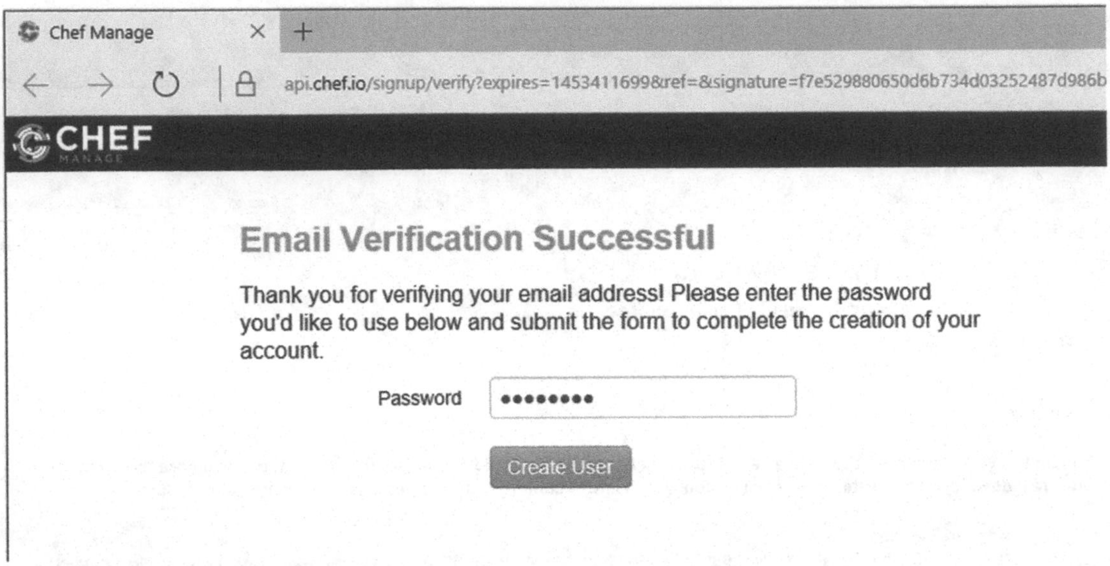

Figure 1-17. Associating a password with your Hosted Chef account

After pressing Create User, you are signed in to the Chef Manage site and a message is displayed (as shown in Figure 1-18):

Figure 1-18. Welcome to Chef Manage (Hosted Chef)

■ **Tip**   I recommend creating an Organization with the name <CompanyName>-<OrganizationName> as this is a shared service and Organizations are named on a first-come-first-served basis.

Press the **Create New Organization** button and enter the requested details as shown in Figure 1-19.

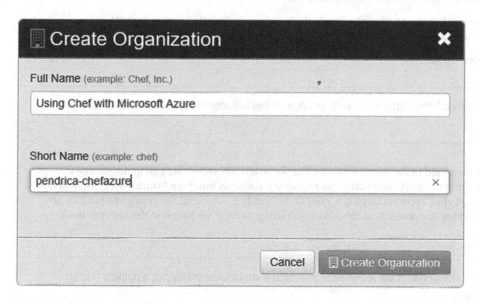

Figure 1-19. Creating an Organization within Hosted Chef

Once the Organization has been created you'll be taken to a page where you can download a 'Starter Kit' as shown in Figure 1-20.

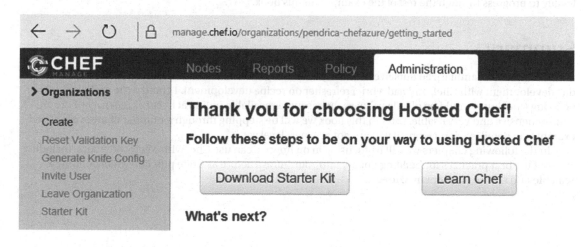

Figure 1-20. Getting Started page on Hosted Chef

The Starter Kit is a zip file that contains a number of files and is by far the quickest way to get your generated keys from the Chef Server. The kit contains:

- A **user private key file** (file name: username.pem) that allows you to perform actions against the organization.

- An **organization validator private key file** (file name: orgname-validator.pem) that allows you to join nodes to the organization.

- A **Knife configuration file** called knife.rb that is used with all commands that talk to the hosted Chef server.

- A 'starter' cookbook.

■ **Note**   Do not download the starter kit more than once as this will reset your access to this Chef organization!

We're not too interested in the starter cookbook as we've already shown we can generate one for ourselves, but download the **chef-starter.zip** and extract the contents into your home folder. You will now have a directory called **chef-repo** containing a **.chef** folder inside it, where all the configuration files are located. We will be taking the contents of this folder and using them as we progress through the book, so keep it safe.

■ **Warning**   Be sure not to check the .chef folder into source control, especially not a publicly hosted Git solution such as GitHub.

In later chapters, we'll be using these keys to connect our repository to the Chef Server, uploading a cookbook, and working through a more advanced scenario in Azure. For now, you have everything you need locally to progress through the rest of the examples in this book.

Summary

In this chapter we familiarized ourselves with Chef's architecture, installed all the tools required for day-to-day development with Chef, and had a brief refresher on recipe development. I could write a whole book on using Chef but it would be of little value as the resources available online at `http://learn.chef.io` are comprehensive and very usable. Later in this book we will be stepping through a number of more advanced examples in detail, so don't worry if you are not at expert level yet.

In the following chapters we will be focusing in on how we can use Chef with Microsoft Azure, including some of the best practices for building quality into your Infrastructure as Code pipeline while building a scalable and secure platform in Azure.

CHAPTER 2

■ ■ ■

Microsoft Azure Terminology and Concepts

Now that we understand the importance of platform automation and had a brief refresher on the key concepts of using Chef for configuration management, let's have a look at what you need to know about the Azure platform in order to get automating!

In this chapter we'll take a brief look at the history of Azure for the newcomer to the platform, then familiarize ourselves with key terminology for deploying to Azure and ensure you have all the tools installed to successfully automate Azure using Chef.

In this book we are focusing on the latest features of Azure, based around Azure Resource Manager (ARM) stack and the latest portal features that are available at https://portal.azure.com

We *won't* be looking at older features of Azure Virtual Machines (sometimes referred to as "Classic" compute resources) such as using the old management portal available from https://manage.windowsazure.com, or using the Service Management APIs although we may mention them from time to time if there is no other way to accomplish a task. These features have mostly been superseded now by the features in Azure Resource Manager (ARM).

■ **Note** The pace of updates to the Azure platform and tools from Microsoft will likely mean that the screenshots seen here may become out of date, so don't be surprised if a button or some text cannot be found or doesn't match the book exactly.

Deploying to the Microsoft Azure Platform

The Windows Azure platform was released in 2010, initially offering Platform-as-a-Service (PaaS) "Hosted services" such as Web and Worker roles, and storage capabilities such as queues and table storage for those organizations who had the capability to develop their solutions based on the .NET stack.

In April 2013, Microsoft released Windows Azure Infrastructure Services to general availability, allowing finally the creation of Infrastructure-as-a-Service (IaaS) solutions. Initially a limited set of Windows Server and Linux operating systems were available and since then more vendors have come to the platform.

In 2014 the platform was renamed to Microsoft Azure, to make it clear that it isn't just Windows resources that you can create on their compute platform. Currently, Linux makes up over 25% of all IaaS compute resource on Azure, and as of November 2015 more than 57% of Fortune 500 companies are using Azure in their environment.

© Stuart Preston 2016
S. Preston, *Using Chef with Microsoft Azure*, DOI 10.1007/978-1-4842-1476-3_2

Much has been written on IaaS versus PaaS and the distinction is fairly well understood (see Figure 2-1 below). In a nutshell, with IaaS you get to manage and operate everything from the OS upwards, whereas with PaaS you only have to worry about deploying your Applications and Data on top of the platform.

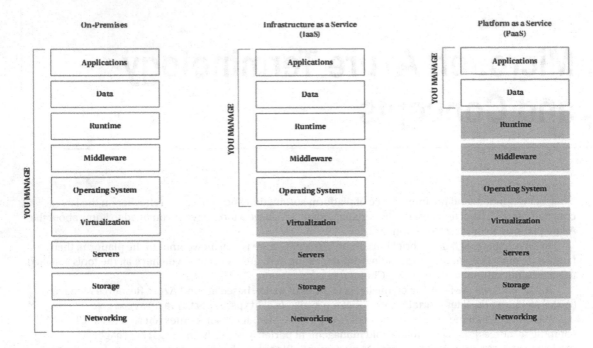

Figure 2-1. *Separation of Responsibilities - On-Premises vs. IaaS vs. PaaS*

One thing that is common to both IaaS and PaaS architectures is that deployment orchestration across different types of resources is the responsibility of the end user and you need automation tooling to help you do this. In Azure the primary way of achieving this orchestration is through the use of Azure Resource Manager (ARM) templates.

The majority of Azure Services are in the PaaS category, and with Azure Resource Manager we can combine IaaS and PaaS based deployments, which means we can deploy web sites or boot up virtual machines using the same set of underlying technologies. We'll cover hybrid deployment scenarios like this in the advanced topics toward the rear of the book.

So remember that while we mostly talk about configuring IaaS environments in this book, the lines are now very much blurred, and it is easy to see how a single deployment can easily be made up of both PaaS and IaaS resources. PaaS generally has a lower surface area for management, which is great because it eliminates the need for patching and upgrading the platform; however it is not so great when you need to customize the underlying platform or manage intricate dependencies.

We're going to use the rest of this chapter to make sure we are familiar with the Azure platform and the components and terminology you will need to work with when automating it.

Subscriptions, Tenants, and Regions

When we start to talk about management of Azure, the terms *Subscription, Tenant,* and *Region* often get confused and we'll be using them quite a bit in this book; so this section will recap the terms. Figure 2-2 shows the relationships between the three terms. At a high level:

- The **subscription** identifies the owner of the subscription and the method of payment (you may see this referred to in Azure-parlance as the Payment Instrument). Subscriptions are given a name and ID and resources you create in Azure can be associated to this subscription. A **subscription** is not tied to a particular region and is associated with a **tenant**.

- The **tenant** is the directory name that was created when you created your first Subscription (unless you added your custom domain already, it probably has a domain name like contoso.onmicrosoft.com).

- The **region** describes the location of the datacenter where you want your primary resources to be located: for example, 'West US' is the region identifier for resources that are hosted in the California datacenter.

Let's drill into each one of these terms a little further.

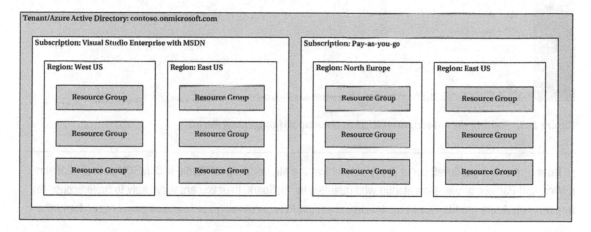

Figure 2-2. *Regions, Tenants, and Subscriptions in Microsoft Azure*

Subscriptions

To follow the exercises and examples in this book, we'll need to use an Azure *subscription*. There are many ways of purchasing Microsoft Azure and we won't cover them here; but if you need a free trial you can visit https://azure.microsoft.com/en-us/pricing/free-trial/

For the examples in the book, you will need the Subscription GUID for the subscription you wish to work with. This can be obtained by following these steps:

1. Navigate to the Azure portal at https://portal.azure.com and log in remembering to use the account you signed up with.

2. Click the **Browse All** icon on the left-hand side of the portal.

3. In the menu that appears, click **Subscriptions**, as shown in Figure 2-3.

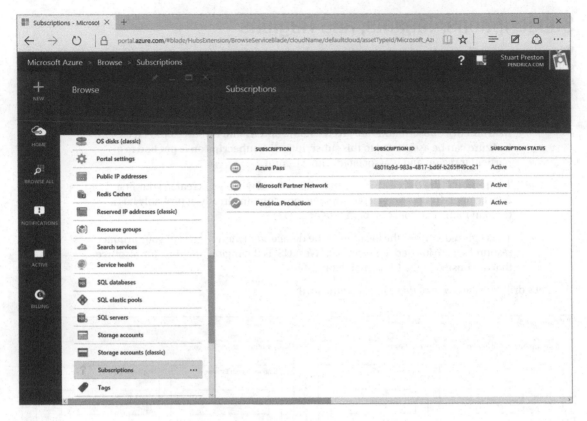

Figure 2-3. *Finding the Subscription GUID in the Azure Management Portal*

■ **Note** If you are a developer or IT professional with a Microsoft Visual Studio with MSDN subscription, are a Microsoft Partner, or you are a startup who qualifies for BizSpark, then you are very likely to have access to free monthly Azure credits. See `http://azure.microsoft.com/en-us/pricing/member-offers/` for further details.

Tenants

A *tenant* refers to a dedicated instance of Azure Active Directory (Azure AD) for your organization. Typically, a tenant is referred to by its default directory name: for example, `contoso.onmicrosoft.com` and it also has a globally unique identifier (GUID) that in general is not used publicly, but is used in automation scenarios.

When you sign up to Microsoft Azure or Office 365, you are allocated a directory automatically, and custom domain names can be added afterwards. Your users and roles are created in the directory.

Active Directory properties are only accessible from the "old" portal at `https://manage.windowazure.com` (as shown in Figure 2-4) so this is one of the few times you may need to access this portal until the functionality can be replicated in the new portal located at `https://portal.azure.com`

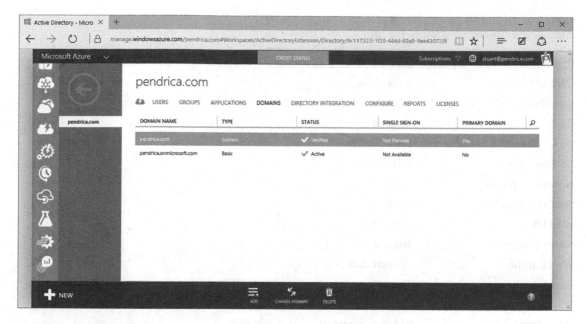

Figure 2-4. *Viewing a tenant in the management portal*

Regions

At the time of writing, Microsoft Azure is available for purchase in 140 countries and from those countries you can provision and deploy compute resource in over 20 *regions* (plus China, which is managed independently and is not generally available unless your company has a legal entity located there). More regions have already been announced for 2016 in the United Kingdom and in Germany.

■ **Note**   Not all machine sizes and services are available in all regions, and this may also influence your decision about where to locate your compute resource. You can view the full list of services by region at `http://azure.microsoft.com/en-us/regions/#services`

When planning to deploy an application to Microsoft Azure it is important to take datacenter location and any usage restrictions into account. Table 2-1 lists the current Microsoft Azure regions. More are being added each year to provide better global coverage and lower latency.

Table 2-1. *Global Microsoft Azure regions and corresponding datacenter locations, as of November 2015*

Azure Region	Location
Central US	Iowa
East US	Virginia
East US	Virginia
US Gov Iowa	Iowa
US Gov Virginia	Virginia
North Central US	Illinois
South Central US	Texas
West US	California
North Europe	Ireland
West Europe	Netherlands
East Asia	Hong Kong
Southeast Asia	Singapore
Japan East	Tokyo, Saitama
Japan West	Osaka
Brazil South	Sao Paulo State
Australia East	New South Wales
Australia Southeast	Victoria
Central India	Pune
South India	Chennai
West India	Mumbai

Note that Australian regions are available only to customers with billing addresses in Australia or New Zealand. For an up-to-date list of regions and service availability, visit `http://azure.microsoft.com/en-us/regions/`

Selecting Your Nearest Region

If you have some experience running applications that consume data from across the Internet, you'll know that *latency* (typically measured as the gap in milliseconds between sending and receiving packets of data) is an important factor in the perceived performance of an application. This is also a key consideration when you select the location of your resources to minimize the latency when using the Microsoft Azure management portal or automation tools. So before we dive in to the exercises it is useful to find out your nearest datacenter location.

We can make an approximation of your nearest datacenter by visiting `http://azurespeed.com` (thank you, Blair Chen) in a web browser as seen in Figure 2-5.

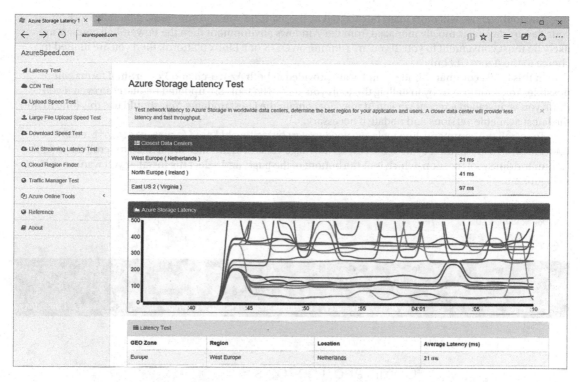

Figure 2-5. *Using azurespeed.com to determine your nearest datacenter*

We can see from the screenshot that my nearest datacenter is in the Netherlands (West Europe). So for my examples I'll be choosing 'West Europe' as the primary location for my resources.

Now we know where we're going to host our resources (region name), the name of our active directory (tenant), and who is paying (subscription); now we can advance through the rest of the chapter and get our environment set up with the right tools.

Managing Azure from the Command Line

There are two ways to manage Azure from the command line - you can either use the *Azure Command-line tools* (referred to as azure-cli), which is a stand-alone, cross-platform (Windows, OS/X and Linux) application written in node.js, or you can use the *Azure PowerShell cmdlets*, which run natively on the Windows platform. There is no explicit feature parity between the two tools, but in general they both release at similar times as new functionality is released in Azure.

■ **Note**   Chef tools such as Chef-Provisioning communicate with Azure's Resource Management API via a separate cross-platform library so these command-line tools are only required on your workstations to help you manage your subscriptions.

The tool you use will most likely be dictated by the platform you and your team generally work on - if your day-to-day job is mostly managed from the Windows environment then the PowerShell cmdlets are likely be most convenient to you. If you are running on OS/X or a Linux platform, then you are limited in choice to the Azure CLI only.

In this book, command-line examples are provided in both **Azure-cli** and **PowerShell** forms where possible. You should start by installing the tools you need. The tools are updated regularly so even if you think you've installed a recent version, it may not contain the latest updates. You should use this time to find the latest available versions and update if necessary.

To install the command-line tools, we need to start by visiting `https://azure.microsoft.com/downloads`, which will direct you to the correct language version of the site. You'll need to scroll down to the Command-line tools section, which is at the bottom of the page, and select the installer you want as shown in Figure 2-6.

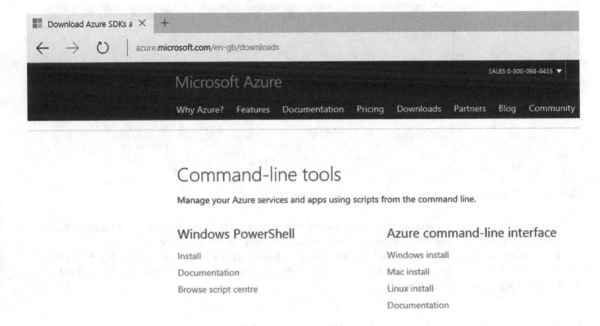

Figure 2-6. Download location for Azure Command-line tools

Installing the Tools (Windows)

In Windows, you can choose to install both the command-line tools and the PowerShell cmdlets via the same WebPI 5.0 installer. It actually doesn't matter which installer you select first, because once installation of the first one is completed you are given the option to install the remaining tools.

Azure-cli

Let's start by installing the command-line tools by running the installer and pressing **Install** (as shown in Figure 2-7).

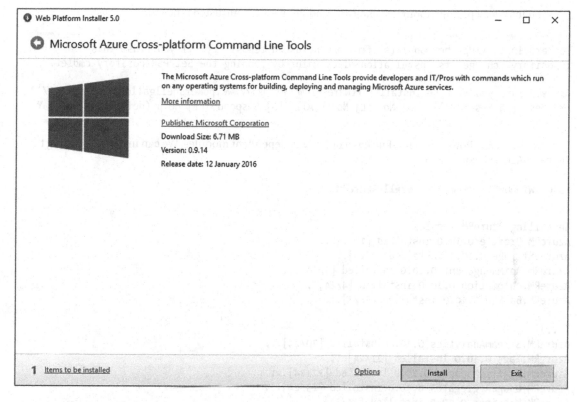

Figure 2-7. Web Platform Installer 5.0 installation of Microsoft Azure Cross-platform Command-line tools

After installation of the command-line tools, you are given the opportunity to add the **Microsoft Azure PowerShell** tools to the installation. I recommend declining this option. Why? Because the PowerShell modules are now available on the PowerShell Gallery, so they are installable and updatable via the excellent PSGet (see http://psget.net).

If you have a copy of Visual Studio installed on your machine, I recommend adding the **Microsoft Azure SDK for .NET** though - this will give you some visual help writing Azure Resource Manager deployment templates in JSON.

Now that we have the tools installed we can skip to the next stage, which is to verify the installation.

PowerShell (PSGet)

■ **Note**   If you do not have PSGet installed, you will need to install it from http://psget.net

---

To install the PowerShell cmdlets via PSGet, open an **administrative/elevated** PowerShell window and use the Install-Module AzureRM cmdlet:

```
PS C:\WINDOWS\system32> Install-Module AzureRM
```

You may get a prompt about installing the modules from an untrusted repository:

```
You are installing the module(s) from an untrusted repository. If you trust this
repository, change its InstallationPolicy value by running the Set-PSRepository cmdlet.

Are you sure you want to install software from 'https://www.powershellgallery.com/api/v2/'?
[Y] Yes  [A] Yes to All  [N] No  [L] No to All  [S] Suspend  [?] Help (default is "N"): Y
```

The AzureRM PowerShell module has a number of dependent modules. We can install these using the Install-AzureRM command:

```
PS C:\WINDOWS\system32> Install-AzureRM
```

```
Installing AzureRM modules.
AzureRM.Profile 0.10.0 installed [1/24]...
Azure.Storage 0.10.1 installed [2/24]...
AzureRM.ApiManagement 0.10.0 installed [3/24]...
AzureRM.Automation 0.10.0 installed [4/24]...
AzureRM.Backup 0.10.0 installed [5/24]...

[...]
AzureRM.StreamAnalytics 0.10.0 installed [20/24]...
AzureRM.Tags 0.10.0 installed [21/24]...
AzureRM.TrafficManager 0.10.0 installed [22/24]...
AzureRM.UsageAggregates 0.10.0 installed [23/24]...
AzureRM.Websites 0.10.0 installed [24/24]...
```

Installing the Tools (Mac OS X)

If you are a Node.js user already, you should be able to install the Azure-cli by using the Node.js package manager, NPM:

```
$ npm install -g azure-cli
```

Otherwise you'll have to install from the downloaded package, as shown in Figure 2-8. After launching the installer, accept all the defaults and proceed to the verification steps.

Install Command Line
Interface

Figure 2-8. Installing the command-line tools on Mac OS X

Installing the Tools (Linux)

On the Linux platform we are basically restricted to the option of installing via the Node.js package manager (NPM) or via a separately downloaded package.

Ubuntu/Debian

```
$ sudo apt-get install nodejs-legacy
$ sudo apt-get install npm
$ sudo npm install -g azure-cli
```

RedHat/CentOS

```
$ sudo yum install nodejs-legacy
$ sudo yum install npm
$ sudo npm install -g azure-cli
```

Logging In and Verifying Command-line Tools Connectivity

Now that we have all tools we need installed, let's see if we can connect to Azure and list the available subscriptions. We do this with the azure-cli by using the **azure login** command. In PowerShell we need to use the **Add-AzureAccount** cmdlet.

Azure-cli

First of all, we need to log in by using the **azure login --username <your-username>** command (note the use of two dashes --). The cli requests the password for your account.

```
PS C:\Users\StuartPreston> azure login --username stuart@pendrica.com
```

```
info:    Executing command login
Password: **********
info:    Added subscription Microsoft Partner Network
info:    Added subscription Pendrica Production
info:    login command OK
```

To list the available subscriptions, use the **azure account list** command:

```
PS C:\Users\StuartPreston> azure account list
```

```
info:    Executing command account list
data:    Name                            Id                                      Current  State
data:    ------------------------------  --------------------------------------  -------  --------
data:    Microsoft Partner Network       b6e7eee9-YOUR-GUID-HERE-03ab624df016    true     Enabled
data:    Pendrica Production             bcf669fc-YOUR-GUID-HERE-e2d1f9f4b1c3    false    Enabled
info:    account list command OK
```

If you want to change the active subscription, you can use the **azure account set** command. Below I am setting the active subscription to my **Microsoft Partner Network** subscription:

```
PS C:\Users\StuartPreston> azure account set "Microsoft Partner Network"
```

```
info:    Executing command account set
info:    Setting subscription to "Microsoft Partner Network" with id
         "b6e7eee9-YOUR-GUID-HERE-03ab624df016".
info:    Changes saved
info:    account set command OK
```

We can view the Tenant ID for a given subscription by using the Subscription ID and passing it into the azure account show command:

```
PS C:\Users\StuartPreston> azure account show b6e7eee9-YOUR-GUID-HERE-03ab624df016
```

```
info:    Executing command account show
data:    Name                   : Microsoft Partner Network
data:    ID                     : b6e7eee9-YOUR-GUID-HERE-03ab624df016
data:    State                  : Enabled
data:    Tenant ID              : 9c117323-YOUR-GUID-HERE-9ee430723ba3
data:    Is Default             : true
data:    Environment            : AzureCloud
data:    Has Certificate        : Yes
data:    Has Access Token       : Yes
data:    User name              : stuart@pendrica.com
data:
```

Finally, to make sure we are creating our resources in Azure Resource Manager mode we need to switch to ARM mode; for this we use the azure config mode arm command:

```
PS C:\Users\StuartPreston> azure config mode arm
```

```
info:    New mode is arm
```

To confirm we are in the correct (ARM) mode, we can use the **azure config list** command:

```
PS C:\Users\StuartPreston> azure config list
```

```
info:    Getting config settings
data:    Setting  Value
data:    -------  -----
data:    mode     arm
```

We now have a fully configured azure-cli installation that we can use for the rest of the examples.

PowerShell

If you're not on Windows, you are free to skip to the next section. We're going to configure Windows PowerShell so we are ready to use it for the remaining examples in the book. First of all, we need to log in by using the Login-AzureRmAccount command. This should launch a browser window (as shown in Figure 2-9) to request credentials. You will need to provide your username and password.

```
PS C:\Users\StuartPreston> Login-AzureRmAccount
```

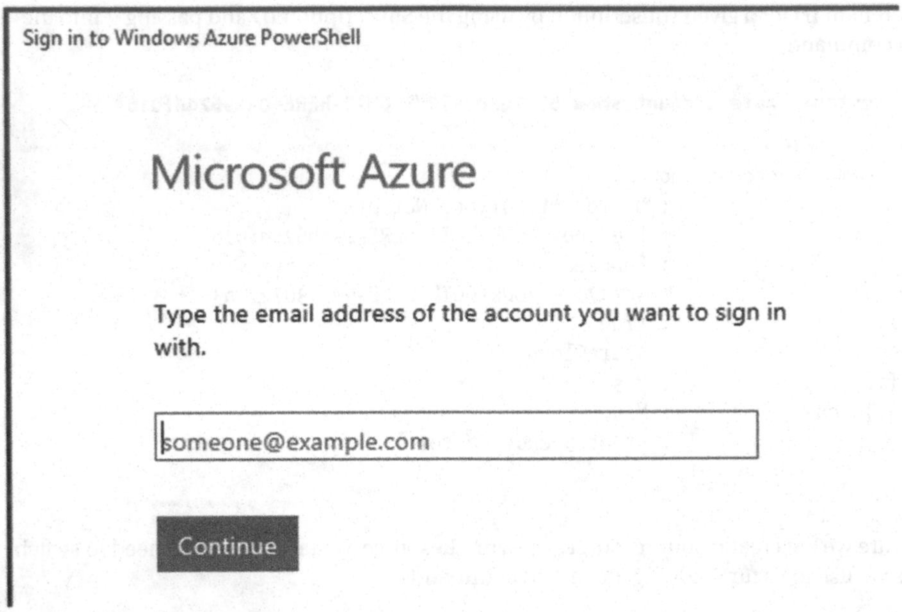

Sign in to Windows Azure PowerShell

Microsoft Azure

Type the email address of the account you want to sign in with.

someone@example.com

Continue

Figure 2-9. *Browser dialog launched during Login-AzureRmAccount cmdlet*

After entering your username and password, you will be logged in and now need to set a subscription to work with. To list the available subscriptions and their state using PowerShell, use the Get-AzureRmSubscription command:

```
PS C:\Users\StuartPreston> Get-AzureRmSubscription | Select SubscriptionId, SubscriptionName


SubscriptionId                       SubscriptionName
--------------                       ----------------
b6e7eee9-YOUR-GUID-HERE-03ab624df016 Microsoft Partner Network
bcf669fc-YOUR-GUID-HERE-e2d1f9f4b1c3 Pendrica Production
```

If you need to change which subscription is the active or current one using PowerShell, use the Select-AzureSubscription command:

```
PS C:\Users\StuartPreston> Select-AzureRmSubscription -SubscriptionName
"Microsoft Partner Network"


Environment        : AzureCloud
Account            : stuart@pendrica.com
TenantId           : 9c117323-YOUR-GUID-HERE-9ee430723ba3
SubscriptionId     : b6e7eee9-YOUR-GUID-HERE-03ab624df016
CurrentStorageAccount :
```

We are now ready to create resources in the cloud with Azure Resource Manager, but before that we need to understand a bit more about Resource groups.

Azure Resource Groups

Resource Groups in Azure let you manage all resources (such as web sites, virtual machines, storage, databases, and networks) for an application together.

A resource group typically include all of the resources for an application, but you can also use them as a container for resources that are logically grouped together: perhaps a set of shared services that other applications use. You can decide how you want to allocate resources to resource groups based on what makes the most sense for your organization.

Resources in Azure are classified into providers, and there are three core providers for IaaS resources - Microsoft.Network, Microsoft.Compute, and Microsoft.Storage. An example of this is shown in Figure 2-10.

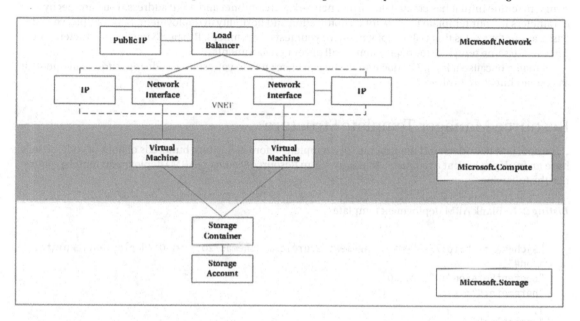

Figure 2-10. Resources inside a single Resource Group for a single application

One of the key benefits of Resource Groups is that you can reuse server names for the same resource but in different resource groups. This is a great advancement for testing purposes as the machine names will not change according to which environment you are in (of course there are some notable exceptions to this such as Storage Accounts and Public IP addresses).

■ **Note** Deleting a resource group will delete all the resources contained within it.

As your application evolves over time you'll need the ability to describe the entire resource group and its dependencies in a way where we can start with the application topology in one shape and end up in another. This is exactly the use case for Azure Resource Manager templates.

Azure Resource Manager Templates

Azure Resource Manager allows you to define a simple template (in JSON format) that defines deployment and configuration of your application. Using the template, you can repeatedly deploy your application throughout the application life cycle and have confidence your resources are deployed in a consistent state.

Resource Manager is *declarative* and *idempotent* - declarative in this case meaning the document describes the target state for each resource, and idempotent in our world means that we can execute the script multiple times and get the same result. Which is very useful for testing, of course!

Resource Manager ensures that the resources for a configuration are created in the correct order to preserve the dependencies and references. For example, Resource Manager will not create the NIC for a virtual machine until it has created the virtual network with a subnet and an IP address. You can specify parameters in your template to allow for customization and flexibility in deployment. For example, you can pass parameter values that tailor deployment for your test environment. By specifying the parameters, you can use the same template for deployment to all of your environments.

Finally, because it is a JSON document, you can check it in to your source code repository and update it as your architecture evolves.

Resource Manager Template Structure

It is important to understand the structure of a template before diving into hundreds of lines of code, so let's have an in-depth look at a template. An empty Azure Resource Manager (ARM) deployment template looks like the following:

Listing 2-1. Blank ARM deployment template

```
{
    "$schema": "http://schema.management.azure.com/schemas/2015-01-01/deploymentTemplate.
    json#",
    "contentVersion": "1.0.0.0",
    "parameters": {
    },
    "variables": {
    },
    "resources": [
    ],
    "outputs": {
    }
}
```

Even if you don't understand JSON just yet, don't worry. A JSON document always has lots of curly brackets that are used to group items together, and brackets not being matched is one of the primary causes of template deployment failure.

There are some tools that will help you ensure you minimize mistakes with the files when you modify them, and we'll discuss these as we get further into the book. For now, we just want to understand how a template is composed as understanding this is key to most of the automation techniques we'll be using.

Table 2-2. *Constituent parts of an ARM deployment template*

Key	Description
Parameters	Used to specify configuration parameters that you wish to expose to the command line or calling process for users to input.
Variables	Used to specify internally scoped variables for use across the deployment template.
Resources	Used to list an array of resources, and their type (identified by a provider name), and their dependencies.
Outputs	Used to relay information back to the caller that is returned by the execution of the deployment (e.g., a generated SQL Server instance name).

Example Resource Manager Template

Here's one of the simplest ARM templates that can be created. It creates a Storage account, Network Interface, A VLAN with two subnets, and a VM in a specified location. Don't worry if this looks daunting right now; there are tools to help ensure you don't make too many mistakes with the file.

Listing 2-2. Populated ARM deployment template

```
{
    "$schema": "http://schema.management.azure.com/schemas/2015-01-01/deploymentTemplate.
    json#",
    "contentVersion": "1.0.0.0",
    "parameters": {
        "vnetLocation": {
            "type": "string",
            "defaultValue": "West US",
            "allowedValues": [
                "East US",
                "West US",
                "West Europe",
                "East Asia",
                "South East Asia"
            ]
        },
        "storageName": {
            "type": "string"
        },
        "storageType": {
            "type": "string",
            "defaultValue": "Standard_LRS",
            "allowedValues": [
                "Standard_LRS",
                "Standard_GRS",
                "Standard_ZRS"
            ]
        },
```

```
        "storageLocation": {
            "type": "string",
            "defaultValue": "West US",
            "allowedValues": [
                "East US",
                "West US",
                "West Europe",
                "East Asia",
                "South East Asia"
            ]
        },
        "vmName": {
            "type": "string"
        },
        "vmAdminUserName": {
            "type": "string"
        },
        "vmAdminPassword": {
            "type": "securestring"
        },
        "vmWindowsOSVersion": {
            "type": "string",
            "defaultValue": "2012-R2-Datacenter",
            "allowedValues": [
                "2008-R2-SP1",
                "2012-Datacenter",
                "2012-R2-Datacenter",
                "Windows-Server-Technical-Preview"
            ]
        }
    },
    "variables": {
        "vnetPrefix": "10.0.0.0/16",
        "vnetSubnet1Name": "Subnet-1",
        "vnetSubnet1Prefix": "10.0.0.0/24",
        "vnetSubnet2Name": "Subnet-2",
        "vnetSubnet2Prefix": "10.0.1.0/24",
        "vmImagePublisher": "MicrosoftWindowsServer",
        "vmImageOffer": "WindowsServer",
        "vmOSDiskName": "vmOSDisk",
        "vmVmSize": "Standard_D1",
        "vmVnetID": "[resourceId('Microsoft.Network/virtualNetworks', 'vnet')]",
        "vmSubnetRef": "[concat(variables('vmVnetID'), '/subnets/',
        variables('vnetSubnet1Name'))]",
        "vmStorageAccountContainerName": "vhds",
        "vmNicName": "[concat(parameters('vmName'), 'NetworkInterface')]"
    },
```

```json
"resources": [
    {
        "name": "vnet",
        "type": "Microsoft.Network/virtualNetworks",
        "location": "[parameters('vnetLocation')]",
        "apiVersion": "2015-05-01-preview",
        "dependsOn": [ ],
        "tags": {
            "displayName": "vnet"
        },
        "properties": {
            "addressSpace": {
                "addressPrefixes": [
                    "[variables('vnetPrefix')]"
                ]
            },
            "subnets": [
                {
                    "name": "[variables('vnetSubnet1Name')]",
                    "properties": {
                        "addressPrefix": "[variables('vnetSubnet1Prefix')]"
                    }
                },
                {
                    "name": "[variables('vnetSubnet2Name')]",
                    "properties": {
                        "addressPrefix": "[variables('vnetSubnet2Prefix')]"
                    }
                }
            ]
        }
    },
    {
        "name": "[parameters('storageName')]",
        "type": "Microsoft.Storage/storageAccounts",
        "location": "[parameters('storageLocation')]",
        "apiVersion": "2015-05-01-preview",
        "dependsOn": [ ],
        "tags": {
            "displayName": "storage"
        },
        "properties": {
            "accountType": "[parameters('storageType')]"
        }
    },
    {
        "name": "[variables('vmNicName')]",
        "type": "Microsoft.Network/networkInterfaces",
        "location": "[parameters('vnetLocation')]",
        "apiVersion": "2015-05-01-preview",
```

```
        "dependsOn": [
            "[concat('Microsoft.Network/virtualNetworks/', 'vnet')]"
        ],
        "tags": {
            "displayName": "vmNic"
        },
        "properties": {
            "ipConfigurations": [
                {
                    "name": "ipconfig1",
                    "properties": {
                        "privateIPAllocationMethod": "Dynamic",
                        "subnet": {
                            "id": "[variables('vmSubnetRef')]"
                        }
                    }
                }
            ]
        }
    },
    {
        "name": "[parameters('vmName')]",
        "type": "Microsoft.Compute/virtualMachines",
        "location": "[parameters('vnetLocation')]",
        "apiVersion": "2015-05-01-preview",
        "dependsOn": [
            "[concat('Microsoft.Storage/storageAccounts/', parameters('storageName'))]",
            "[concat('Microsoft.Network/networkInterfaces/', variables('vmNicName'))]"
        ],
        "tags": {
            "displayName": "vm"
        },
        "properties": {
            "hardwareProfile": {
                "vmSize": "[variables('vmVmSize')]"
            },
            "osProfile": {
                "computername": "[parameters('vmName')]",
                "adminUsername": "[parameters('vmAdminUsername')]",
                "adminPassword": "[parameters('vmAdminPassword')]"
            },
            "storageProfile": {
                "imageReference": {
                    "publisher": "[variables('vmImagePublisher')]",
                    "offer": "[variables('vmImageOffer')]",
                    "sku": "[parameters('vmWindowsOSVersion')]",
                    "version": "latest"
                },
```

```
                    "osDisk": {
                        "name": "vmOSDisk",
                        "vhd": {
                            "uri": "[concat('http://', parameters('storageName'),
                            '.blob.core.windows.net/', variables('vmStorageAccount
                            ContainerName'), '/', variables('vmOSDiskName'), '.vhd')]"
                        },
                        "caching": "ReadWrite",
                        "createOption": "FromImage"
                    }
                },
                "networkProfile": {
                    "networkInterfaces": [
                        {
                            "id": "[resourceId('Microsoft.Network/networkInterfaces',
                            variables('vmNicName'))]"
                        }
                    ]
                }
            }
        }
    ],
    "outputs": {
    }
}
```

Let's now go through the constituent parts of this template to get an understanding of the patterns involved.

Parameters

Parameters are the **external** inputs to the template and can be set externally by both the command-line tools and Windows PowerShell. We can see in this case there are eight parameters added - vnetLocation, storageName, storageType, storageLocation, vmName, vmAdminUserName, vmAdminPassword, vmWindowsOSVersion.

```
"parameters": {
        "vnetLocation": {
            "type": "string",
            "defaultValue": "West US",
            "allowedValues": [
                "East US",
                "West US",
                "West Europe",
                "East Asia",
                "South East Asia"
            ]
        },
```

```json
        "storageName": {
            "type": "string"
        },
        "storageType": {
            "type": "string",
            "defaultValue": "Standard_LRS",
            "allowedValues": [
                "Standard_LRS",
                "Standard_GRS",
                "Standard_ZRS"
            ]
        },
        "storageLocation": {
            "type": "string",
            "defaultValue": "West US",
            "allowedValues": [
                "East US",
                "West US",
                "West Europe",
                "East Asia",
                "South East Asia"
            ]
        },
        "vmName": {
            "type": "string"
        },
        "vmAdminUserName": {
            "type": "string"
        },
        "vmAdminPassword": {
            "type": "securestring"
        },
        "vmWindowsOSVersion": {
            "type": "string",
            "defaultValue": "2012-R2-Datacenter",
            "allowedValues": [
                "2008-R2-SP1",
                "2012-Datacenter",
                "2012-R2-Datacenter",
                "Windows-Server-Technical-Preview"
            ]
        }
    }
```

Each parameter has a *type*, a *default value*, and optionally a list of *allowed values*. For example, the **vmWindowsOSVersion** parameter is a string type and has a default value of **2012-R2-Datacenter**. It also has values that can be selected from the allowedValues list shown.

Variables

Variables are **internally** scoped to the template: that is, they are only settable from within the template. In the variables section, you construct values that can be used to simplify template language expressions. Typically, these variables will be based on values provided from the parameters. The example below demonstrates how to reference other elements, as well as introducing the concat() function:

```
"variables": {
        "vnetPrefix": "10.0.0.0/16",
        "vnetSubnet1Name": "Subnet-1",
        "vnetSubnet1Prefix": "10.0.0.0/24",
        "vnetSubnet2Name": "Subnet-2",
        "vnetSubnet2Prefix": "10.0.1.0/24",
        "vmImagePublisher": "MicrosoftWindowsServer",
        "vmImageOffer": "WindowsServer",
        "vmOSDiskName": "vmOSDisk",
        "vmVmSize": "Standard_D1",
        "vmVnetID": "[resourceId('Microsoft.Network/virtualNetworks', 'vnet')]",
        "vmSubnetRef": "[concat(variables('vmVnetID'), '/subnets/',
        variables('vnetSubnet1Name'))]",
        "vmStorageAccountContainerName": "vhds",
        "vmNicName": "[concat(parameters('vmName'), 'NetworkInterface')]"
    },
```

Resources

As you can see, a blank template requires one or more Resources added to it so that it has some work to do. Each resource follows a very similar structure. Let's examine the resource for the Storage account in the example template:

```
{
    "name": "[parameters('storageName')]",
    "type": "Microsoft.Storage/storageAccounts",
    "location": "[parameters('storageLocation')]",
    "apiVersion": "2015-05-01-preview",
    "dependsOn": [ ],
    "tags": {
        "displayName": "storage"
    },
    "properties": {
        "accountType": "[parameters('storageType')]"
    }
},
```

Each resource has a *name, type, location*, and *properties*. It also defines any dependencies it has so that Resource Manager can provision resources in order. As we spend more time with Resource Manager with more complex examples, we'll delve deeper into how things work.

Outputs

In the Outputs section, you specify values that are returned from deployment. For example, you could return the URI to access a deployed resource.

The following example shows a value that is returned in the Outputs section.

```
{
    "outputs": {
        "siteUri" : {
            "type" : "string",
            "value": "[concat('http://',reference(resourceId('Microsoft.Web/sites',
            parameters('siteName'))).hostNames[0])]"
        }
    }
}
```

Expressions and Functions

Expressions and functions extend the JSON that is available in the template and allow you to create values that are not strict literal values. Expressions are enclosed with brackets ([and]), and are evaluated at deployment time.

Listed in Table 2-3 are some common expression functions:

Table 2-3. *Common Resource Manager template functions (from https://azure.microsoft.com/en-gb/ documentation/articles/resource-group-template-functions)*

Function	Description
base64	Returns the base64 representation of the input string.
concat	Combines multiple string values and returns the resulting string value. This function can take any number of arguments.
copyIndex	Returns the current index of an iteration loop. For examples of using this function, see Create multiple instances of resources in Azure Resource Manager.
deployment	Returns information about the current deployment operation.
listKeys	Returns the keys of a storage account. The resourceId can be specified by using the resourceId function or by using the format providerNamespace/resourceType/ resourceName. You can use the function to get the primaryKey and secondaryKey.
padLeft	Returns a right-aligned string by adding characters to the left until reaching the total specified length.
parameters	Returns a parameter value. The specified parameter name must be defined in the parameters section of the template.
provider	Return information about a resource provider and its supported resource types. If no type is provided, all of the supported types are returned.
reference	Enables an expression to derive its value from another resource's runtime state.
replace	Returns a new string with all instances of one character in the specified string replaced by another character.

(continued)

Table 2-3. (*continued*)

Function	Description
resourceGroup	Returns a structured object that represents the current resource group.
resourceId	Returns the unique identifier of a resource. You use this function when the resource name is ambiguous or not provisioned within the same template.
subscription	Returns details about the subscription.
toLower	Converts the specified string to lower case.
toUpper	Converts the specified string to upper case.
variables	Returns the value of variable. The specified variable name must be defined in the variables section of the template.

The following example shows how to use several of the functions when constructing values:

```
"variables": {
    "location": "[resourceGroup().location]",
    "usernameAndPassword": "[concat('parameters('username'), ':', parameters('password'))]",
    "authorizationHeader": "[concat('Basic ', base64(variables('usernameAndPassword')))]"
}
```

We can see the **usernameAndPassword** value uses the concat() function to join together the username and password, which are passed in as parameters. We also see the **authorizationHeader** key uses the base64() function to generate the base64 version of the **usernamcAndPassword** variable.

For now, you know enough about expressions and functions to understand the sections of the template. For more detailed information about all of the template functions, including parameters and the format of returned values, see https://azure.microsoft.com/en-gb/documentation/articles/resource-group-template-functions/

Summary

In this chapter we learned about some of the key Microsoft terminology that will be required to automate the provisioning and configuration management of Azure using Chef. There is obviously a lot more to learn about Azure than I have covered in this chapter. There are some great resources available already so I have only touched on the basics here.

If you were able to follow through the examples and installations, then you have everything you need for the upcoming chapters.

CHAPTER 3

■ ■ ■

Chef Azure VM Extensions

Whether you have many years' experience with Chef or just followed the online training material at `http://learn.chef.io` you will know that one of the first things you need to do when setting up an environment is to *bootstrap* the machines you are working with. This means installing the Chef client onto the target machines over the network. This chapter introduces the Chef VM Extensions for Azure, a more efficient method of applying the Chef client onto a virtual machine and registering that node with your Chef server.

We'll start by looking at the mechanics of Azure VM Extensions and discuss the benefits of using the Chef VM Extension in place of the traditional Chef bootstrap process. We will then step through what you need to do to install, configure, and troubleshoot the Chef VM Extensions in your environment.

What Are Azure VM Extensions?

Azure VM Extensions are lightweight pieces of software that extend VM functionality in some way. They are managed by a process running on each compute resource called the VM Agent, which is installed by default when creating a VM. If you've used a Windows virtual machine on Azure and ever had to reset an administrator password through the portal, you'll have used the features of the VM Agent.

VM Extensions are stored in an Extension Gallery that is accessible to the VM at provisioning time. The gallery is geo-replicated so that it is available in all regions. The VM Agent on each machine is responsible for retrieving the extension to the local VM and then calling an Install, Update, or Uninstall command, which then executes logic contained in scripts within the extension.

During installation and once the Extension has been installed the status of the extension is reported into an area of blob storage alongside the VM. This location can be read by the Resource Manager API (and including the Portal) to give feedback.

VM Extensions are useful because their state can be made visible externally without logging onto the machine; they are also provisioned and de-provisioned independently of the machine itself, all of which mean they lend themselves well to be used in configuration management scenarios. Figure 3-1 shows the components of an Azure VM Extension.

© Stuart Preston 2016
S. Preston, *Using Chef with Microsoft Azure*, DOI 10.1007/978-1-4842-1476-3_3

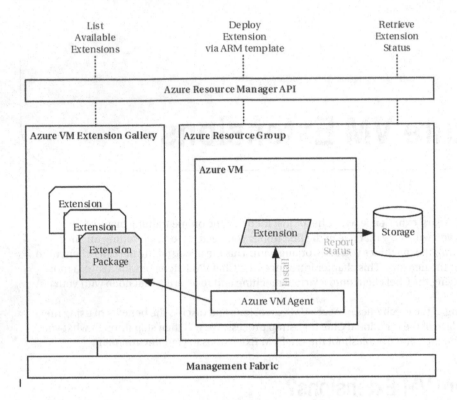

Figure 3-1. *Components of Azure VM Extensions*

■ **Note** VM extensions can technically be added to any compute (VM) resource including those servicing PaaS roles (such as web and worker processes); however we will focus on adding resource to IaaS resources only.

Introducing Chef VM Extensions

Chef worked with Microsoft to build and certify the Chef VM Extension as a more efficient way of enabling the Chef client on a machine, demonstrating the integration points of Azure with vendor-based solutions such as Chef.

Azure Resource Manager (ARM) allows us to define complete infrastructure stacks and architectures to be provisioned within Azure, including storage, network interfaces, public IP addresses, and load balancers. One assumption that is often made that because the cloud is 'public' that all resources created on it are public and therefore the only surface for management is through the front end. This is not the case for many cloud providers - it is also possible to create virtual machines that are not externally accessible with a public IP address.

To bootstrap a VM with a Chef client in Azure the following requirements must be met:

- The target machine must have WinRM (Windows) or SSH (Linux) protocol enabled and configured to be listening.

- You must be able to route to the machine directly, either over the Internet, VPN, or ExpressRoute.

- Firewalls must be opened to allow connections to the target machine from your client on ports TCP/5985-5986 (WinRM) or port TCP/22 (SSH).

- The target machine must have access to the Chef Server via HTTPS.

But what if the nodes you wish to bootstrap are not directly accessible to the Internet or via a private (VPN or ExpressRoute) network? We need an alternative approach. The Azure VM Extension is deployed as a resource, so the prerequisites to use the extension are much simpler:

- The target machine only requires outbound network connectivity via an Internet gateway to retrieve the installer files (enabled by default).

- The target machine must have access to the Chef Server via HTTPS.

Enabling the client is attractive in an automation sense, as we can declare the extension at the machine definition time, making it a time-saving option, too, when you are building many machines in parallel.

To start working with the Chef VM Extension, we first need to find a suitable version from the Extension Gallery so we can provision it.

Chef Azure VM Extension Compatibility

There are three different types of extensions published to the gallery; in fact we are probably only interested in two of them. **ChefClient** is the name of the extension for Windows and **LinuxChefClient** is the name of the extension for Linux. **CentosChefClient** only provides a Chef version 11 client and is not recommended unless you are using a very old Chef server. You can see a list of the version compatibility for the Chef VM Extension in Table 3-1:

Table 3-1. *Chef VM Extension compatibility*

Extension Name	Supported Operating Systems
CentosChefClient	CentOS 6.5+ (NB: Installs Chef Client version 11 only)
ChefClient	Windows Server 2008 (all variants including R2), Windows Server 2012 (all variants including R2), Windows Server 2016 Technical Preview (experimental)
LinuxChefClient	Ubuntu 12.04+, CentOS 6.5+

To get started let's see which VM Extensions are available to us from the VM Extension Gallery.

Listing the Available Chef VM Extension Versions from the VM Extension Gallery

The easiest way to accomplish this is by using either the Azure command line interface (CLI) or Azure PowerShell cmdlets *(see chapter 2 if you have not installed or configured either tool yet)*. Let's start with demonstrating how to do this using the Azure-cli.

Azure-cli

First we need to ensure we have a valid session by signing in using the azure login command and following the instructions displayed on the screen:

```
PS C:\Users\StuartPreston> azure login --username stuart@pendrica.com
```

```
info:     Executing command login
Password: **********
info:     Added subscription Microsoft Partner Network
info:     Added subscription Pendrica Production
info:     login command OK
```

Once we have logged in, ensure that you are in ARM mode by using the azure config mode arm command:

```
PS C:\Users\StuartPreston> azure config mode arm
```

```
info:     New mode is arm
```

The Azure-cli has a number of commands that relate to VM resource extensions. These can be seen by typing azure vm extension-image at the command line:

```
PS C:\Users\StuartPreston> azure vm extension-image
```

```
help:     Commands to manage VM resource extension images
help:
help:     Lists virtual machine/extension image publishers
help:       vm extension-image list-publishers [options] <location>
help:
help:     Lists virtual machine extension image types by a publisher
help:       vm extension-image list-types [options] <location> <publisher>
help:
help:     Lists virtual machine extension image versions by publisher and type input
help:       vm extension-image list-versions [options] <location> <publisher> <typeName>
help:
help:     Lists virtual machine extension images by publisher, and type input
help:       vm extension-image list [options] <location> <publisher> <typeName>
help:
help:     Lists virtual machine extension image versions by publisher, type and version
input
help:       vm extension-image show [options] <location> <publisher> <typeName> <version>
help:
help:     Options:
help:       -h, --help  output usage information
help:
help:     Current Mode: arm (Azure Resource Management)
```

We're interested first in using the azure `vm extension-image list-types` command to get a list of the image types that can be assigned to our VM. For this we need to know the datacenter location (e.g., **West Europe**) and the publisher name, which in our case is **Chef.Bootstrap.WindowsAzure**:

```
PS C:\Users\StuartPreston> azure vm extension-image list-types
```

```
info:     Executing command vm extension-image list-types
Location: West Europe
Publisher: Chef.Bootstrap.WindowsAzure
+ Getting virtual machine extension image types (Publisher: "Chef.Bootstrap.WindowsAzure"
Location:"westeurope")
data:     Publisher                        Type                 Location
data:     --------------------------       ----------------     ----------
data:     Chef.Bootstrap.WindowsAzure      CentosChefClient     westeurope
data:     Chef.Bootstrap.WindowsAzure      ChefClient           westeurope
data:     Chef.Bootstrap.WindowsAzure      LinuxChefClient      westeurope
info:     vm extension-image list-types command OK
```

We can see the three types of VM Extension are available to us; but to use the VM Extension in our ARM templates, we need the version number too. This is retrieved by the use of the azure `vm extension-image list-versions` command. In addition to the datacenter location and publisher, we also now need to supply the VM extension type name:

```
PS C:\Users\StuartPreston> azure vm extension-image list-versions
```

```
info:     Executing command vm extension-image list-versions
Location: West Europe
Publisher: Chef.Bootstrap.WindowsAzure
TypeName: ChefClient
- Getting virtual machine extension image verions (Publisher: "Chef.Bootstrap.
WindowsAzure" Type:"ChefClient" Location:"westeurope")
data:     Publisher                        Type          Version             Location
data:     --------------------------       ----------    ----------------    ----------
data:     Chef.Bootstrap.WindowsAzure      ChefClient    11.10.4             westeurope
data:     Chef.Bootstrap.WindowsAzure      ChefClient    11.12.0.0           westeurope
data:     Chef.Bootstrap.WindowsAzure      ChefClient    11.18.6.2           westeurope
data:     Chef.Bootstrap.WindowsAzure      ChefClient    1207.12.3.0         westeurope
data:     Chef.Bootstrap.WindowsAzure      ChefClient    1210.12.100.1000    westeurope
data:     Chef.Bootstrap.WindowsAzure      ChefClient    1210.12.4.1000      westeurope
info:     vm extension-image list-versions command OK
```

PowerShell

For PowerShell, we need to use the combination of the Get-AzureVMImagePublisher, Get-AzureVMExtensionImageType, and Get-AzureVMExtensionImage cmdlets to retrieve a list of valid extension versions:

First of all, we need to ensure we are logged in with the correct account:

```
PS C:\Users\StuartPreston> Login-AzureRmAccount
```

A web page will be presented, allowing you to sign in with your Organizational ID. You should then be logged in, and presented your account information:

```
Environment          : AzureCloud
Account              : stuart@pendrica.com
Tenant               : 9c117323-abab-abab-abab-9ee430723ba3
Subscription         : 4801fa9d-cdcd-cdcd-cdcd-b265ff49ce21
CurrentStorageAccount :
```

We can now run the following command to get a list of the available Chef Azure VM Extension versions (you will need to substitute the -Location parameter value with the *region* you are interested in):

```
PS C:\Users\StuartPreston> Get-AzureRmVMImagePublisher -Location "West Europe" | where
PublisherName -eq 'Chef.Bootstrap.WindowsAzure' | Get-AzureRmVMExtensionImageType |
Get-AzureRmVmExtensionImage | Select Type, Version | Format-Table -AutoSize
```

```
Type             Version
----             -------
CentosChefClient 11.12.4.2
CentosChefClient 11.14.6.1
ChefClient       11.10.4
ChefClient       11.12.0.0
ChefClient       11.18.6.2
ChefClient       1207.12.3.0
ChefClient       1210.12.100.1000
ChefClient       1210.12.4.1000
LinuxChefClient  11.18.6.2
LinuxChefClient  1207.12.3.0
LinuxChefClient  1210.12.100.1000
LinuxChefClient  1210.12.4.2000
```

■ **Note**   If you have been paying close attention, you will see that both Azure-cli and PowerShell approaches return the full version number of the extension (e.g., 1210.12.100.1000). When specifying the version in an ARM template, we need to specify only the Major and Minor versions in the template (e.g., 1210.12).

Adding a Chef VM Extension to an Existing Virtual Machine

The Chef VM extension can be added to machines individually from the command line using either the Azure-cli or PowerShell.

■ **Note** At the time of writing there is no way of achieving this through the management portal.

To add a Chef VM extension to an existing VM from the command line we will need to supply two configuration files, one called `publicSettings.config` and one called `privateSettings.config`. The difference between the two files is that `privateSettings.config` contains values you would like to keep secret - any settings entered here are hidden from all Azure logging and only made available to the target machine.

■ **Hint** Many of the values required for the configuration files can be found in the knife.rb file that you downloaded with the Starter Kit (see chapter 1 for more details).

---

publicSettings.config

Here is the template that needs to be used for the `publicSettings.config` file, and the description of each key can be seen in Table 3-2:

```
{
  "bootstrap_options": {
    "chef_node_name":"<your node name>",
    "chef_server_url":"<your chef server url>",
    "validation_client_name":"<your chef organization validation client name>"
  },
  "runlist":"<your run list>"
}
```

Table 3-2. Chef VM Extensions publicSettings.config settings

Key Name	Description	Example Value
chef_node_name	This needs to be set to the name you wish to register with the Chef Server.	VM
chef_server_url	This is the Chef server URL to register the node with.	`https://api.chef.io/organizations/myorganization`
validation_client_name	This is the name of the validation key (usually the same as the filename without -validator.pem).	`myorganization`
runlist	This is the initial runlist to add to the node. This runlist will be deployed when the machine has first run.	`recipe[starter::default]`

privateSettings.config

Here is the template that needs to be used for the `privateSettings.config` file, the description of each key can be seen in Table 3-3:

```
{
    "validation_key": "<your chef organization validation key>"
}
```

Table 3-3. *Chef VM Extensions privateSettings.config settings*

Key Name	Description	Example Value
validation_key	This is the extracted text from the organization-validator.pem file. Each line ending should be replaced with "\n" so that it fits into a single string	`<see example>`

Converting a Multiline Key to a String Suitable for JSON

The JSON format does not deal well with the concept of multiline strings, so we must convert our key to a single line string that is delimited with "\n". Ruby offers a quick way of accomplishing this, by using the following snippet. Simply replace cert.pem with the path to the certificate you wish to convert to a single line with explicit line breaks.

```
PS C:\Users\StuartPreston> chef exec ruby -e 'p ARGF.read' cert.pem
```

"-----BEGIN RSA PRIVATE KEY-----\nMIIEpAIBAAKCAQEAlSvQ/TcQVLHlGAo5im3eS79BbtJJ5j/
CON5aXF7IwjnMOLtw\nMsn/i1qdV1mMUTuPrCFkQYaOcK5gIkqld15DXjv7y6tnvxlxkCUHaALfNx23Q9J/\nJR
2o3INyliGgW9RlBBTSZ916Lm1ur+K35fDn3TmPKszVnPwpPmqn7aWSbjd8MhMc\nISlTawIUaYVNadEK6ba4bf6
uztOVekP6RGw68O7dOqnO+YFNuuclqyMDoozXrHsc\nzpd6jNEMvlzGrUTlP+6jhvDACOQsoNq1sONNdTXsABce
c6TmTNy/1REeGiFOAxfT\nlB1vo3Z2On34oFbmYLUlsqzRhmtdXmAy7MBOgwIDAQABAoIBAF8BhR2AOHngw1RI\
nTtWHnCkKKpZ2gHKQ8Xct5scl5x8syPG4L4FpfcQ3djaH5gJmuN6cdcn19Qp3ROsS\nN8iK1MVT1s6k4HKptdZ
kfw8TpS7pUitOCV6OQVoQrg5IZGWYJK4wxME6IfMn53NG\nJnHguQwA+Nn9k59kSrBiJYoKBfUDkLq8CzRLKXDF
QtfFwxUO+Gei7ClB6dPcUADC\nbvti/crAK3n/6MXoxTGyRNZvKYdxTwV2ZKd2QWT/2oiAnOzS6Qo4mnTMPQvH
T93h\nbqcm58ELJAEaUkmb/h/7rMdH7mDmKBv4wr8LRyqPIiLDcGF/88UzkdgxxVu/Il09\ng92qnqECgYEAxV1
B5ta4LfmNwPhEu9e9JVpYY73ONWteV+TbZHC1pwLZy6SnSLa8\nScgu7t+wcJ/\nZX7nNkwybuNmVOh+iCwQUVN
92zbOcytDvRF/ODrzkh/px5RIXqF+pP3pXMbNbyRF\nOxYpv6JyNo94NJI5h114s4HDTogeyq82A2pm5Bs2YO/
iFINJIlW/nyB+OixxM+C5\n5sqFWrWmaEulo67tuDTGGXMiArSQYI/ItJdWn7cCgYEAmW36QX5DCFqsvItEw9Lf\
nlB48AK4ZlKW3XhToCZklXoRO1D9YXMrSbXlWIxV6kNOLXuXJXGoIEoVPJgP98NO\nGIO56HmqQNmiV48yTTit
YWG9detxa2LXHCPQLXqwAxAkagmR7G1evGH9JXbGVmWX\nKLJUWqmvVG2OsNYcg8u4ylECgYBrK7cjKKNQg+v7V6E
6rnxHWIDBSwmO/mVv1Srz\n8lllMQHwkhSfIxbis3i+UpWLeeIYCXL/QOtkhcnVRqpCFCwhOji81MclHGhRw7Kb\
nObg76Ia6MqR6OCOWA4Db1teTyUH6hiLyHoK2t56wbhYVD7NEMJb5Sbgw32qIOZtN\nny/WDCQKBgQC+adlpcO6RQuL
EuyxXH9aFQi3FRXBjK3Op+8nN1IlW7kfLNkkkKsez\nZII47UkrboVTxaZRmEfTkcJzANNft9gxMz9EjiSJOXOKG/+
v4bNiP1mjUJlIfhlQ\n9Tq7asOu8NV5BCds/S6VKiVoznhVCzkSH5mwczJSgoJwMeg4QVAHDw==\n-----END RSA
PRIVATE KEY-----"

You can now copy and paste this single string into the correct location in the privateSetting.config JSON file.

Now that we have our settings files we can use the azure vm extension set command (Azure-cli) or Set-AzureRmVMExtension cmdlet (PowerShell) to add the extension to an existing VM:

Azure-cli

Assuming we have a resource group named **chefazure-ch03** and a VM named **ch03-vm**, then the command to execute to add the Windows **ChefClient** would look similar to the following:

```
PS C:\Users\StuartPreston\chefazure-ch03> azure vm extension set --public-config-path pu
blicsettings.config --private-config-path privatesettings.config chefazure-ch03 ch03-vm
ChefClient Chef.Bootstrap.WindowsAzure 1210.12
```

```
info:    Executing command vm extension set
+ Looking up the VM "ch03-vm"
+ Installing extension "ChefClient", VM: "ch03-vm"
info:    vm extension set command OK
```

PowerShell

To add the Chef VM Extension using PowerShell we use the Set-AzureRmVMExtension cmdlet. Again, with an existing resource group named **chefazure-ch03** and a VM named **ch03-vm**, then the command to execute to add the Windows **ChefClient** would look similar to the following:

```
PS C:\Users\StuartPreston\chefazure-ch03> $settings = gc .\publicSettings.config -raw
PS C:\Users\StuartPreston\chefazure-ch03> $protectedSettings =
gc .\privateSettings.config -raw
PS C:\Users\StuartPreston\chefazure-ch03> Set-AzureRmVMExtension -ResourceGroupName
chefazure-ch03 -Name ChefClient -VMName ch03-vm -Publisher Chef.Bootstrap.WindowsAzure
-ExtensionType ChefClient -TypeHandlerVersion 1210.12 -Location "West Europe" -SettingString
$settings -ProtectedSettingString $protectedSettings
```

Note that there will be a delay before the result is returned:

```
Status               : Succeeded
StatusCode           : OK
RequestId            : f2a51388-93a8-4fd7-858d-d30864f3e98b
Output               :
Error                :
StartTime            : 19/10/2015 21:52:15 +01:00
EndTime              : 19/10/2015 21:55:08 +01:00
TrackingOperationId  : cd985541-fec4-4e43-88e2-91825f35f616
```

Validating a Chef VM Extension is successfully installed at the Command Line

Next you will want to ensure that the Chef VM Extension is successfully installed. There are a variety of ways this can be achieved. First of all, the extension status can be viewed in the portal. From the command line, the azure vm extension command allows us to retrieve properties about a provisioned Chef VM Extension:

Azure Management Portal

If all went well you should be able to navigate via **Browse All** to your VM, navigate to **All Settings** and then **Extensions** to see that the Chef Client extension is installed successfully, as shown in Figure 3-2 below.

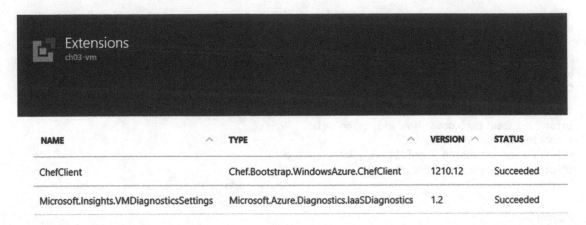

NAME	TYPE	VERSION	STATUS
ChefClient	Chef.Bootstrap.WindowsAzure.ChefClient	1210.12	Succeeded
Microsoft.Insights.VMDiagnosticsSettings	Microsoft.Azure.Diagnostics.IaaSDiagnostics	1.2	Succeeded

Figure 3-2. *Viewing the status of VM Extensions in the management portal*

To verify that the node has registered itself, we can visit the Hosted Chef management portal in a browser, and the default tab *Nodes* should be showing the new node. Figure 3-3 shows this.

Figure 3-3. *Chef Server showing registered node*

There are many more options available in the Chef management portal for configuring your nodes; for example, you may be asking yourself why is Environment set to _default? We will discuss this when we look at productionizing your workloads in chapter 7.

Azure-cli

In order to verify the installation of a Chef VM Extension using Azure-cli we use the `azure vm extension get` command:

```
PS C:\Users\StuartPreston\chefazure-ch03> azure vm extension get chefazure-ch03 ch03-vm
```

```
info: Executing command vm extension get
+ Looking up the VM "ch03-vm"
data: Publisher                   Name                                   Version
State
data: -------------------------   -------------------------------       -------  ---------
data: Chef.Bootstrap.WindowsAzure ChefClient                            1210.12 Succeeded
data: Microsoft.Azure.Diagnostics Microsoft.Insights.VMDiagnosticsSettings 1.2     Succeeded
info: vm extension get command OK
```

To get more detailed information such as the provisioning state of the extension, we need to use the `--json` flag, which returns us full details of the resource:

```
PS C:\Users\StuartPreston\chefazure-ch03> azure vm extension get chefazure-ch03 ch03-vm
--json
```

```
[
  {
    "tags": {},
    "publisher": "Chef.Bootstrap.WindowsAzure",
    "extensionType": "ChefClient",
    "typeHandlerVersion": "1210.12",
    "autoUpgradeMinorVersion": false,
    "settings": {
      "bootstrap_options": {
        "chef_node_name": "ch03-vm",
        "chef_server_url": "https://api.chef.io/organizations/pendemowin",
        "validation_client_name": "pendemowin-validator"
      },
      "runlist": "recipe[dscdemo::default]"
    },
    "provisioningState": "Succeeded",
    "id": "/subscriptions/b6e7eee9-YOUR-GUID-HERE-03ab624df016/resourceGroups/chefazure-
ch03/providers/Microsoft.Compute/virtualMachines/ch03-vm/extensions/ChefClient",
    "name": "ChefClient",
    "type": "Microsoft.Compute/virtualMachines/extensions",
    "location": "westeurope"
  },
```

```
{
    "tags": {},
    "publisher": "Microsoft.Azure.Diagnostics",
    "extensionType": "IaaSDiagnostics",
    "typeHandlerVersion": "1.2",
    "autoUpgradeMinorVersion": false,
    "settings": {
        "xmlCfg": "removed for brevity"",
        "storageAccount": "chefazurech033545"
    },
    "provisioningState": "Succeeded",
    "id": "/subscriptions/b6e7eee9-YOUR-GUID-HERE-03ab624df016/resourceGroups/chefazure-
    ch03/providers/Microsoft.Compute/virtualMachines/ch03-vm/extensions/Microsoft.
    Insights.VMDiagnosticsSettings",
    "name": "Microsoft.Insights.VMDiagnosticsSettings",
    "type": "Microsoft.Compute/virtualMachines/extensions",
    "location": "westeurope"
}
]
```

From the output, we are able to validate all the non-protected settings (protected settings are settable only, and not retrievable after deployment). We can identify from the **provisioningState** key that the deployment of the Chef VM Extensions was successful.

PowerShell

When using PowerShell, we can verify the extension is installed by using the Get-AzureRmVMExtension cmdlet, as follows (again it is assumed the Resource Group Name is **chefazure-ch03** and the VM Name is **ch03-vm**).

```
PS C:\Users\StuartPreston\chefazure-ch03> Get-AzureRmVMExtension -ResourceGroupName chef
azure-ch03 -VMName ch03-vm -Name ChefClient | Select Name, TypeHandlerVersion,
ProvisioningState
```

Name	TypeHandlerVersion	ProvisioningState
ChefClient	1210.12	Succeeded

Removing a Chef VM Extension from a Virtual Machine

Let's assume that we wish to remove the extension from a VM again. To accomplish this task, we can use either Azure-cli or PowerShell:

Azure-cli

To remove the Chef extension using the Azure-cli we use the azure vm extension set command with the -u parameter:

```
PS C:\Users\StuartPreston\chefazure-ch03> azure vm extension set -u -q chefazure-ch03
ch03-vm ChefClient Chef.Bootstrap.WindowsAzure 1210.12
```

```
info:    Executing command vm extension set
+ Looking up the VM "ch03-vm"
+ Looking up extension "ChefClient", VM: "ch03-vm"
+ Uninstalling extension "ChefClient", VM: "ch03-vm"
info:    vm extension set command OK
```

PowerShell

To remove the Chef extension using PowerShell we use the Remove-AzureRmVMExtension cmdlet:

```
PS C:\Users\StuartPreston\chefazure-ch03> Remove-AzureRmVMExtension -ResourceGroupName
chefazure-ch03 -VMName ch03-vm -Name ChefClient -Force
```

After a few minutes, this should succeed with the following message:

```
Status               : Succeeded
StatusCode           : OK
RequestId            : e0202987-d642-4698-9f2a-c6eb0f59c7cd
Output               :
Error                :
StartTime            : 19/10/2015 22:15:32 +01:00
EndTime              : 19/10/2015 22:19:22 +01:00
TrackingOperationId  : 7cd45cf9-702d-437-b314-66ca2cc2e27f
```

Installing a Chef VM Extension at the Command Line Using Azure Resource Manager Template Language

Although it is relatively simple to deploy the Chef VM Extension from within the management portal, you are more likely to want to automate this from the command line. We can do this by using Azure Resource Manager. Remember that the Chef VM Extension is essentially another resource so we can define it in the JSON and add it to the collection of resources to deploy.

Here's a template that shows us the options available with the Chef VM Extension:

```
{
    "type": "Microsoft.Compute/virtualMachines/extensions",
    "name": "[concat(parameters('vmName'),'/', 'chefExtension')]",
    "apiVersion": "2015-05-01-preview",
    "location": "[parameters('location')]",
    "dependsOn": [
      "[concat('Microsoft.Compute/virtualMachines/', parameters('vmName'))]"
    ],
```

```
"properties": {
    "publisher": "Chef.Bootstrap.WindowsAzure",
    "type": "<configurable>",
    "typeHandlerVersion": "<configurable>",
    "settings": {
        "bootstrap_options": {
            "chef_node_name" : "<configurable>",
            "chef_server_url" : "<configurable>",
            "validation_client_name" : "<configurable>"
        },
        "runlist": "<configurable>"
    },
    "protectedSettings": {
            "validation_key": "<configurable>"
    }
}
}
```

This fragment of JSON can then be taken and inserted as a resource in a Resource Manager template. The configurable options are shown in Table 3-4:

Table 3-4. *Chef VM Extensions configuration options*

Key Name	Description	Example Value
type	One of *ChefClient*, *LinuxChefClient*, or *CentosChefClient* depending on whether you use Windows, Ubuntu/Debian, or RedHat/CentOS.	ChefClient
typeHandlerVersion	This is the version of the extension, just the major and minor parts.	1210.12
chef_node_name	This needs to be set to the name you wish to register with the Chef Server.	VM
chef_server_url	This is the Chef server URL to register the node with.	https://api.chef.io/organizations/myorganization
validation_client_name	This is the name of the validation key (usually the same as the filename without -validator.pem).	myorganization
runlist	This is the initial runlist to add to the node. This runlist will be deployed when the machine has first run.	recipe[starter::default]
validation_key	This is the extracted text from the organization-validator.pem file.	<see example>

You can then use either the Azure-cli or PowerShell or one of the methods shown later in this book to deploy this template. Remember that the Chef VM Extensions install themselves as a service by default on the Windows platform. Chef VM Extensions are used extensively in the Chef Provisioning driver so we will be referring to terminology from this chapter later in the book.

Summary

In this chapter, we showed you how using the Chef VM Extensions can save you time and effort when compared to bootstrapping virtual machines via their public IP address. We demonstrated how to add, verify, and remove the VM Extension from Azure-cli and PowerShell and showed you how to build an ARM resource that adds the extension to an existing VM.

■ ■ ■

## CHAPTER 4

Using Chef Provisioning to Provision Machines

Chef Provisioning is a part of the Chef toolset that orchestrates the creation of machines and supporting infrastructure, particularly in the cloud but also for on-premises infrastructure too. It lets you define your application topology in an infrastructure-as-code way via one or more Chef recipes. This is particularly powerful in today's world of continuous delivery where we need fast feedback cycles - the ability to create, destroy, and re-create entire environments from scratch gives us flexibility, reliability, and repeatability; and as we know this eventually helps organizations reduce their time to market and lower support overheads by reducing recovery times.

Chef Provisioning operates a driver model so that it can communicate with different cloud providers and software platforms. There are Chef Provisioning drivers not only for Microsoft Azure but for Amazon Web Services (AWS), OpenStack, VMWare vSphere, Docker, and others too. See https://github.com/chef/chef-provisioning for a comprehensive list.

In this chapter we'll make sure your local machine is configured for Chef Provisioning, describe the resources available for use, explore the options that are configurable on Azure, and run a couple of recipes to demonstrate the concepts of provisioning resources in Azure using Chef.

In chapter 5 we'll enhance these recipes and look at examples of more sophisticated architectures that you can deploy using Chef Provisioning. Once you've mastered all that, in chapter 8 we'll explore the end-to-end world of continuous provisioning and set up a continuous delivery pipeline using Chef on Azure.

About Chef Provisioning on Azure

Before we delve into the implementation specifics of the driver, Figure 4-1 shows the architecture of the Chef Provisioning driver for Azure Resource Manager.

© Stuart Preston 2016
S. Preston, *Using Chef with Microsoft Azure*, DOI 10.1007/978-1-4842-1476-3_4

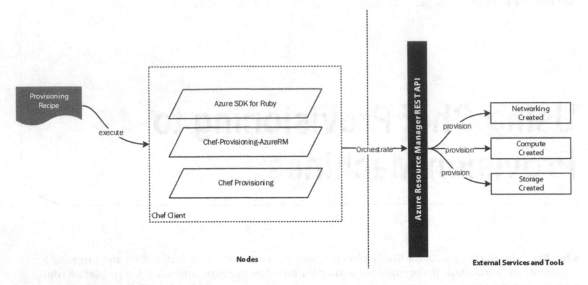

Figure 4-1. *Overview of Chef Provisioning and Azure*

The Chef Provisioning driver for Azure is heavily dependent on the Azure SDK for Ruby, which provides helpful functionality to support modeling, authentication, threading, and error handling. The driver communicates with the Azure Resource Manager REST APIs, which then take on the hard work of dealing with idempotency, creating resources in the correct order and reporting status. Behind the scenes a set of Resource Providers are responsible for each operation they are handed to do. The Azure SDK for Ruby runs on Windows, OS X, and Linux.

Installation and Configuration

We're going to be using our local workstation as a 'provisioning node' for this example, and we'll configure it to talk to the organization on the hosted Chef server that you created in chapter 1. This is so that we can upload provisioning recipes and have the provisioned resources communicate with that same organization continuously after that. The provisioning node will be communicating with both the Chef Server and the Azure Management API over TLS (port TCP/443).

Installing the Chef Provisioning for Azure Resource Manager Ruby Gem

Chef Provisioning for Azure Resource Manager has the following dependencies that must be installed before we can start to build our recipes:

- Chef Client

- Chef Provisioning

Both of the above components were installed when we installed the ChefDK in chapter 1. So if you are reading this and don't have the ChefDK installed, now would be a good time to go back and install it.

To verify we have all the required components, we can use the `chef gem list` command to view the Ruby gems that are installed:

```
PS C:\Users\StuartPreston> chef gem list --local chef
```

```
*** LOCAL GEMS ***

chef (12.5.1 universal-mingw32)
chef-config (12.5.1)
chef-dk (0.10.0)
chef-provisioning (1.5.0)
chef-provisioning-aws (1.6.1)
chef-provisioning-azure (0.4.0)
chef-provisioning-fog (0.15.0)
chef-provisioning-vagrant (0.10.0)
chef-vault (2.6.1)
chef-zero (4.3.2, 1.5.6)
cheffish (1.6.0)
chefspec (4.4.0)
```

If you see **chef** and **chef-provisioning** in the list, we're ready to carry on. Otherwise, you'll need to investigate why, and possibly reinstall the ChefDK (see chapter 1 for detailed instructions on how to do this).

We can now install the **chef-provisioning-azurerm** gem and its dependencies by using the following command:

```
PS C:\Users\StuartPreston> chef gem install chef-provisioning-azurerm
```

```
Fetching: concurrent-ruby-1.0.0.pre1.gem (100%)
Successfully installed concurrent-ruby-1.0.0.pre1
Fetching: timeliness-0.3.7.gem (100%)
Successfully installed timeliness-0.3.7
Fetching: ms_rest-0.1.1.gem (100%)
Successfully installed ms_rest-0.1.1
Fetching: faraday-cookie_jar-0.0.6.gem (100%)
Successfully installed faraday-cookie_jar-0.0.6
Fetching: ms_rest_azure-0.1.1.gem (100%)
Successfully installed ms_rest_azure-0.1.1
Fetching: azure_mgmt_resources-0.1.0.gem (100%)
Successfully installed azure_mgmt_resources-0.1.0
Successfully installed chef-provisioning-azurerm-0.3.1
Parsing documentation for concurrent-ruby-1.0.0.pre1
Installing ri documentation for concurrent-ruby-1.0.0.pre1
Parsing documentation for timeliness-0.3.7
Installing ri documentation for timeliness-0.3.7
Parsing documentation for ms_rest-0.1.1
Installing ri documentation for ms_rest-0.1.1
```

```
Parsing documentation for faraday-cookie_jar-0.0.6
Installing ri documentation for faraday-cookie_jar-0.0.6
Parsing documentation for ms_rest_azure-0.1.1
Installing ri documentation for ms_rest_azure-0.1.1
Parsing documentation for azure_mgmt_resources-0.1.0
Installing ri documentation for azure_mgmt_resources-0.1.0
Parsing documentation for chef-provisioning-azurerm-0.3.1
Installing ri documentation for chef-provisioning-azurerm-0.3.1
Done installing documentation for concurrent-ruby, timeliness, ms_rest,
faraday-cookie_jar, ms_rest_azure, azure_mgmt_resources, chef-provisioning-azurerm
after 12 seconds
7 gems installed
```

If you see output similar to the above, then that's all we need from an installation perspective, and we can now progress on to configuring our node with the credentials required to connect to Azure. If not, you'll need to stop at this point and troubleshoot.

Authenticating to Azure Resource Manager

Azure Resource Manager operates a claims-based authorization, meaning that every request sent to Azure needs to be accompanied with a token. Luckily for us this is dealt with behind the scenes; however we do need to configure a special type of object in Azure Active Directory for automation called a Service Principal.

A Service Principal is able to have permissions delegated to it so it can perform actions on your Azure subscription. Why can't we just use a username and password? The primary advantage a Service Principal has over using a standard User object in Azure Active Directory is that a Service Principal is not subject to any restrictions when multifactor authentication is enabled.

Azure Resource Manager has Role-based Access Control (RBAC) measures built into it; this is a flexible system that allows fine-grained access management and allows only the necessary access required to perform tasks. RBAC can be applied to individual resources, to a Resource Group, or to a Subscription if required. That is what we are most interested in.

So in the following example, we're going to grant our **Service Principal** the **Owner** permission on our **Subscription A**. This is depicted in Figure 4-2 below.

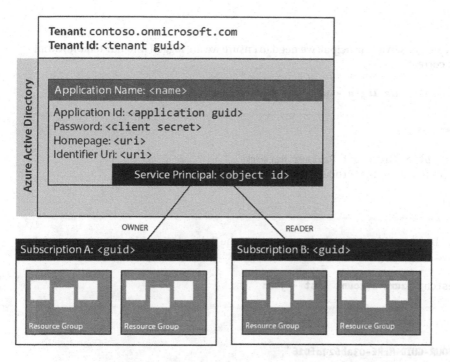

Figure 4-2. *Service Principal in Azure Directory with specific rights against Subscriptions*

■ **Note**   If you are interested in reading up on Role-based Access Control, have a read of
https://azure.microsoft.com/en-us/documentation/articles/role-based-access-control-configure

---

Service Principals are objects that are attached to Applications within Azure Active Directory, and we use the ID of the Service Principal to assign a role against the relevant Subscription. So we have four things to achieve in order to complete this task:

1. **Authenticate**/Log in to Azure

2. Create an **Application**

3. Create a **Service Principal** for the Application

4. Assign the Service Principal to a valid **Role** on a Subscription

Configuring the Application and Service Principal

We can use either the cross-platform Azure-cli tool or PowerShell to configure the Application and add a Service Principal. In this section we will demonstrate both approaches.

Azure-cli

To use the Azure-cli to create our service principal, we need to ensure we are logged into our tenant within Azure Resource Manager correctly:

```
PS C:\Users\StuartPreston> azure login --username stuart@pendrica.com
```

```
info:     Executing command login
Password: **********
/ info:     Added subscription Microsoft Partner Network
info:     Added subscription Pendrica Production
+
info:     login command OK
```

At this point, it would be a good idea to get the **Tenant Id** and the **Subscription Id** and make a note of them. This can be achieved by running azure account list --json and inspecting the output:

```
PS C:\Users\StuartPreston> azure account list --json
```

```
[
  {
    "id": "b6e7eee9-YOUR-GUID-HERE-03ab624df016",
    "name": "Microsoft Partner Network",
    "user": {
      "name": "stuart@pendrica.com",
      "type": "user"
    },
    "tenantId": "9c117323-YOUR-GUID-HERE-9ee430723ba3",
    "state": "Enabled",
    "isDefault": true,
    "registeredProviders": [],
    "environmentName": "AzureCloud",
    "managementEndpointUrl": https://management.core.windows.net
  },
  {
    "id": "bcf669fc-YOUR-GUID-HERE-e2d1f9f4b1c3",
    "name": "Pendrica Production",
    "user": {
      "name": "stuart@pendrica.com",
      "type": "user"
    },
    "tenantId": "9c117323-YOUR-GUID-HERE-9ee430723ba3",
    "state": "Enabled",
    "isDefault": false,
    "registeredProviders": [],
    "environmentName": "AzureCloud",
    "managementEndpointUrl": https://management.core.windows.net
  }
]
```

As we can see the **Tenant ID** is **9c117323-YOUR-GUID-HERE-9ee430723ba3** and the **Subscription ID** we are interested in is **b6e7eee9-YOUR-GUID-HERE-03ab624df016**. Keep these values safe as we'll use them shortly.

We can then create the new application by using the azure `ad app create` command; note that the --home-page and --identified-uris must be specified even though we won't actually use them later on. The --password option is used to set a shared secret and will be used later on so make a note of it.

```
PS C:\Users\StuartPreston> azure ad app create --name "automation-chef" --home-page
"http://chef.io" --identifier-uris "https://pendrica.com/automation-chef" --password
"my-top-secret-password"
```

```
info:    Executing command ad app create
+ Creating application automation-chef
data:    Application Id:            02a2ba0d-YOUR-GUID-HERE-0e7cd312d62b
data:    Application Object Id:     cafac4ae-YOUR-GUID-HERE-2d8b6eb2d21c
data:    Application Permissions:
data:                              claimValue:  user_impersonation
data:                              description:  Allow the application to access
                                   automation-chef on behalf of the signed-in user.
data:                              directAccessGrantTypes:
data:                              displayName:  Access automation-chef
data:                              impersonationAccessGrantTypes:  impersonated=User,
                                   impersonator=Application
data:                              isDisabled:
data:                              origin:  Application
data:                              permissionId:  6c98e9b7-YOUR-GUID-HERE-6c62693c5c4
data:                              resourceScopeType:  Personal
data:                              userConsentDescription:  Allow the application to access
                                   automation-chef on your behalf.
data:                              userConsentDisplayName:  Access automation-chef
data:                              lang:
info:    ad app create command OK
```

By creating an application, we are returned an **Application Id**; we'll need this to configure Chef Provisioning later on, so make a note of it. The next thing we'll need to do is create our Service Principal for our application. For this we need to pass in the **Application Id** at the command line:

```
PS C:\Users\StuartPreston> azure ad sp create 02a2ba0d-YOUR-GUID-HERE-0e7cd312d62b
```

```
info:    Executing command ad sp create
+ Creating service principal for application 02a2ba0d-YOUR-GUID-HERE-0e7cd312d62b
data:    Object Id:                 c49c3e61-70a9-4af4-86d1-86c61ab2f428
data:    Display Name:              automation-chef
data:    Service Principal Names:
data:                              02a2ba0d-YOUR-GUID-HERE-0e7cd312d62b
data:                              https://pendrica.com/automation-chef
info:    ad sp create command OK
```

This time, we were returned an **Object Id** for our Service Principal, which we will use to assign a role. For this we need azure role assignment create command passing in the **Object Id** and **Subscription Id** as shown below:

```
PS C:\Users\StuartPreston> azure role assignment create --objectId c49c3e61-70a9-4af4-8
6d1-86c61ab2f428 -o Owner -c /subscriptions/b6e7eee9-YOUR-GUID-HERE-03ab624df016
```

```
info:    Executing command role assignment create
+ Finding role with specified name
data:    RoleAssignmentId    : /subscriptions/b6e7eee9-YOUR-GUID-HERE-03ab624df016/
providers/Microsoft.Authorization/roleAssignments/53c94040-YOUR-GUID-HERE-cabe8abd6560
data:    RoleDefinitionName  : Owner
data:    RoleDefinitionId    : 8e3af657-YOUR-GUID-HERE-2fe8c4bcb635
data:    Scope               : /subscriptions/b6e7eee9-YOUR-GUID-HERE-03ab624df016
data:    Display Name        : automation-chef
data:    SignInName          :
data:    ObjectId            : c49c3e61-YOUR-GUID-HERE-86c61ab2f428
data:    ObjectType          : ServicePrincipal
```

We should now have a working Service Principal with access to the subscription. To verify that we can log in, we use the **Application Id** and **Tenant Id** (obtained from azure account list) along with the password for the application and the --service-principal option:

```
PS C:\Users\StuartPreston> azure login -u 02a2ba0d-YOUR-GUID-HERE-0e7cd312d62b -p "my-top-
secret-password" --service-principal --tenant 9c117323-YOUR-GUID-HERE-9ee430723ba3
```

```
info:    Executing command login
/info:       Added subscription Microsoft Partner Network
+
info:    login command OK
```

PowerShell

Let's set up a Service Principal using PowerShell now, following the same pattern as described above. First of all, we need to log in to Azure using the **Login-AzureRmAccount** cmdlet:

```
PS C:\Users\StuartPreston> Login-AzureRmAccount
```

You will be asked to authenticate using a browser-based form; then you should receive the below output or similar:

```
Environment           : AzureCloud
Account               : stuart@pendrica.com
TenantId              : 9c117323-YOUR-GUID-HERE-9ee430723ba3
SubscriptionId        : b6e7eee9-YOUR-GUID-HERE-03ab624df016
CurrentStorageAccount :
```

As you can see, we are presented the TenantId and the SubscriptionId upon login; we'll need both of these later so make a note of them. We can now progress to create an application using the New-AzureRmADApplication cmdlet:

```
PS C:\Users\StuartPreston> $app = New-AzureRmADApplication -DisplayName "automation-chef2"
-HomePage "http://chef.io" -IdentifierUris "https://pendrica.com/automation-chef2" -Password
"my-top-secret-password"
```

If we examine **$app** we can see we are returned an ApplicationId that we can use:

```
PS C:\Users\StuartPreston> $app
```

```
Type                   : Application
ApplicationId          : 5f2536db-YOUR-GUID-HERE-db080287b58a
ApplicationObjectId    : 094a1477-YOUR-GUID-HERE-291432050fdb
AvailableToOtherTenants : False
AppPermissions         : {{
                             "claimValue": "user_impersonation",
                             "description": "Allow the application to access automation-chef2
on behalf of the
                         signed-in user.",
                             "directAccessGrantTypes": [],
                             "displayName": "Access automation-chef2",
                             "impersonationAccessGrantTypes": [
                               {
                                 "impersonated": "User",
                                 "impersonator": "Application"
                               }
                             ],
                             "isDisabled": false,
                             "origin": "Application",
                             "permissionId": "43869379-YOUR-GUID-HERE-6f0fc7bfeae7",
                             "resourceScopeType": "Personal",
                             "userConsentDescription": "Allow the application to access
                         automation-chef2 on your behalf.",
                             "userConsentDisplayName": "Access automation-chef2",
                             "lang": null
                         }}
```

We can now create a service principal for the application using the New-AzureRmADServicePrincipal cmdlet:

```
PS C:\Users\StuartPreston> New-AzureRmADServicePrincipal -ApplicationId $app.ApplicationId
```

DisplayName	Type	ObjectId
automation-chef2		924895ba-YOUR-GUID-HERE-d1c8b4e208f2

Now we can assign the Owner role on the current subscription to the Service Principal using the New-AzureRmRoleAssignment cmdlet:

■ **Tip** Use the Select-AzureRmSubscription cmdlet if the subscription you want to grant access to is not the current one.

```
PS C:\Users\StuartPreston> New-AzureRmRoleAssignment -RoleDefinitionName Owner
-ServicePrincipalName $app. ApplicationId
```

```
RoleAssignmentId   : /subscriptions/b6e7eee9-YOUR-GUID-HERE-03ab624df016/providers/
                     Microsoft.Authorization/roleAssignme
                     nts/c3ee69b5-YOUR-GUID-HERE-afb8f5179d60
Scope              : /subscriptions/b6e7eee9-YOUR-GUID-HERE-03ab624df016
DisplayName        : automation-chef2
SignInName         :
RoleDefinitionName : Owner
RoleDefinitionId   : 8e3af657-YOUR-GUID-HERE-2fe8c4bcb635
ObjectId           : 924895ba-YOUR-GUID-HERE-d1c8b4e208f2
ObjectType         : ServicePrincipal
```

We can test this using Login-AzureRMAccount. We use the Application ID and the Password to create a credentials object:

```
PS C:\Users\StuartPreston> $creds = Get-Credentials
```

Then we can use these credentials as part of the Login request, passing in the **TenantId** we noted down earlier:

```
PS C:\Users\StuartPreston> Login-AzureRmAccount -Credential $creds -ServicePrincipal -Tenant
9c117323-YOUR-GUID-HERE-9ee430723ba3
```

```
Environment           : AzureCloud
Account               : 5f2536db-YOUR-GUID-HERE-db080287b58a
TenantId              : 9c117323-YOUR-GUID-HERE-9ee430723ba3
SubscriptionId        : b6e7eee9-YOUR-GUID-HERE-03ab624df016
CurrentStorageAccount :
```

We have completed the four stages to creating a Service Principal using the command-line tools. We now can proceed to use the values captured above in order to configure our provisioning node so it can authenticate correctly and gain access to the requested resources. We'll need the **Tenant Id**, **Subscription Id**, **Application Id** (otherwise known as a Client Id), and the **Password** (otherwise known as a Client Secret) from above.

Configuring Chef Provisioning for Authentication

Now that we have a Service Principal with delegated ownership permission on our Subscription, we need to configure the Chef Provisioning for Azure Resource Manager driver. The driver can read credentials from one of two locations:

1. A file located beneath the home directory of the user executing Chef Client

2. By reading in a set of environment variables

Here's how:

Configuring the Credentials File

Our credentials are stored in the ~/**.azure**/**credentials** file; let's create it and add a section for our subscription:

```
[b6e7eee9-YOUR-GUID-HERE-03ab624df016]          Do not enter these:
tenant_id = "9c117323-YOUR-GUID-HERE-9ee430723ba3"   <- Subscription ID
client_id = "02a2ba0d-YOUR-GUID-HERE-0e7cd312d62b"   <- Tenant ID
client_secret = "my-top-secret-password"        <- Application ID
                                                <- Application Password
```

Breaking this down, the first line [b6e7eee9-YOUR-GUID-HERE-03ab624df016] represents the **Subscription Id**, and is the connection between the Chef Provisioning recipe and Azure. The Tenant ID you will have already. In the credentials file the **client_id** and **client _secret** values are the Application Id and Password that were created above respectively. The Azure SDK for Ruby uses client_id and client_secret in its terminology (and error messages), which is why they are named like that.

■ **Note**   ~ (tilde) is an alias in most shells (including PowerShell) for the user's home directory. This is the equivalent of using $env:USERPROFILE in Windows PowerShell or $HOME in OS X or a Unix shell.

Environment Variable-based Configuration

If it is preferable in your environment to set up some Environment variables, the following can be used. In this case we do not need to set the Subscription ID, because we will be passed it by the recipe. However, it means we can only support one Subscription per host, unless your Service Principal is granted access to multiple subscriptions:

```
AZURE_CLIENT_ID="02a2ba0d-YOUR-GUID-HERE-0e7cd312d62b"
AZURE_CLIENT_SECRET="my-top-secret-password"
AZURE_TENANT_ID="9c117323-YOUR-GUID-HERE-9ee430723ba3"
```

All done? Great. Now we can progress onto writing recipes!

Preparing the Chef-Repo

To follow the examples, we will need the **.chef** folder from the Starter Kit that you downloaded in chapter 1, which is preconfigured with the private keys required to talk to the hosted Chef server and the validation key that allows us to register newly provisioned nodes against it.

Starting from your home directory, let's create a new repo for this chapter:

```
PS C:\Users\StuartPreston> chef generate app chefazure-ch04 --copyright "Stuart Preston"
--email "stuart@pendrica.com"
```

Copy the **.chef** folder from the Starter Kit zip file into the chefazure-ch04 folder.

We can now generate a new cookbook called **provision**. We do this with the chef generate cookbook command. Note that we start in the **chefazure-ch04** folder:

```
PS C:\Users\StuartPreston> cd chefazure-ch04
PS C:\Users\StuartPreston\chefazure-ch04> chef generate cookbook cookbooks/provision
--copyright "Stuart Preston" --email "stuart@pendrica.com"
```

```
Compiling Cookbooks...
Recipe: code_generator::cookbook
  * directory[C:/Users/StuartPreston/chefazure-ch04/cookbooks/provision] action create
    - create new directory C:/Users/StuartPreston/chefazure-ch04/cookbooks/provision
[...]
  * directory[C:/Users/StuartPreston/chefazure-ch04/cookbooks/provision/recipes] action
create
    - create new directory C:/Users/StuartPreston/chefazure-ch04/cookbooks/provision/recipes
  * template[C:/Users/StuartPreston/chefazure-ch04/cookbooks/provision/recipes/default.rb]
  action create_if_missing
    - create new file C:/Users/StuartPreston/chefazure-ch04/cookbooks/provision/recipes/
      default.rb
    - update content in file C:/Users/StuartPreston/chefazure-ch04/cookbooks/provision/
      recipes/default.rb from none to 505148
  (diff output suppressed by config)

PS C:\Users\StuartPreston\chefazure-ch04>
```

We can see by inspecting the output that a number of folders and files were created, including a **default.rb** recipe file. We'll be using that to describe the machines we want to create using Chef Provisioning.

When we want to begin integrating some quality tooling with Chef we'll need to use some more of these generated files, this will be covered later in chapter 6. For now, let's open the whole repo in our code editor of choice. I use Microsoft's **Visual Studio Code** but feel free to use your favorite editor:

```
PS C:\Users\StuartPreston\chef-repo> code .
```

Once the editor has launched, we can navigate to **cookbooks/provision/recipes/default.rb** as shown in the screenshot below and we're ready to add some provisioning code. Figure 4-3 shows the default.rb recipe opened in our text editor:

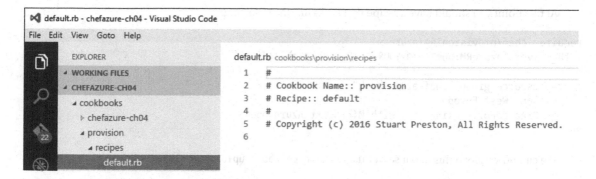

Figure 4-3. Visual Studio Code showing the default recipe in the provision cookbook

Chef Provisioning Recipes

In this section, we'll add to the blank recipe that is open and add the code required to define the resources we want to deploy. First of all, we need to tell Chef Provisioning that we're interested in the **AzureRM** driver and provide it the **Subscription ID** of the subscription we want to work with. This is accomplished by adding the following two lines to **default.rb**:

```
require 'chef/provisioning/azurerm'
with_driver 'AzureRM:b6e7eee9-YOUR-GUID-HERE-03ab624df016'
```

We're now ready to add our resources to our recipe. To start off with, let's create an **Azure Resource Group** in our subscription:

```
azure_resource_group "chef-azure-book" do
  location 'West Europe'
  tags CreatedFor: 'Using Chef with Microsoft Azure book'
end
```

The resource actually defines two actions **:create** and **:destroy** - we will cover the destroy action later in the chapter. **:create** is the default action so does not need to be specified in the recipe. The full list of parameters is shown below in Table 4-1:

Table 4-1. azure_resource_group resource options

Parameter Name	Description	Example Value
location	This is the location where the machine and storage account should be created. See chapter 2 for a list of all regions.	'West Europe'
tags	This is a comma-separated list of tag values to be applied to the resource group. Note that this field is not incremental - the tags on the target resource will be overwritten with the contents of this parameter each time the Chef client converges.	CreatedFor: 'Using Chef with Microsoft Azure book'

At this point you should have a recipe that looks like the following:

```
require 'chef/provisioning/azurerm'
with_driver 'AzureRM:b6e7eee9-YOUR-GUID-HERE-03ab624df016'

azure_resource_group "chef-azure-book" do
  location 'West Europe'
  tags CreatedFor: 'Using Chef with Microsoft Azure book'
end
```

We can now upload this to our server using `knife cookbook upload`:

```
PS C:\Users\StuartPreston\chefazure-ch04> knife cookbook upload provision
```

```
Uploading provision       [0.1.0]
Uploaded 1 cookbook.
```

Configuring the Provisioning Node as a Chef Client

We need to configure our workstation as a provisioning node in order to work with Azure. This is because when we send instructions to create resources in Azure, those resources need a real Chef Server to talk to. Unfortunately, we cannot use Chef Client in local mode for this scenario. So we're going to set up our workstation as a full Chef Client. Don't worry though: Chef Client will only run when we tell it to do so from the command line. There are three things we need to accomplish:

1. Copy the **organization-validator.pem** file from within your **.chef** folder to **c:\ chef** (Windows) or **/etc/chef** (OS X/Linux) depending on which platform you are on.

2. Copy the following lines from your **knife.rb** to **c:\chef\client.rb** or **/etc/chef/ client.rb** depending on your platform:

   ```
   current_dir = File.dirname(__FILE__)
   validation_client_name   "pendrica-chefazure-validator"
   validation_key           "#{current_dir}/pendrica-chefazure-validator.pem"
   chef_server_url          https://api.chef.io/organizations/pendrica-chefazure
   ```

3. At an administrative command prompt on Windows or via sudo on OS X and Linux, run `chef-client` once:

```
C:\WINDOWS\system32> chef-client
```

```
Starting Chef Client, version 12.5.1
Creating a new client identity for DESKTOP-TIDJ3S8 using the validator key.
resolving cookbooks for run list: []
Synchronizing Cookbooks:
Compiling Cookbooks...
[2015-11-15T09:48:47+00:00] WARN: Node DESKTOP-TIDJ3S8 has an empty run list.
Converging 0 resources
```

```
Running handlers:
Running handlers complete
Chef Client finished, 0/0 resources updated in 20 seconds
```

We can see that a new client identity has been created. Behind the scenes a new key, **client.pem,** was generated and stored locally in either **c:\chef** or **/etc/chef** depending on your platform.

If we log on to the hosted Chef Management interface at https://manage.chef.io with the credentials you created in chapter 1, then you'll be able to see our new 'node' created successfully as shown in Figure 4-4:

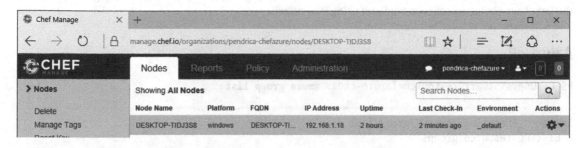

Figure 4-4. *Chef Management interface showing a new node has been created*

We can now proceed to use our local node to provision cloud resources.

Executing the Provisioning Recipe

We now have a cookbook that has been uploaded to the server, and a client that talks to the same server. But how does the provisioning node know which recipe to run?

Chef Client lets us specify the items that should be in the runlist itself using the -r or -o options. The -r option will persist the run-list to the server so that it would run next time whereas the -o option simply overrides the run-list for that run.

At this point we want the ability to control the run list from the client so we will specify the -o option to override the runlist for this run.

PS C:\Users\StuartPreston\chefazure-ch04> **chef-client -o recipe[provision::default]**

```
Starting Chef Client, version 12.5.1
[2015-11-15T10:12:49+00:00] WARN: Run List override has been provided.
[2015-11-15T10:12:49+00:00] WARN: Original Run List: []
[2015-11-15T10:12:49+00:00] WARN: Overridden Run List: [recipe[provision::default]]
[2015-11-15T10:12:50+00:00] WARN: chef-client doesn't have administrator privileges on node
DESKTOP-TIDJ3S8. This might cause unexpected resource failures.
resolving cookbooks for run list: ["provision::default"]
Synchronizing Cookbooks:
  - provision (0.1.0)
Compiling Cookbooks...
Converging 1 resources
Recipe: provision::default
  * azure_resource_group[chef-azure-book] action create
```

```
    - create or update Resource Group chef-azure-book
[2015-11-15T10:12:54+00:00] WARN: Skipping final node save because override_runlist
was given

Running handlers:
Running handlers complete
Chef Client finished, 1/1 resources updated in 27 seconds
```

We can see that our recipe was executed and the **azure_resource_group** resource took the **:create** action. To verify from the command line, we can use the azure group list command if using Azure-cli or the Get-AzureRmResourceGroup cmdlet if using PowerShell.

Azure-cli

```
PS C:\Users\StuartPreston\chefazure-ch04> azure group list
```

```
info:    Executing command group list
+ Listing resource groups
data:    Name            Location    Provisioning State    Tags:
data:    --------------  ----------  --------------------  ------------------------
data:    chef-azure-book  westeurope  Succeeded            CreatedFor=Using Chef with
                                                           Microsoft Azure book
[...]
info:    group list command OK
```

PowerShell

```
PS C:\Users\StuartPreston\chefazure-ch04> Get-AzureRmResourceGroup | Format-Table
```

```
ResourceGroupName         Location    ProvisioningState
-----------------         --------    -----------------
chef-azure-book           westeurope  Succeeded
```

Management Portal

We can also verify the creation of our resource group via the Azure Management Portal, as shown in Figure 4-5.

Figure 4-5. *Azure Management Portal showing the chef-azure-book Resource Group and tags*

It should be noted that if you were to change the tags option, and re-upload the cookbook and re-run the Chef client, the new tags would overwrite the first set that were uploaded. Now that we have verified the Resource Group exists, we can now add a Resource Template to our repository and execute it using the Chef client.

Chef Provisioning a Windows VM with Remote Desktop Enabled

We're ready to add an Azure Resource Manager template to our recipe and watch resources from it get provisioned.

There are many sources of Azure Resource Manager templates, from creating your own from scratch using the documentation, to predefined templates that others have created. A good library of predefined templates is available at `https://github.com/Azure/azure-quickstart-templates`

Let's find a template that we can use to demonstrate provisioning from Chef. In my example I use the one from `https://github.com/Azure/azure-quickstart-templates/tree/master/101-vm-with-rdp-port` as shown in Figure 4-6.

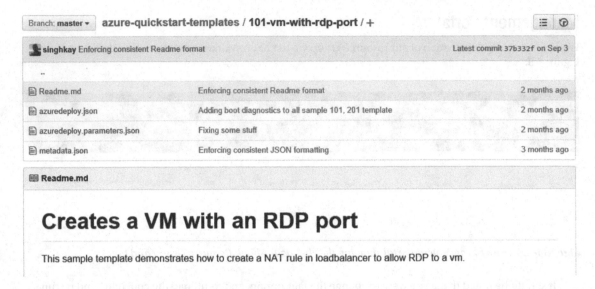

Figure 4-6. *GitHub page for our sample Windows VM*

Downloading the Template

Each template in the gallery has a file **azuredeploy.json** that contains the ARM template; let's download it by clicking on the link, making sure you click on the Raw button as shown in Figure 4-7. Then save the entire file into the location **cookbooks/provision/files/default/azuredeploy.json** within your repo.

Figure 4-7. *GitHub "Raw" button used to display the contents of a file in your browser*

We should now be able to navigate to and inspect the **azuredeploy.json** file in our code editor, as shown in Figure 4-8.

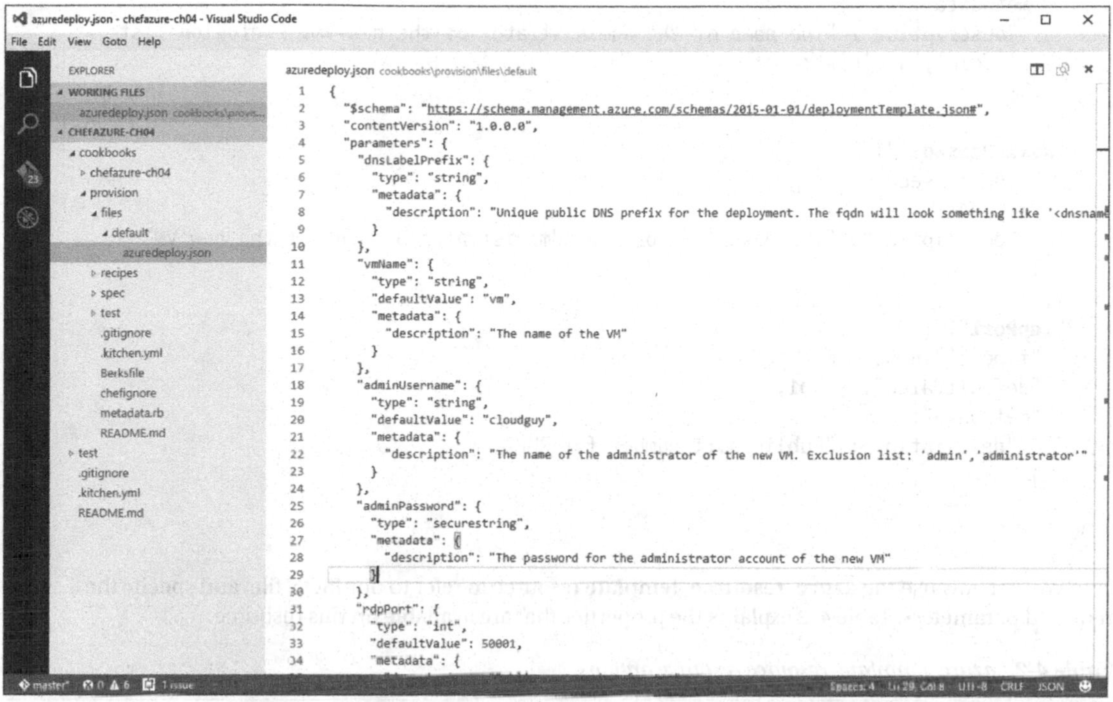

Figure 4-8. Viewing azuredeploy.json in a code editor

We shouldn't need to modify the **azuredeploy.json** file after this point; what we are interested in is the parameters. We need the names of all the parameters in order to add a resource to our Chef recipe. If we examine the parameters section of JSON we can see all the keys are the names of the parameters that we want to put in our recipe. I've highlighted them in bold below.

```
"parameters": {
    "dnsLabelPrefix": {
      "type": "string",
      "metadata": {
        "description": "Unique public DNS prefix for the deployment. The fqdn will look
          something like '<dnsname>.westus.cloudapp.azure.com'. Up to 62 chars, digits or
          dashes, lowercase, should start with a letter: must conform to '^[a-z][a-z0-9-]
          {1,61}[a-z0-9]$'."
      }
    },
    "vmName": {
      "type": "string",
      "defaultValue": "vm",
      "metadata": {
        "description": "The name of the VM"
      }
    },
```

```
"adminUsername": {
  "type": "string",
  "defaultValue": "cloudguy",
  "metadata": {
    "description": "The name of the administrator of the new VM. Exclusion list:
    'admin','administrator'"
  }
},
"adminPassword": {
  "type": "securestring",
  "metadata": {
    "description": "The password for the administrator account of the new VM"
  }
},
"rdpPort": {
  "type": "int",
  "defaultValue": 50001,
  "metadata": {
    "description": "Public port number for RDP"
  }
}
}
}
```

We can now use the **azure_resource_template** resource to refer to our JSON file, and specify the required parameters. Table 4-2 explains the properties that are available on this resource.

Table 4-2. *azure_template_resource resource options*

Parameter Name	Description	Example Value
resource_group	This is the name of the Azure Resource Group you want to provision your resources in.	'chef-azure-book'
template_source	This is the path to the ARM template you wish to deploy, relative to the root of the repo.	'cookbooks/provision/files/ default/azuredeploy.json'
parameters	This is an array of key/value pairs used to define parameters. The key names match the parameter names in the ARM template.	username: 'test', password: 'P2ssw0rd'
chef_extension	This is an array of key/value pairs used to determine whether a Chef VM Extension should be added to each Compute resource found in the ARM template.	client_type: 'ChefClient', version: '1210.12', runlist: 'role[webserver]'

Here's what our **azure_resource_template** recipe should look like after modifiation:

```
azure_resource_template "chef-azure-deployment" do
  resource_group "chef-azure-book"
  template_source "cookbooks/provision/files/default/azuredeploy.json"
  parameters  dnsLabelPrefix: 'chef-azure-book',
              vmName: 'chefazurevm',
              adminUsername: 'azure',
              adminPassword: 'P2ssw0rd',
              rdpPort: 3389
end
```

Let's go through each of the parameters in turn to explain them and some of the Azure naming rules that apply.

- **dnsLabelPrefix** - this is an Azure DNS entry that will be created dynamically. Only the first part of the name needs to be specified as. **<location>.cloudapp.azure.com** will be added automatically. In our case 'chef-azure-book'.

- **vmName** - the name assigned to the VM itself. In our case 'chefazurevm'.

- **adminUsername**/**adminPassword** - credentials for the VM.

- **rdpPort** - TCP port number that will be used to create a rule allowing access to the machine on the RDP port. In our case we will use the default RDP port '3389'.

Ensure that you have saved both the recipe file and the template and we can now upload this to our server using knife cookbook upload:

```
PS C:\Users\StuartPreston\chefazure-ch04> knife cookbook upload provision
```

```
Uploading provision        [0.1.0]
Uploaded 1 cookbook.
```

We can now run our recipe again from our workstation:

```
PS C:\Users\StuartPreston\chefazure-ch04> chef-client -o recipe[provision::default]
```

The output should follow a similar pattern to below (I have shortened the output):

```
resolving cookbooks for run list: ["provision::default"]
Synchronizing Cookbooks:
  - provision
Compiling Cookbooks...
Converging 2 resources
Recipe: provision::default
  * azure_resource_group[chef-azure-book] action create
    - create or update Resource Group chef-azure-book
  * azure_resource_template[chef-azure-deployment] action deploy
    - Result: Accepted
    - Resource Microsoft.Network/virtualNetworks 'VNET' provisioning status is Running
    - Resource Microsoft.Storage/storageAccounts 'chefazure2015' provisioning status is Running
    - Resource Microsoft.Storage/storageAccounts 'chefazure2015' provisioning status is Running
    - Resource Microsoft.Storage/storageAccounts 'chefazure2015' provisioning status is Running
[...]
    - Resource Template deployment reached end state of 'Succeeded'.
    - deploy or re-deploy Resource Manager template 'my-deployment'
Running handlers:
Running handlers complete
Chef Client finished, 2/2 resources updated in 428.605428 seconds
```

We can verify that our resources have been created using the Azure-cli, PowerShell. or in the Management Portal:

Azure-cli

```
PS C:\Users\StuartPreston\chefazure-ch04> azure group show chef-azure-book
```

```
{
  "tags": {
    "CreatedFor": "Using Chef with Microsoft Azure book"
  },
  "id": "/subscriptions/b6e7eee9-YOUR-GUID-HERE-03ab624df016/resourceGroups/chef-azure-
  book",
  "name": "chef-azure-book",
  "provisioningState": "Succeeded",
  "location": "westeurope",
  "properties": {
    "provisioningState": "Succeeded"
  },
  "resources": [
    {
      "id": "/subscriptions/b6e7eee9-YOUR-GUID-HERE-03ab624df016/resourceGroups/chef-
      azure-book/providers/Microsoft.Compute/virtualMachines/vm",
      "name": "vm",
      "type": "virtualMachines",
      "location": "westeurope",
      "tags": null
    },
[...]
```

PowerShell

```
PS C:\Users\StuartPreston\chefazure-ch04> Get-AzureRmResource | where {$_.ResourceGroupName
-eq "chef-azure-book" } | Select Name, ResourceType
```

```
Name               ResourceType
----               ------------
vm                 Microsoft.Compute/virtualMachines
loadBalancer       Microsoft.Network/loadBalancers
chefazurevm-nif    Microsoft.Network/networkInterfaces
publicIp           Microsoft.Network/publicIPAddresses
VNET               Microsoft.Network/virtualNetworks
chefazure2015      Microsoft.Storage/storageAccounts
```

Management Portal

Figure 4-9 shows the Resource Group with the resources available after Chef Provisioning has run.

Figure 4-9. *Resource Group showing created Resources in the Management portal*

We can now connect to the machine by RDP if we wish. In our particular deployment, we have a load balancer with a NAT rule enabled that allows us to connect to the target VM on the standard port. Figure 4-10 shows the configuration that was created, entirely based on the JSON template combined with the parameters we specified.

Figure 4-10. *Inbound NAT rules through a load balancer as seen in the Azure Management portal*

Chef Provisioning and the Chef VM Extensions

If you recall from chapter 3, we have the ability to add the Chef VM Extension to compute resource in Azure as a 'bootstrapless' mechanism to get the Chef client installed and enabled on the machine. Chef Provisioning for Azure Resource Manager has a feature that allows this VM Extension to be automatically added to compute resources.

To enable the feature, we need to change the **azure_resource_template** resource to add a property **chef_extension**, which in turn has a couple of properties that are settable, such as the machine's initial run_list on provision, and the version of the extension to deploy.

The additional property looks like this:

```
chef_extension client_type: 'ChefClient',
               version: '1210.12'
               runlist: 'role[webserver]'
```

If we add this property to our existing resource, our entire recipe now looks like this:

```
require 'chef/provisioning/azurerm'
with_driver 'AzureRM:b6e7eee9-YOUR-GUID-HERE-03ab624df016'

azure_resource_group "chef-azure-book" do
  location 'West Europe'
  tags CreatedFor: 'Using Chef with Microsoft Azure book'
end
```

```
azure_resource_template "chef-azure-deployment" do
  resource_group "chef-azure-book"
  template_source "cookbooks/provision/files/default/azuredeploy.json"
  parameters  dnsLabelPrefix: 'chef-azure-book',
              vmName: 'chefazurevm',
              adminUsername: 'azure',
              adminPassword: 'P2ssw0rd',
              rdpPort: 3389
  chef_extension  client_type: 'ChefClient',
                  version: '1210.12'
end
```

Having made these changes can now upload this recipe to our server using knife cookbook upload:

```
PS C:\Users\StuartPreston\chefazure-ch04> knife cookbook upload provision
```

```
Uploading provision       [0.1.0]
Uploaded 1 cookbook.
```

We can now run our recipe again from our workstation:

```
PS C:\Users\StuartPreston\chefazure-ch04> chef-client -o recipe[provision::default]
```

The output should follow a similar pattern to below (I have shortened the output):

```
resolving cookbooks for run list: ["provision::default"]
Synchronizing Cookbooks:
  - provision (0.1.0)
Compiling Cookbooks...
Converging 2 resources
Recipe: provision::default
  * azure_resource_group[chef-azure-book] action create
    - create or update Resource Group chef-azure-book
  * azure_resource_template[chef-azure-deployment] action deploy
    - adding a Chef VM Extension with name: vm and location: [parameters('location')]
    - Result: Accepted
    - Resource Microsoft.Compute/virtualMachines 'vm' provisioning status is Running
    - Resource Microsoft.Compute/virtualMachines 'vm' provisioning status is Running
    - Resource Microsoft.Compute/virtualMachines/extensions 'vm/chefExtension'
      provisioning status is Running
    - Resource Microsoft.Compute/virtualMachines/extensions 'vm/chefExtension'
      provisioning status is Running
    - Resource Microsoft.Compute/virtualMachines/extensions 'vm/chefExtension'
      provisioning status is Running
```

```
    - Resource Microsoft.Compute/virtualMachines/extensions 'vm/chefExtension'
      provisioning status is Running
[...]
    - Resource Template deployment reached end state of 'Succeeded'.
    - deploy or re-deploy Resource Manager template 'chef-azure-deployment'
[2015-11-15T13:41:53+00:00] WARN: Skipping final node save because override_runlist was given
```

We have now provisioned our first server via Chef Provisioning and enabled it to talk to the hosted Chef server via the Chef VM Extension. We are now able to manage the node like any other node in the organization.

What happened here? Via the Azure Resource Manager driver, we instructed Azure to add a Virtual Machine extension of type chefExtension to the existing VM that was created. We picked up the organization validator key from the local Chef client, and used the settings from our client to point our new node to the hosted Chef server.

If you navigate to the Hosted Chef management portal at **`https://manage.chef.io`** we can see that our node has registered successfully, as shown in Figure 4-11. You'll note the machine is called **<vm>.<resource group name>** - this is so that the server can disambiguate the machines when they connect.

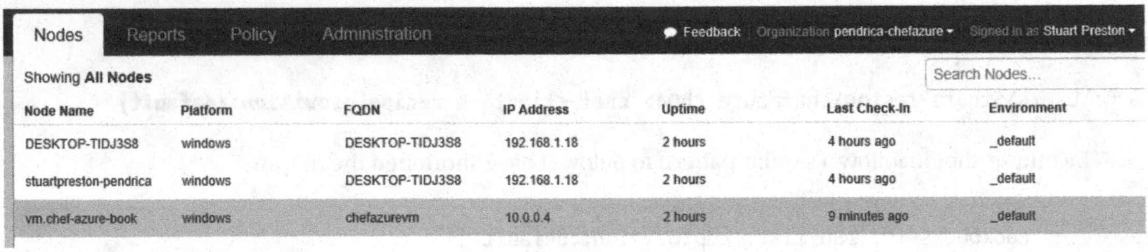
Nodes
Reports
Policy
Administration
Feedback
Organization pendrica-chefazure
Signed in as Stuart Preston
Showing All Nodes
Search Nodes...
Node Name
Platform
FQDN
IP Address
Uptime
Last Check-In
Environment
DESKTOP-TIDJ3S8 windows DESKTOP-TIDJ3S8 192.168.1.18 2 hours 4 hours ago _default
stuartpreston-pendrica windows DESKTOP-TIDJ3S8 192.168.1.18 2 hours 4 hours ago _default
vm.chef-azure-book windows chefazurevm 10.0.0.4 2 hours 9 minutes ago _default

Figure 4-11. *Hosted Chef portal showing vm.chef-azure-book is registered correctly*

We can also check via Remote Desktop to the server that the settings in **client.rb** are as we expect them, as shown in Figure 4-12.

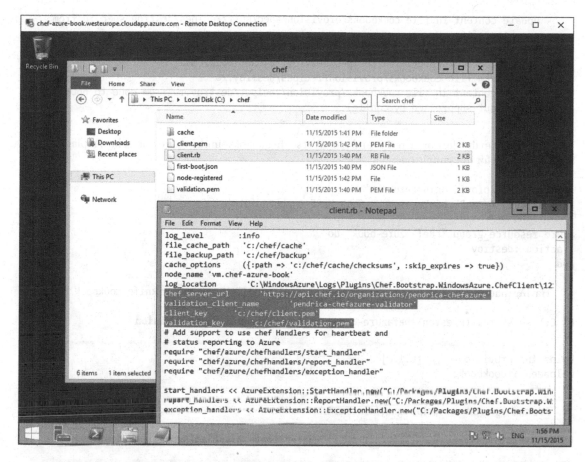

Figure 4-12. *Confirming the configuration values set in client.rb are set correctly*

Destroying Azure Resources

Now we have seen how to create resources in Azure, we had better work out how to remove them or else someone within your organization will get a large bill at the end of the month! Luckily we can simply destroy our resource group.

To destroy the resource group after use, we need to create a new recipe that destroys our resources by specifying the **:destroy** action on the **azure_resource_group** resource. We can generate the recipe using the chef generate recipe command:

```
PS C:\Users\StuartPreston\chefazure-ch04> chef generate recipe cookbooks/provision destroy
--copyright "Stuart Preston" --email stuart@pendrica.com
```

```
Compiling Cookbooks...
Recipe: code_generator::recipe
  * directory[cookbooks/provision/spec/unit/recipes] action create (up to date)
  * cookbook_file[cookbooks/provision/spec/spec_helper.rb] action create_if_missing (up to date)
  * template[cookbooks/provision/spec/unit/recipes/destroy_spec.rb] action create_if_missing
    - create new file cookbooks/provision/spec/unit/recipes/destroy_spec.rb
```

```
    - update content in file cookbooks/provision/spec/unit/recipes/destroy_spec.rb from
      none to 0ef16e
    (diff output suppressed by config)
  * template[cookbooks/provision/recipes/destroy.rb] action create
    - create new file cookbooks/provision/recipes/destroy.rb
    - update content in file cookbooks/provision/recipes/destroy.rb from none to 660c50
    (diff output suppressed by config)
```

Now open up the destroy.rb recipe and modify it so that it looks similar to the one below, replacing your Subscription ID for the sample one:

```
require 'chef/provisioning/azurerm'
with_driver 'AzureRM:b6e7eee9-YOUR-GUID-HERE-03ab624df016'

azure_resource_group "chef-azure-book" do
  action :destroy
end
```

Having made these changes, upload this recipe to the hosted Chef server using knife cookbook upload:

PS C:\Users\StuartPreston\chefazure-ch04> **knife cookbook upload provision**

```
Uploading provision        [0.1.0]
Uploaded 1 cookbook.
```

We can now run our recipe again from our workstation:

PS C:\Users\StuartPreston\chefazure-ch04> **chef-client -o recipe[provision::destroy]**

```
Starting Chef Client, version 12.5.1
[2015-11-15T14:57:15+00:00] WARN: Run List override has been provided.
[2015-11-15T14:57:15+00:00] WARN: Original Run List: []
[2015-11-15T14:57:15+00:00] WARN: Overridden Run List: [recipe[provision::destroy]]
[2015-11-15T14:57:16+00:00] WARN: chef-client doesn't have administrator privileges on
node DESKTOP-TIDJ3S8. This might cause unexpected resource failures.
resolving cookbooks for run list: ["provision::destroy"]
Synchronizing Cookbooks:
  - provision (0.1.0)
Compiling Cookbooks...
Converging 1 resources
Recipe: provision::destroy
  * azure_resource_group[chef-azure-book] action destroy
    - destroy Resource Group chef-azure-book
[2015-11-15T15:01:52+00:00] WARN: Skipping final node save because override_runlist was given

Running handlers:
Running handlers complete
Chef Client finished, 1/1 resources updated in 04 minutes 58 seconds
```

The recipe can take up to five minutes to execute while locks are freed on all of the resources within the Resource Group. Chef Provisioning will wait for this to complete in case anything further down the recipe is dependent on the Resource Group being deleted.

While the resource group is being destroyed it is given the status of Deleting as seen in the portal in Figure 4-13.

Figure 4-13. *Azure Resource Group in Deleting state as seen in the Management portal*

We can see how an operation that would have taken quite a few clicks – refreshing and waiting in the portal – can be accomplished with a single line, and we don't have to worry about shutting resources down in the correct order.

Summary

In this chapter we made sure your workstation was configured correctly to support Chef Provisioning and the Chef Provisioning Azure Resource Manager driver (**chef-provisioning-azurerm**). We went into detail on how to set up a Service Principal to allow us to configure Chef Provisioning correctly. We then looked at examples of ARM templates and showed you how to build a Windows Server using the framework. On top of that we looked at how to enable the Chef VM Extension so that every machine you boot up in Azure is configuration managed from Day 1.

By this point you will may be starting to see how this all comes together to express an entire Azure environment as code, using Chef to orchestrate the provisioning and the configuration management of the environment. Now that you understand the basics, we'll move on to some more complex real-world scenarios.

■ ■ ■

## CHAPTER 5

Advanced Chef Provisioning Techniques

In this chapter, we're going to have a look at some of the more advanced things you might want to do when provisioning resources in Azure via Chef Provisioning. We'll start by looking at how to ensure your secrets can be stored securely using Azure's Key Vault PaaS service, use that service to securely configure WinRM on a VM running in Azure, and then look at some ways in which you can leverage some of the newest PaaS services in Azure.

Explaining VM Image Naming within Azure Resource Manager JSON

In the previous chapter we saw how we could use an Azure Resource Manager template to create a Windows Server compute resource, but how did we know which version of Windows Server to deploy? The basic answer is that the image used was baked into the template. But what if we want to use a different version of Windows Server? That's what we'll explain shortly.

We saw in the template we were using, downloaded from https://github.com/Azure/azure-quickstart-templates/tree/master/101-vm-with-rdp-port, that the Virtual Machine is a type of Compute resource that has some internal variables that include **publisher**, **offer**, **sku**, and **version**. Here's the fragment of template that defines the Virtual Machine:

```
{
  "apiVersion": "[variables('apiVersion')]",
  "type": "Microsoft.Compute/virtualMachines",
  "name": "vm",
  "location": "[variables('location')]",
  "dependsOn": [
    "[resourceId('Microsoft.Storage/storageAccounts',variables('storageAccountName'))]",
    "[concat('Microsoft.Network/networkInterfaces/',parameters('vmName'),'-nic')]"
  ],
  "properties": {
    "hardwareProfile": {
      "vmSize": "Standard_D2"
    },
```

```
    "osProfile": {
      "computerName": "[parameters('vmName')]",
      "adminUsername": "[parameters('adminUserName')]",
      "adminPassword": "[parameters('adminPassword')]"
    },
    "storageProfile": {
      "imageReference": {
        "publisher": "[variables('imagePublisher')]",
        "offer": "[variables('imageOffer')]",
        "sku": "[variables('imageSku')]",
        "version": "latest"
      },
      "osDisk": {
        "name": "osdisk",
        "vhd": {
          "uri": "[concat('http://',variables('storageAccountName'),'.blob.core.
          windows.net/vhds/',parameters('vmName'),'-osdisk.vhd')]"
        },
        "caching": "ReadWrite",
        "createOption": "FromImage"
      }
    },
    "networkProfile": {
      "networkInterfaces": [
        {
          "id": "[resourceId('Microsoft.Network/networkInterfaces',concat(parameters
          ('vmName'),'-nic'))]"
        }
      ]
    },
    "diagnosticsProfile": {
      "bootDiagnostics": {
        "enabled": "true",
        "storageUri": "[concat('http://',variables('storageAccountName'),
        '.blob.core.windows.net')]"
      }
    }
  }
}
```

The template above expects these properties to be provided to it, so how do we discover the correct values for the template? Let's have a look at how to retrieve the **publishers**, **offers**, and **skus** for any public VM image.

Identifying and Retrieving VM Images

There's a particular sequence of events you must go through in order to list the publicly available VM images:

- To get a list of the **Publishers** you need to execute azure vm image list-publishers (Azure-cli) or Get-AzureRmVMImagePublisher (PowerShell).

- Then you can retrieve the **Offers** with azure vm image list-offers (Azure-cli) or Get-AzureRmVMImageOffer (PowerShell).

- Only then can you retrieve the **Sku** with azure vm image list-skus (Azure-cli) or Get-AzureRmVMImageSku (PowerShell).

As the specific images available can possibly vary by region, the datacenter **location** must be passed in as a parameter to each command or cmdlet too. Let's step through the process of 'discovering' the **Windows 2012 R2 Datacenter** image in both Azure-cli and PowerShell, noting that I am using **West Europe** as my region (as it is my nearest datacenter).

Azure-cli

To discover images using Azure-cli we use the following commands:

```
PS C:\Users\StuartPreston> azure vm image list-publishers "West Europe"
```

```
info:    Executing command vm image list-publishers
+ Getting virtual machine and/or extension image publishers (Location: "westeurope")
data:    Publisher                                          Location
data:    -------------------------------------------------- ----------
[...]

data:    MicrosoftWindowsServer                             westeurope

[...]
info:    vm image list-publishers command OK
```

Now we can use the azure vm image list-offers command and specify the publisher:

```
PS C:\Users\StuartPreston> azure vm image list-offers "West Europe" MicrosoftWindowsServer
```

```
info:    Executing command vm image list-offers
+ Getting virtual machine image offers (Publisher: "MicrosoftWindowsServer"
Location:"westeurope")
data:    Publisher              Offer          Location
data:    ---------------------- -------------- ----------
data:    MicrosoftWindowsServer WindowsServer  westeurope
info:    vm image list-offers command OK
```

Now armed with the Publisher and the Offer we can retrieve the Skus:

```
PS C:\Users\StuartPreston> azure vm image list-skus "West Europe" MicrosoftWindowsServer
WindowsServer
```

```
info:    Executing command vm image list-skus
+ Getting virtual machine image skus (Publisher:"MicrosoftWindowsServer"
Offer:"WindowsServer" Location:"westeurope")
data:    Publisher              Offer          sku
data:    ---------------------  -------------  ---------------------------------------
data:    MicrosoftWindowsServer WindowsServer  2008-R2-SP1
data:    MicrosoftWindowsServer WindowsServer  2012-Datacenter
data:    MicrosoftWindowsServer WindowsServer  2012-R2-Datacenter
data:    MicrosoftWindowsServer WindowsServer  2016-Technical-Preview-3-with-Containers
data:    MicrosoftWindowsServer WindowsServer  2016-Technical-Preview-4-Nano-Server
data:    MicrosoftWindowsServer WindowsServer  2016-Technical-Preview-Nano-Server
data:    MicrosoftWindowsServer WindowsServer  Windows-Server-Technical-Preview
info:    vm image list-skus command OK
```

Let's see how to do the same using PowerShell.

PowerShell

To discover images using PowerShell we use the following commands:

```
PS C:\Users\StuartPreston> Get-AzureRmVMImageOffer -Location "West Europe"
```

```
PublisherName
-------------
[...]
MicrosoftWindowsServer
```

Now we can use the Get-AzureRmVMImageOffer command and specify the publisher:

```
PS C:\Users\StuartPreston> Get-AzureRmVMImageOffer -Location "West Europe" -PublisherName
"MicrosoftWindowsServer" | Select Offer
```

```
Offer
-----
WindowsServer
```

Armed with the Publisher and the Offer we can retrieve the list of available Skus:

```
PS C:\Users\StuartPreston> Get-AzureRMImageSku -Location "West Europe" -PublisherName
"MicrosoftWindowsServer" -Offer "WindowsServer" | Select PublisherName, Offer, Skus
```

```
PublisherName          Offer           Skus
-------------          -----           ----
MicrosoftWindowsServer WindowsServer   2008-R2-SP1
MicrosoftWindowsServer WindowsServer   2012-Datacenter
MicrosoftWindowsServer WindowsServer   2012-R2-Datacenter
MicrosoftWindowsServer WindowsServer   2016-Technical-Preview-3-with-Containers
MicrosoftWindowsServer WindowsServer   2016-Technical-Preview-4-Nano-Server
MicrosoftWindowsServer WindowsServer   2016-Technical-Preview-Nano-Server
MicrosoftWindowsServer WindowsServer   Windows-Server-Technical-Preview
```

Now we have all the constituent values, these can be passed in as parameters in your provisioning recipes or used for other purposes, such as with Test Kitchen (you can read more about this in chapter 6).

Using Azure Key Vault to Store Secrets

As we know, it's not just VMs that you can create with Azure Resource Manager. We can also provision PaaS resources too. One of the PaaS solutions within Azure is KeyVault (see https://azure.microsoft.com/en-us/services/key-vault/), which is best described as a scalable Key Management solution that allows the storage of cryptographic keys without the cost normally associated with the implementation of HSMs (Hardware Security Modules) on premises.

The retrieval of a certificate from Key Vault is currently required if you wish to enable WinRM in a secure configuration on a Windows Server at provisioning time. So let's cover how to provision the Key Vault itself, along with the command-line tools used to manage it. Later examples in this chapter will show you how to provision machines that rely on secrets stored in the Key Vault.

You may create many Key Vault per subscription if you wish. Let's go through the process of provisioning a Key Vault. Azure Key Vault is quite simple to provision using Azure-cli, PowerShell, or Chef Provisioning, so you may be asking yourself why you would want to use Chef. The main reason to do so is for consistency, so that we can keep all our provisioned resources in the same repo. Now let's go through the process of provisioning a Key Vault using Chef.

As this is the first example in this chapter, we'll need a repo in which to work in:

```
PS C:\Users\StuartPreston> chef generate app chefazure-ch05
```

```
Compiling Cookbooks...
Recipe: code_generator::app
[output truncated]
```

You'll now want to copy in the **.chef** folder from our **chef-starter** repo (as created in chapter 1), so that our keys and knife.rb configuration are available in our new repo.

Now we can enter our repo and open the folder in our code editor:

```
PS C:\Users\StuartPreston> cd chefazure-ch05
PS C:\Users\StuartPreston\chefazure-ch05> code .
```

Azure Key Vault ARM Template

We need to create a file **cookbooks/chefazure-ch05/files/keyvault/deploy.json** within our repository representing the ARM template that creates a Key Vault so that we can refer to it from a provisioning recipe.

■ **Note** This ARM template can be downloaded from `https://raw.githubusercontent.com/Azure/azure-quickstart-templates/master/101-key-vault-create/azuredeploy.json`, and you can find this and the associated recipes in the book's accompanying download.

Here's the template reproduced in its entirety. We can see there are nine parameters that I have highlighted in bold that we will need to supply in our Chef Provisioning recipe and finally the resource contained within it:

```
{
  "$schema": "https://schema.management.azure.com/schemas/2015-01-01/deploymentTemplate.
  json#",
  "contentVersion": "1.0.0.0",
  "parameters": {
    "keyVaultName": {
      "type": "string",
      "metadata": {
        "description": "Name of the Vault"
      }
    },
    "location": {
      "type": "string",
      "allowedValues": [
        "Central US",
        "East US",
        "East US 2",
        "North Central US",
        "South Central US",
        "West US",
        "North Europe",
        "West Europe",
        "East Asia",
        "Southeast Asia",
        "Japan East",
        "Japan West",
        "Brazil South",
        "Australia East",
        "Australia Southeast"
      ],
      "metadata": {
        "description": "Key Vault location"
      }
    },
    "tenantId": {
      "type": "string",
```

```
    "metadata": {
      "description": "Tenant Id of the subscription. Get using Get-AzureSubscription
      cmdlet or Get Subscription API"
    }
},
"objectId": {
  "type": "string",
  "metadata": {
    "description": "Object Id of the AD user. Get using Get-AzureADUser or
    Get-AzureADServicePrincipal cmdlets"
  }
},
"keysPermissions": {
  "type": "array",
  "defaultValue": [ ],
  "metadata": {
    "description": "Permissions to keys in the vault. Valid values are: all, create,
    import, update, get, list, delete, backup, restore, encrypt, decrypt, wrapkey,
    unwrapkey, sign, and verify."
  }
},
"secretsPermissions": {
  "type": "array",
  "defaultValue": [ ],
  "metadata": {
    "description": "Permissions to secrets in the vault. Valid values are: all, get,
    set, list, and delete."
  }
},
"skuName": {
  "type": "string",
  "defaultValue": "Standard",
  "allowedValues": [
    "Standard",
    "Premium"
  ],
  "metadata": {
    "description": "SKU for the vault"
  }
},
"enableVaultForDeployment": {
  "type": "bool",
  "defaultValue": false,
  "allowedValues": [
    true,
    false
  ],
  "metadata": {
    "description": "Specifies if the vault is enabled for a VM deployment"
  }
},
```

```json
      "enableVaultForDiskEncryption": {
        "type": "bool",
        "defaultValue": false,
        "allowedValues": [
          true,
          false
        ],
        "metadata": {
          "description": "Specifies if the azure platform has access to the vault for enabling
          disk encryption scenarios."
        }
      }
    },
    "resources": [
      {
        "type": "Microsoft.KeyVault/vaults",
        "name": "[parameters('keyVaultName')]",
        "apiVersion": "2015-06-01",
        "location": "[parameters('location')]",
        "properties": {
          "enabledForDeployment": "[parameters('enableVaultForDeployment')]",
          "enabledForDiskEncryption": "[parameters('enableVaultForDiskEncryption')]",
          "tenantId": "[parameters('tenantId')]",
          "accessPolicies": [
            {
              "tenantId": "[parameters('tenantId')]",
              "objectId": "[parameters('objectId')]",
              "permissions": {
                "keys": "[parameters('keysPermissions')]",
                "secrets": "[parameters('secretsPermissions')]"
              }
            }
          ],
          "sku": {
            "name": "[parameters('skuName')]",
            "family": "A"
          }
        }
      }
    ]
}
```

Retrieving the Object ID for an Azure Active Directory User

When we create the Key Vault, we will need to add permissions so that our normal user (not the application Service Principal) has access to be able to create keys. Luckily this is something that the Key Vault provider can do for us. To configure that, we need the Object Id of the Azure Active Directory user we want to grant access to, which can be retrieved using Azure-cli and PowerShell.

Azure-cli

In Azure-cli we can use the `azure ad user show --upn` command and pass in the UPN of the user we want to grant access to:

```
PS C:\Users\StuartPreston\chefazure-ch05> azure ad user show --upn stuart@pendrica.com
```

```
info:    Executing command ad user show
+ Getting active directory user
data:    Object Id:        38e8a50f-YOUR-GUID-HERE-a605e06e9695
data:    Principal Name:   stuart@pendrica.com
data:    Display Name:     Stuart Preston
data:    E-Mail:           stuart@pendrica.com
data:
```

PowerShell

In PowerShell we can use the `Get-AzureRmADUser -UserPrincipalName` cmdlet and pass in the UPN of the user we want to grant access to:

```
PS C:\Users\StuartPreston> Get-AzureRmADUser -UserPrincipalName stuart@pendrica.com
```

```
DisplayName              ObjectId
-----------              --------
Stuart Preston           38e8a50f-YOUR-GUID-HERE-a605e06e9695
```

Azure Key Vault Provisioning Recipe

To provision our Key Vault, we need to create a new file to contain our recipe in the following path: **cookbooks/chefazure-ch05/recipes/keyvault.rb** and add the below recipe to it. Now that we have the ObjectId for the user who should have permission to the Key Vault, this can be substituted into the **objectId** parameter.

■ **Tip** If you cannot locate your TenantId, the quickest way might be to have a look in your credentials file located at **~/.azure/credentials**.

```
require 'chef/provisioning/azurerm'
with_driver 'AzureRM:b6e7eee9-YOUR-GUID-HERE-03ab624df016'

azure_resource_group 'chefazure-shared' do
  location 'West Europe'
  tags CreatedFor: 'Using Chef with Microsoft Azure book'
end
```

```
azure_resource_template 'keyvault-deployment' do
  resource_group 'chefazure-shared'
  template_source 'cookbooks/chefazure-ch05/files/keyvault/deploy.json'
  parameters keyVaultName: 'chefazure-keyvault',
             location: 'West Europe',
             tenantId: '48b9bba3-YOUR-GUID-HERE-90f0b68ce8ba',
             objectId: '38e8a50f-YOUR-GUID-HERE-a605e06e9695',
             keysPermissions: ['all'],
             secretsPermissions: ['all'],
             skuName: 'Standard',
             enableVaultForDeployment: true,
             enableVaultForDiskEncryption: false
end
```

Upload the cookbook using knife cookbook upload:

```
PS C:\Users\StuartPreston\chefazure-ch05> knife cookbook upload chefazure-ch05
```

```
Uploading chefazure-ch05 [0.1.0]
Uploaded 1 cookbook.
```

Now let's provision this recipe using our local chef-client:

```
PS C:\Users\StuartPreston\chefazure-ch05> chef-client -o recipe[chefazure-ch05::keyvault]
```

```
Starting Chef Client, version 12.5.1
[2015-11-21T17:20:24+00:00] WARN: Run List override has been provided.
[2015-11-21T17:20:24+00:00] WARN: Original Run List: []
[2015-11-21T17:20:24+00:00] WARN: Overridden Run List: [recipe[chefazure-ch05::keyvault]]
resolving cookbooks for run list: ["chefazure-ch05::keyvault"]
Synchronizing Cookbooks:
  - chefazure-ch05 (0.1.0)
Compiling Cookbooks...
Converging 2 resources
Recipe: chefazure-ch05::keyvault
  * azure_resource_group[chefazure-shared] action create
    - create or update Resource Group chefazure-shared
  * azure_resource_template[keyvault-deployment] action deploy
    - Result: Accepted
    - Resource Template deployment reached end state of 'Succeeded'.
    - deploy or re-deploy Resource Manager template 'keyvault-deployment'
[2015-11-21T17:20:39+00:00] WARN: Skipping final node save because override_runlist was
given

Running handlers:
Running handlers complete
Chef Client finished, 2/2 resources updated in 31 seconds
```

We have now successfully created a Key Vault and provided access to our Service Principal. Let's have a look at how a Windows Server might use Key Vault in the process of enabling WinRM securely.

Creating a Windows Server with WinRM Securely Enabled via Key Vault

Now that we have uploaded our certificates into a Key Vault, we can refer to the Key Vault in an Azure Resource Manager template. This opens up certain scenarios such as this one where the WinRM endpoint is correctly configured on a new VM that we create in a Resource Group. There are three stages to the process:

1. Creating a self-signed certificate

2. Uploading the self-signed certificate to the Key Vault

3. Provisioning a WinRM-enabled Windows Server using the certificate in the Key Vault

Let's go through the process in detail.

Creating a Self-signed Certificate

To get started we need to generate a self-signed certificate to upload to our Key Vault.

Mac OS X/Linux (Azure-cli)

If you are running on Mac or Linux, we can use the OpenSSL tools to generate a certificate in PFX format by following the commands below in bold:

```
$ openssl genrsa 2048 > private.pem
Generating RSA private key, 2048 bit long modulus
...............................................+++
..+++
e is 65537 (0x10001)

$ openssl req -x509 -new -key private.pem -out public.key
You are about to be asked to enter information that will be incorporated
into your certificate request.
What you are about to enter is what is called a Distinguished Name or a DN.
There are quite a few fields but you can leave some blank
For some fields there will be a default value,
If you enter '.', the field will be left blank.
-----
Country Name (2 letter code) [AU]:GB
State or Province Name (full name) [Some-State]:London
Locality Name (eg, city) []:London
Organization Name (eg, company) [Internet Widgits Pty Ltd]:Pendrica Ltd
Organizational Unit Name (eg, section) []:IT
Common Name (e.g. server FQDN or YOUR name) []:vm
Email Address []:stuart@pendrica.com

$ openssl pkcs12 -export -in public.key -inkey private.pem -out vm.pfx
Enter Export Password:
Verifying - Enter Export Password:
```

We how have a .pfx suitable for uploading to Key Vault.

Windows (PowerShell)

If you are running on Windows 8.1, Windows 2012 R2 or higher, the New-SelfSignedCertificate cmdlet can be used to generate a certificate that can then be exported to a .pfx suitable for uploading to the Key Vault:

```
PS C:\Users\StuartPreston\chefazure-ch05> New-SelfSignedCertificate -DnsName
vm.mydomain.local
```

```
    Directory: Microsoft.PowerShell.Security\Certificate::LocalMachine\MY

Thumbprint                                Subject
----------                                -------
434A322583F2903880B27FED0E6AA1E0AB68E000  CN=vm.mydomain.local
```

```
C:\Users\StuartPreston\chefazure-ch05> $certPassword = ConvertTo-SecureString -String
"P2ssw0rd" -Force -AsPlainText
C:\Users\StuartPreston\chefazure-ch05> $cert = Get-ChildItem -Path cert:\localMachine\my |
where { $_.Subject -eq 'CN=vm.mydomain.local' }
C:\Users\StuartPreston\chefazure-ch05> Export-PfxCertificate -Cert $cert -Password
$certPassword -FilePath vm.pfx
```

```
    Directory: C:\Users\StuartPreston\chefazure-ch05
Mode                LastWriteTime         Length Name
----                -------------         ------ ----
-a----        21/11/2015     23:20          2615 vm.pfx
```

Uploading the Certificate to Key Vault

To upload our certificate into the Key Vault so it is ready for use later, we can use the Azure-cli or PowerShell. Both paths follow the same approach - a temporary file is needed as our payload that we upload to Key Vault. The payload is a JSON document that contains our PFX data (which needs to be base64 encoded), and then the whole document needs to be base64 encoded before uploading it.

Mac OS X/Linux (Azure-cli)

To manually create the required payload, we'll start by base64 encoding our PFX file:

```
$ base64 -i vm.pfx
```

```
MIIKMwIBAzCCCe8GCSqGSIb3DQEHAaCCCeAEggncMIIJ2DCCBg8GCSqGSIb3DQEHAaCCBgAEggX8MIIF+
DCCBfQGCyqGSIb3DQEMCgECoIIE/jCCBPowHAYKKoZIhvcNAQwBAzAOBAhFmO4v4OiE9wICB9AEgg
TYz4nFVhhVpiKqD6+DZ8TLd837
[...] full output not shown
RzEiBCBEAEUAUwBLAFQATwBQACoAVABJAEQASgAzAFMAOAAAADA7MB8wBwYFKw4DAhoEFNZlC7N1gOrgUIuGWBuo
Sa31UbHcBBTtCIWsbWB/qgWl31zEK4kmwKQUbQICB9A=
```

Now we can create a temporary file called **secret.json** using the following as a template and pasting in your base64 encoded data and password if you set one:

```
{
"data": "[paste your base64 encoded content from above]",
"dataType" :"pfx",
"password": "[pfx password]"
}
```

Now we need to base64 encode this secret.json:

```
$ base64 -i secret.json
```

ewoiZGF0YSI6ICJNSUlLSVFJQkF6QONDZWNHQ1NxR1NJYjNEUUVIQWFDQONkZoVnZ25VTUlJSjBEQONCSWNHQ1Nx
R1NJYjNEUUVIQnFDQoJIZ3dnZ1IwQWdFQU1JSUViUVlKS29aSWh2Y05BUWNCTUJ3RONpcUdTWIzRFFFTU
FRWXdEZZ1FJVHIv
[...] full output not shown
Yk1GaXpFTXBTWUUvODVnS0ZvSDk4T1BHc3dNVEFoTUFrR0JTc09BdOlhQlFBRUZBdWFzdjlVM2gx
Ri8wL2NWK0EvSWx4eDhkMFhCQWdvc2NUbkpwWMEZ4QUlDQoQFBPSIsCiJkYXRhVHlwZSI6ICJwZngiLAoicGF
zc3dvcmQiOiAiIgp9Cg==

We can then use the azure keyvault secret set command to upload this secret:

```
$ azure keyvault secret set --vault-name "chefazure" --secret-name "vmselfcert" --value
"ewoiZGF0YSI6ICJNSUlLSVFJQkF6QONDZWNHQ1NxR1NJYjNEUUVIQWFDQONkZoVnZ25VTUlJSj
BEQONCSWNHQ1NxR1NJYjNEUUVIQnFDQoJIZ3dnZ1IwQWdFQU1JSUViUVlKS29aSWh2Y05BUWNCTUJ3
RONpcUdTWIzRFFFTUFRWXdEZZ1FJVHIvdOppOE5QcHNDQWdnQWdJSUVRRHNldzZVaVM4SHg2el
dOWHN2c1E1WGFiMDJsNUZkOE5aZjhEeEVFzOCtYOHBOVGlZNUJSOGFMaDd5UVJ

[...] full input not shown

GaXpFTXBTWUUvODVnS0ZvSDk4T1BHc3dNVEFoTUFrR0JTc09BdOlhQlFBRUZBdWFzdjlVM2gxRi8wL2NWK0EvSWx4e
DdhMFhCQWdvc2NUbkpwWMEZ4QUlDQoQFBPSIsCiJkYXRhVHlwZSI6ICJwZngiLAoicGFzc3dvcmQiOiAiIgp9Cg=="
```

```
info:    Executing command keyvault secret set
+ Creating secret https://chefazure.vault.azure.net/secrets/vmselfcert
data:    value
"ewoiZGF0YSI6ICJNSUlLSVFJQkF6QONDZWNHQ1NxR1NJYjNEUUVIQWFDQONkZoVnZ25VTUlJSjBEQONCSWNHQ1Nx
R1NJYjNEUUVIQnFDQoJIZ3dnZ1IwQWdFQU1JSUViUVlKS29aSWh2Y05BUWNCTUJ3RONpcUdTWIzRFF
FTUFRWXdEZZ1FJVHI
[...] full output not shown
aYk1GaXpFTXBTWUUvODVnS0ZvSDk4T1BHc3dNVEFoTUFrR0JTc09BdOlhQlFBRUZBdWFzdjlVM2gxRi8wL2NWK0Ev
SWx4eDhkMFhCQWdvc2NUbkpwWMEZ4QUlDQoQFBPSIsCiJkYXRhVHlwZSI6ICJwZngiLAoicGFzc3dvcmQiOiAiIgp9Cg=="
data:    id https://chefazure.vault.azure.net/secrets/vmselfcert/3772db676efd407b89f8fdd86bb545f5
data:    attributes enabled true
data:    attributes created "2016-01-28T22:34:51.000Z"
data:    attributes updated "2016-01-28T22:34:51.000Z"
info:    keyvault secret set command OK
```

Windows (PowerShell)

Here's a PowerShell script to create our temporary payload in the correct format and upload it:

```
$fileName = "vm_mydomain_com.pfx"
$certPassword = "your-cert-password"
$fileContentBytes = get-content $fileName -Encoding Byte
$fileContentEncoded = [System.Convert]::ToBase64String($fileContentBytes)
$jsonObject = @"
{
"data": "$filecontentencoded",
"dataType" :"pfx",
"password": "$certPassword"
}
"@
$jsonObjectBytes = [System.Text.Encoding]::UTF8.GetBytes($jsonObject)
$jsonEncoded = [System.Convert]::ToBase64String($jsonObjectBytes)
$secret = ConvertTo-SecureString -String $jsonEncoded -AsPlainText -Force
```

Save the file as **encodeCertificate.ps1** and execute it. Now we can execute the Set-AzureKeyVaultSecret cmdlet to upload the secret to the Key Vault:

PS C:\Users\StuartPreston\chefazure-ch05> **Set-AzureKeyVaultSecret -VaultName "chefazure" -Name "vmselfcert" -SecretValue $secret**

```
Vault Name     : chefazure
Name           : vmselfcert
Version        : f4233e85f0c94bd987b337a7e329fa48
Id             : https://chefazure.vault.azure.net:443/secrets/vmselfcert/
                 f4233e85f0c94bd987b337a7e329fa48
Enabled        : True
Expires        :
Not Before     :
Created        : 22/11/2015 00:20:23
Updated        : 22/11/2015 00:20:23
Content Type   :
Tags           :
```

We'll need the URL to the secret (the Id field) for the next section.

Provisioning a WinRM-Enabled Windows Server

Here's the **deploy.json** file you will need to provision a WinRM-enabled Windows Server. You can save this JSON in **cookbooks/chefazure-ch05/files/winrm_winserver/deploy.json**

```
{
  "$schema": "http://schema.management.azure.com/schemas/2014-04-01-preview/
deploymentTemplate.json",
  "contentVersion": "1.0.0.0",
  "parameters": {
```

```
    "newStorageAccountName": {
      "type": "string",
      "metadata": {
        "description": "This is the name of the storage account"
      }
    },
    "dnsNameForPublicIP": {
      "type": "string",
      "metadata": {
        "description": "DNS Name for the Public IP. Must be lowercase."
      }
    },
    "adminUserName": {
      "type": "string",
      "metadata": {
        "description": "Admin username"
      }
    },
    "adminPassword": {
      "type": "securestring",
      "metadata": {
        "description": "Admin password"
      }
    },
    "imagePublisher": {
      "type": "string",
      "defaultValue": "MicrosoftWindowsServer",
      "metadata": {
        "description": "Image Publisher"
      }
    },
    "imageOffer": {
      "type": "string",
      "defaultValue": "WindowsServer",
      "metadata": {
        "description": "Image Offer"
      }
    },
    "imageSKU": {
      "type": "string",
      "defaultValue": "2012-R2-Datacenter",
      "metadata": {
        "description": "Image SKU"
      }
    },
    "location": {
      "type": "String",
      "metadata": {
        "description": "Location where resources will be deployed"
      }
    },
```

```json
      "vmSize": {
        "type": "string",
        "metadata": {
          "description": "Size of the VM"
        }
      },
      "vmName": {
        "type": "string",
        "metadata": {
          "description": "Name of the VM"
        }
      },
      "vaultName": {
        "type": "string",
        "metadata": {
          "description": "Name of the KeyVault"
        }
      },
      "vaultResourceGroup": {
        "type": "string",
        "metadata": {
          "description": "Resource Group of the KeyVault"
        }
      },
      "certificateUrl": {
        "type": "string",
        "metadata": {
          "description": "Url of the certificate with version in KeyVault e.g.
          https://testault.vault.azure.net/secrets/testcert/b621es1db241e56a72d037479xab1r7"
        }
      }
    },
    "variables": {
      "addressPrefix": "10.0.0.0/16",
      "subnet1Name": "Subnet-1",
      "subnet1Prefix": "10.0.0.0/24",
      "vmStorageAccountContainerName": "vhds",
      "publicIPAddressName": "myPublicIP",
      "publicIPAddressType": "Dynamic",
      "storageAccountType": "Standard_LRS",
      "virtualNetworkName": "myVNET",
      "nicName": "myNIC",
      "vnetID": "[resourceId('Microsoft.Network/virtualNetworks', variables('virtualNetworkName'))]",
      "subnet1Ref": "[concat(variables('vnetID'),'/subnets/',variables('subnet1Name'))]"
    },
    "resources": [
      {
        "type": "Microsoft.Storage/storageAccounts",
        "name": "[parameters('newStorageAccountName')]",
        "apiVersion": "2015-05-01-preview",
        "location": "[parameters('location')]",
```

```
    "properties": {
      "accountType": "[variables('storageAccountType')]"
    }
  },
  {
    "apiVersion": "2015-05-01-preview",
    "type": "Microsoft.Network/publicIPAddresses",
    "name": "[variables('publicIPAddressName')]",
    "location": "[parameters('location')]",
    "properties": {
      "publicIPAllocationMethod": "[variables('publicIPAddressType')]",
      "dnsSettings": {
        "domainNameLabel": "[parameters('dnsNameForPublicIP')]"
      }
    }
  },
  {
    "apiVersion": "2015-05-01-preview",
    "type": "Microsoft.Network/virtualNetworks",
    "name": "[variables('virtualNetworkName')]",
    "location": "[parameters('location')]",
    "properties": {
      "addressSpace": {
        "addressPrefixes": [
          "[variables('addressPrefix')]"
        ]
      },
      "subnets": [
        {
          "name": "[variables('subnet1Name')]",
          "properties": {
            "addressPrefix": "[variables('subnet1Prefix')]"
          }
        }
      ]
    }
  },
  {
    "apiVersion": "2015-05-01-preview",
    "type": "Microsoft.Network/networkInterfaces",
    "name": "[variables('nicName')]",
    "location": "[parameters('location')]",
    "dependsOn": [
      "[concat('Microsoft.Network/publicIPAddresses/', variables('publicIPAddressName'))]",
      "[concat('Microsoft.Network/virtualNetworks/', variables('virtualNetworkName'))]"
    ],
    "properties": {
      "ipConfigurations": [
        {
          "name": "ipconfig1",
          "properties": {
```

```json
        "privateIPAllocationMethod": "Dynamic",
        "publicIPAddress": {
          "id": "[resourceId('Microsoft.Network/publicIPAddresses',variables
          ('publicIPAddressName'))]"
        },
        "subnet": {
          "id": "[variables('subnet1Ref')]"
        }
      }
    }
  ]
}
},
{
  "apiVersion": "2015-06-15",
  "type": "Microsoft.Compute/virtualMachines",
  "name": "[parameters('vmName')]",
  "location": "[parameters('location')]",
  "dependsOn": [
    "[concat('Microsoft.Storage/storageAccounts/', parameters('newStorageAccountName'))]",
    "[concat('Microsoft.Network/networkInterfaces/', variables('nicName'))]"
  ],
  "properties": {
    "hardwareProfile": {
      "vmSize": "[parameters('vmSize')]"
    },
    "osProfile": {
      "computername": "[parameters('vmName')]",
      "adminUsername": "[parameters('adminUsername')]",
      "adminPassword": "[parameters('adminPassword')]",
      "secrets": [
        {
          "sourceVault": {
            "id": "[resourceId(parameters('vaultResourceGroup'), 'Microsoft.KeyVault/
            vaults', parameters('vaultName'))]"
          },
          "vaultCertificates": [
            {
              "certificateUrl": "[parameters('certificateUrl')]",
              "certificateStore": "My"
            }
          ]
        }
      ],
      "windowsConfiguration": {
        "provisionVMAgent": "true",
        "winRM": {
          "listeners": [
            {
              "protocol": "http"
            },
```

```json
              {
                "protocol": "https",
                "certificateUrl": "[parameters('certificateUrl')]"
              }
            ]
          },
          "enableAutomaticUpdates": "true"
        }
      },
      "storageProfile": {
        "imageReference": {
          "publisher": "[parameters('imagePublisher')]",
          "offer": "[parameters('imageOffer')]",
          "sku": "[parameters('imageSKU')]",
          "version": "latest"
        },
        "osDisk": {
          "name": "osdisk",
          "vhd": {
            "uri": "[concat('http://',parameters('newStorageAccountName'),'.blob.core.
            windows.net/vhds/','osdisk.vhd')]"
          },
          "caching": "ReadWrite",
          "createOption": "FromImage"
        }
      },
      "networkProfile": {
        "networkInterfaces": [
          {
            "id": "[resourceId('Microsoft.Network/networkInterfaces',variables('nicName'))]"
          }
        ]
      },
      "diagnosticsProfile": {
        "bootDiagnostics": {
          "enabled": "true",
          "storageUri": "[concat('http://',parameters('newStorageAccountName'),'.blob.
          core.windows.net')]"
        }
      }
    }
  }
 ]
}
```

Here's an example recipe that would be required. You can tweak it as required for your environment and save it as **cookbooks/chefazure-ch05/recipes/winrm_winserver.rb**.

```
require 'chef/provisioning/azurerm'
with_driver 'AzureRM:b6e7eee9-YOUR-GUID-HERE-03ab624df016'

azure_resource_group 'chefazure-ch05' do
  location 'West Europe'
  tags CreatedFor: 'Using Chef with Microsoft Azure book'
end

azure_resource_template 'keyvault-deployment' do
  resource_group 'chefazure-ch05'
  template_source 'cookbooks/chefazure-ch05/files/winrm_winserver/deploy.json'
  parameters newStorageAccountName: 'chefazurech05',
             dnsNameForPublicIP: 'chefazure-ch05-vm',
             adminUsername: 'azure',
             adminPassword: 'P2ssw0rd',
             imagePublisher: 'MicrosoftWindowsServer',
             imageOffer: 'WindowsServer',
             imageSKU: '2012-R2-Datacenter',
             location: 'West Europe',
             vmName: 'ch05vm',
             vmSize: 'Standard_D2',
             vaultName: 'chefazure',
             vaultResourceGroup: 'chefazure-shared',
             certificateUrl: 'https://chefazure.vault.azure.net:443/secrets/vmselfcert/02a48
             bca5dbf42228a170c6ebab476af'
end
```

We can see that this is a fairly standard ARM template that will produce a Windows 2012 R2 Datacenter server, but also configured to point at the Key Vault we created earlier. This allows the template to retrieve the certificate, store it in the VM's certificate store, and then configure WinRM securely.

Upload the cookbook using knife cookbook upload:

```
PS C:\Users\StuartPreston\chefazure-ch05> knife cookbook upload chefazure-ch05
```

```
Uploading chefazure-ch05 [0.1.0]
Uploaded 1 cookbook.
```

We can now execute this by running chef-client -o recipe[chefazure-ch05::winrm_winserver]:

```
PS C:\Users\StuartPreston\chefazure-ch05> chef-client -o recipe[chefazure-ch05::winrm_
winserver]
```

```
Starting Chef Client, version 12.5.1
[2015-11-22T07:43:45+00:00] WARN: Run List override has been provided.
[2015-11-22T07:43:45+00:00] WARN: Original Run List: []
[2015-11-22T07:43:45+00:00] WARN: Overridden Run List: [recipe[chefazure-ch05::winrm_winserver]]
[2015-11-22T07:43:46+00:00] WARN: chef-client doesn't have administrator privileges on node
DESKTOP-TIDJ3S8. This might cause unexpected resource failures.
resolving cookbooks for run list: ["chefazure-ch05::winrm_winserver"]
```

```
Synchronizing Cookbooks:
  - chefazure-ch05 (0.1.0)
Compiling Cookbooks...
Converging 2 resources
Recipe: chefazure-ch05::winrm_winserver
  * azure_resource_group[chefazure-ch05] action create
    - create or update Resource Group chefazure-ch05
  * azure_resource_template[chefazure-ch05-vm-deployment] action deploy
    - Result: Accepted
    - Resource Microsoft.Network/virtualNetworks 'myVNET' provisioning status is Running
    - Resource Microsoft.Network/publicIPAddresses 'myPublicIP' provisioning status is Running
    - Resource Microsoft.Storage/storageAccounts 'chefazurech05' provisioning status is Running
    - Resource Microsoft.Network/virtualNetworks 'myVNET' provisioning status is Running
    - Resource Microsoft.Network/publicIPAddresses 'myPublicIP' provisioning status is Running
    - Resource Microsoft.Storage/storageAccounts 'chefazurech05' provisioning status is Running
    - Resource Microsoft.Storage/storageAccounts 'chefazurech05' provisioning status is Running
    - Resource Microsoft.Storage/storageAccounts 'chefazurech05' provisioning status is Running
    - Resource Microsoft.Storage/storageAccounts 'chefazurech05' provisioning status is Running
    - Resource Microsoft.Storage/storageAccounts 'chefazurech05' provisioning status is Running
    - Resource Microsoft.Storage/storageAccounts 'chefazurech05' provisioning status is Running
    - Resource Microsoft.Storage/storageAccounts 'chefazurech05' provisioning status is Running
    - Resource Microsoft.Compute/virtualMachines 'ch05vm' provisioning status is Running
    - Resource Microsoft.Compute/virtualMachines 'ch05vm' provisioning status is Running
    - Resource Microsoft.Compute/virtualMachines 'ch05vm' provisioning status is Running
    - Resource Microsoft.Compute/virtualMachines 'ch05vm' provisioning status is Running
    - Resource Microsoft.Compute/virtualMachines 'ch05vm' provisioning status is Running
    - Resource Microsoft.Compute/virtualMachines 'ch05vm' provisioning status is Running
    - Resource Template deployment reached end state of 'Succeeded'.
    - deploy or re-deploy Resource Manager template 'chefazure-ch05-vm-deployment'
[2015-11-22T07:59:37+00:00] WARN: Skipping final node save because override_runlist was
given

Running handlers:
Running handlers complete
Chef Client finished, 2/2 resources updated in 6 minutes 13 seconds
```

Verifying WinRM Status

We can verify the status by using the Test-NetConnection cmdlet, which checks whether the specified port is open. When configured securely, WinRM runs on port 5986.

```
PS C:\Users\StuartPreston\chefazure-ch05> Test-NetConnection chefazure-ch05-vm.westeurope.
cloudapp.azure.com -Port 5986
```

```
WARNING: Ping to chefazure-ch05-vm.westeurope.cloudapp.azure.com failed -- Status:
TimedOut
ComputerName            : chefazure-ch05-vm.westeurope.cloudapp.azure.com
RemoteAddress           : 23.97.185.157
RemotePort              : 5986
InterfaceAlias          : Ethernet 2
SourceAddress           : 192.168.1.13
PingSucceeded           : False
PingReplyDetails (RTT)  : 0 ms
TcpTestSucceeded        : True
```

We can also RDP to the machine to verify that the WinRM server is configured correctly by typing the command `winrm get winrm/config/service` at an administrative command prompt as shown in Figure 5-1:

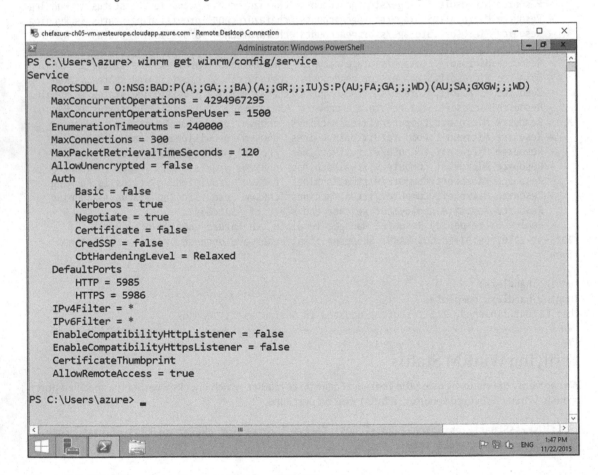

Figure 5-1. *WinRM configuration on a Windows 2012 R2 server*

That covers the server side, but what about the client side? First of all, depending on your operating system, you may find that the WinRM service is not started, so let's start it. At an administrative PowerShell session, type `Start-Service winrm`:

```
PS C:\Users\StuartPreston\chefazure-ch05> Start-Service winrm
```

As the certificate we uploaded wasn't signed by a trusted certificate authority, and neither does the name of the certificate match the hostname we are connecting to, we need to specify a couple of options so that we can skip this checking when WinRM connects:

```
PS C:\Users\StuartPreston\chefazure-ch05> $PSSessionOptions = New-PSSessionOption
-SkipCACheck -SkipCNCheck
PS C:\Users\StuartPreston\chefazure-ch05> Enter-PSSession -UseSSL -ComputerName
chefazure-ch05-vm.westeurope.cloudapp.azure.com -Credential ch05vm\azure -SessionOption
$PSSessionOptions
```

After entering the password, you will be presented with a remote session:

```
[chefazure-ch05-vm.westeurope.cloudapp.azure.com]: PS C:\Users\azure\Documents> hostname
ch05vm
```

■ **Note** Don't forget to destroy your Resource Group after each exercise in the book!

We have now used Chef Provisioning and Azure to provision and Key Vault and used it to securely enable WinRM. Let's have a look at the other types of resources that can be created in Azure.

Creating Other PaaS Resources via Chef Provisioning and Resource Explorer

Let's imagine we wanted to use a brand new Azure PaaS resource that has just been announced publicly at a conference. We could wait until the API gets documented. Or we could use a tool called **Resource Explorer** to inspect and explore resources that have already been created in your subscription.

Let's have a look at the process needed to automate the creation of any resource you can create through the Management Portal today.

Azure Data Factory describes itself as "a fully managed service for composing data storage, processing, and movement services into streamlined, scalable, and reliable data production pipelines." (see https://azure.microsoft.com/en-us/documentation/videos/azure-data-factory-overview for more detail).

Immediately I can imagine hundreds of use cases for such a PaaS service as part of a larger architecture, so it sounds like a good candidate for our lesson in provisioning generic resources from Chef Provisioning. Azure has some useful tools for quickly creating provisioning templates for anything available in the gallery, if you know where to look. We'll start from scratch, assuming no prior knowledge of this resource and work through the process for rapidly creating an Azure Resource Manager template and Chef Provisioning recipe.

Creating a Dummy Resource

The first thing I do when I want to have a play with new resources in Azure is to head to the Azure Management Portal (https://portal.azure.com). Every time I click **New**, I am overwhelmed with a list of new shiny things I can play with!

An example of this can be seen in Figure 5-2. The analytics space is clearly a fast-moving area with plenty of solutions already integrated into Azure and no doubt more to come. Let's create a Data Factory.

Figure 5-2. *Example services that can be deployed from the Azure Marketplace*

When we create a resource using the portal in Azure, there is a predictable process with a pattern to it. We select our resource, pick a subscription and resource group, add some settings/properties, and then press **Create**. Moments later we have a provisioned resource. Taking Data Factory as an example, Figure 5-3 shows the options that need to be supplied to provision a Data Factory.

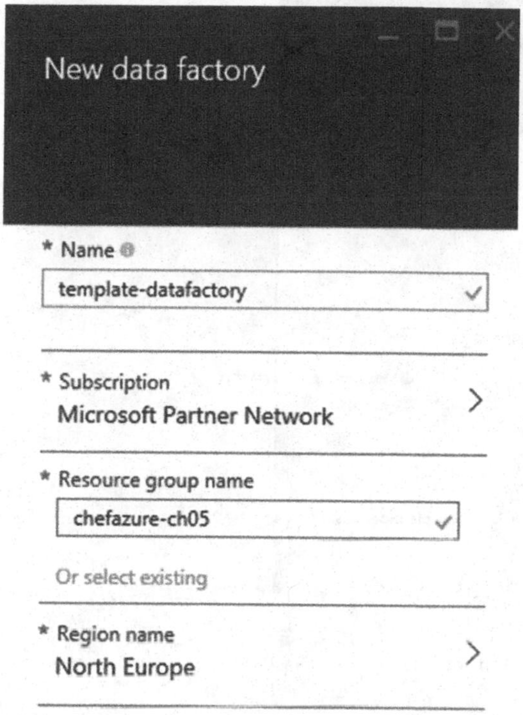

Figure 5-3. New Data Factory options

We simply need to supply the name, a Resource Group, and a Region to provision the resource. Once the resource has been provisioned we can view the Data Factory blade, as shown in Figure 5-4.

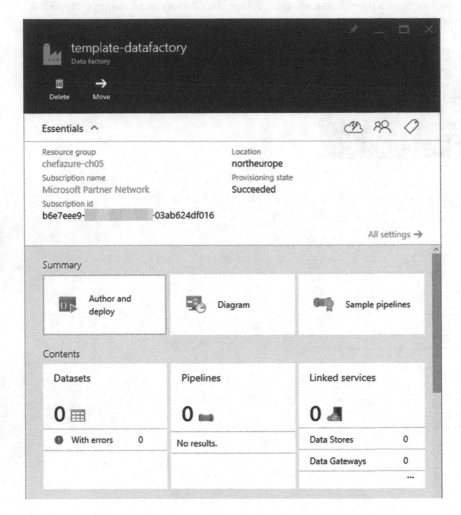

Figure 5-4. *Viewing our template data factory that has been provisioned*

Viewing the Resource in Resource Explorer

Now the resource has been provisioned we can use the Resource Explorer tool, which can be found from the Portal by pressing Browse, then navigating to Resource Explorer (as shown in Figure 5-5).

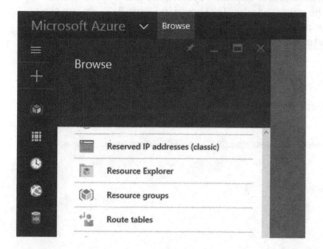

Figure 5-5. *Finding the Resource Explorer in the Browse list in the Azure Management Portal*

You are presented here with a tree-view containing all the Providers and importantly, Subscriptions available. Drilling into the Subscription we can see a list of all the available Resource Groups, from which we can further expand and see the Resources that have been provisioned in that Resource Group.

This can be seen in Figure 5-6, where we have expanded the **chefazure-ch05** Resource Group to find a Resource of type **Microsoft.DataFactory/dataFactories** called **template-datafactory**.

```
[Microsoft.DataFactory/dataFactories] template-datafactory   (Response Time 212ms)

Open blade   /subscriptions/b6e7eee9-          -03ab624df016/resourceGroups/chefazure-ch05/providers/Microsoft.DataFactory/d

 1 {
 2     "name": "template-datafactory",
 3     "id": "/subscriptions/b6e7eee9-          -03ab624df016/resourcegroups/chefazure-ch05,
 4     "type": "Microsoft.DataFactory/datafactories",
 5     "location": "northeurope",
 6     "tags": {},
 7     "properties": {
 8         "dataFactoryId": "ca18c176-          -e11b421d2a79",
 9         "provisioningState": "Succeeded",
10         "error": null,
11         "errorMessage": null
12     }
13 }
```

Figure 5-6. *Resource Explorer showing the tempate-datafactory resource*

Extracting the Template

As before, we need an ARM template and a Recipe so that we can use Chef Provisioning to provision our Data Factory.

Let's start with the Resource definition found in Resource Explorer, by navigating to Deployments/ Microsoft.DataFactory-template-datafactory. In the output window (as shown in Figure 5-7), we can see a **templateLink** element, in our case the URL: `https://gallery.azure.com/artifact/20151001/Microsoft. DataFactory.0.9.3-preview/DeploymentTemplates/DataFactory.json` and we can use this to retrieve the complete template used, and the parameters.

```
1  {
2      "id": "/subscriptions/b6e7eee9-          -03ab624df016/resourceGroups/chefazurech05/deployments/Microsoft.DataFactory-template-dat
3      "name": "Microsoft.DataFactory-template-datafactory",
4      "properties": {
5          "templateLink": {
6              "uri": "https://gallery.azure.com/artifact/20151001/Microsoft.DataFactory.0.9.3-preview/DeploymentTemplates/DataFactory.json",
7              "contentVersion": "1.0.0.0"
8          },
9          "parameters": {
10             "name": {
11                 "type": "String",
12                 "value": "template-datafactory"
13             },
14             "location": {
15                 "type": "String",
16                 "value": "northeurope"
17             },
18             "apiVersion": {
19                 "type": "String",
20                 "value": "2015-05-01-preview"
21             }
22         },
```

Figure 5-7. Viewing the deployment JSON within Resource Explorer

Now we can proceed to create the required files for our deployment; we'll need to store the deploy.json and a data_factory.rb in our cookbook as follows:

cookbooks/chefazure-ch05/files/data_factory/deploy.json:

```
{
    "$schema": "http://schema.management.azure.com/schemas/2014-04-01-preview/
    deploymentTemplate.json#",
    "contentVersion": "1.0.0.0",
    "parameters": {
        "name": {
            "type": "string"
        },
        "location": {
            "type": "string"
        },
        "apiVersion": {
            "type": "string",
            "defaultValue": "2015-01-01-preview"
        }
    },
    "resources": [
        {
```

```
                "apiVersion": "[parameters('apiVersion')]",
                "name": "[parameters('name')]",
                "location": "[parameters('location')]",
                "type": "Microsoft.DataFactory/dataFactories",
                "properties": {}
        }
    ]
}
```

cookbooks/chefazure-ch05/recipes/data_factory.rb:

```
require 'chef/provisioning/azurerm'
with_driver 'AzureRM:b6e7eee9-YOUR-GUID-HERE-03ab624df016'

azure_resource_group 'chefazure-ch05-ne' do
  location 'North Europe'
  tags CreatedFor: 'Using Chef with Microsoft Azure book'
end

azure_resource_template 'chefazure-ch05-datafactory-deployment' do
  resource_group 'chefazure-ch05-ne'
  template_source 'cookbooks/chefazure-ch05/files/data_factory/deploy.json'
  parameters name: 'chefazure-ch05-datafactory',
             location: 'North Europe'
end
```

Running a Custom Deployment

Now that we have retrieved our Resource Manager template, stored it in our cookbook, and created a recipe that uses it, we can execute it using the Chef Client as follows:

```
PS C:\Users\StuartPreston\chefazure-ch05> knife cookbook upload chefazure-ch05
```

```
Uploading chefazure-ch05 [0.1.0]
Uploaded 1 cookbook.
```

```
PS C:\Users\StuartPreston\chefazure-ch05> chef-client -o recipe[chefazure-ch05::data_factory]
```

```
Starting Chef Client, version 12.5.1
[2015-11-22T17:16:51+00:00] WARN: Run List override has been provided.
[2015-11-22T17:16:51+00:00] WARN: Original Run List: []
[2015-11-22T17:16:51+00:00] WARN: Overridden Run List: [recipe[chefazure-ch05::data_factory]]
resolving cookbooks for run list: ["chefazure-ch05::data_factory"]
Synchronizing Cookbooks:
  - chefazure-ch05 (0.1.0)
Compiling Cookbooks...
Converging 2 resources
Recipe: chefazure-ch05::data_factory
  * azure_resource_group[chefazure-ch05-ne] action create
    - create or update Resource Group chefazure-ch05-ne
  * azure_resource_template[chefazure-ch05-datafactory-deployment] action deploy
```

```
- Result: Accepted
- Resource Microsoft.DataFactory/dataFactories 'chefazure-ch05-datafactory' provisioning
    Status is Running
- Resource Microsoft.DataFactory/dataFactories 'chefazure-ch05-datafactory' provisioning
    Status is Running
- Resource Template deployment reached end state of 'Succeeded'.
- deploy or re-deploy Resource Manager template 'chefazure-ch05-datafactory-deployment'
[2015-11-22T17:17:27+00:00] WARN: Skipping final node save because override_runlist was given

Running handlers:
Running handlers complete
Chef Client finished, 2/2 resources updated in 01 minutes 16 seconds
```

Having converged, we can now view that our Resource was provisioned correctly, as seen in Figure 5-8.

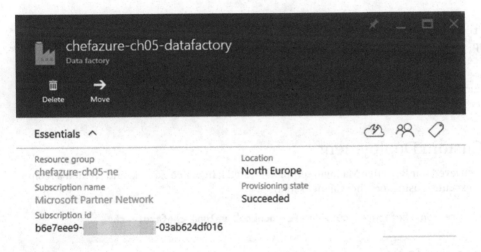

Figure 5-8. *A Data Factory created via Chef Provisioning and Azure Resource Manager*

This was a very simple example, but we can now combine PaaS and IaaS resources when using Chef Provisioning and Azure, and this opens up many possibilities for the creation of hybrid environments.

Summary

In this chapter we explored Azure Resource Manager and demonstrated how to use it with all the features of Chef Provisioning. As we have been able to see - integrating Chef with Azure is not just about provisioning compute (VM) resources, and this enables Chef to be used to provision hybrid PaaS and IaaS environments in a reliable, repeatable way.

The number of services in Azure grows weekly, a pace far faster than this book can keep up with. So we demonstrated how to interpret Resource Explorer and create your own templates as and when new services become available.

In the next chapter we're going to take a look how we can use Azure as part of our quest for quality when using the Chef toolset.

CHAPTER 6

■ ■ ■

Integrating Quality Tooling into the Chef Development Life Cycle

The Chef ecosystem is fortunate to have many tools available to it to help in the quest for quality. This chapter introduces some of the tools that are publicly available to help. Eventually we will be using these tools as part of a Continuous Delivery pipeline, and it is important to get an understanding of how each tool can be executed individually.

In this chapter we're going to take a tour around some of the most popular code analysis and testing tools that are distributed with the ChefDK. First we'll have a look at cookbook linting using tools such as Rubocop and FoodCritic, before turning our attention to the different types of unit and integration testing tools out there.

As the purpose of this chapter is to introduce the tools, we'll show you one or two working examples for each tool, focusing on how they are used in the context of Chef and Azure and then provide some further resources for you to go and explore at your own pace.

Cookbook Linting

Linting is the process of checking source code for problems before execution. Two tools have emerged as the most popular in this area: Rubocop and FoodCritic. Rubocop is a static code analyzer that focuses on Ruby code style errors, FoodCritic focuses on common errors in Chef recipes, and both are powerful tools when used as part of a development workflow. Writing code in a consistent manner makes it easier for other team members to read your code and extend it confidently. It also reduces the amount of difference from commit to commit in your source code repository, making it easier to review.

It takes just a few seconds to run Rubocop and FoodCritic, so there's no reason not to run both regularly against your cookbooks as part of your development process. These tools also return standard return codes meaning they are very suitable for use in automated pipelines. We'll be covering this in chapter 8.

■ **Note**   Rubocop and FoodCritic are installed with the Chef Development Kit (ChefDK) by default. See chapter 1 if you have not installed ChefDK yet.

Using RuboCop

Most of the code that is authored when working with Chef is written as Ruby. Just about every file within a cookbook (with few exceptions) is a Ruby file. So we can use Rubocop to do the following:

- Enforce style conventions and best practices
- Evaluate the code in a cookbook against metrics such as "line length" and "function size"
- Help every member of a team to author similarly structured code
- Establish uniformity of source code
- Set expectations for fellow (and future) project contributors

The Rubocop ruleset was borne out of the **Ruby Style Guide** (see `https://github.com/bbatsov/ruby-style-guide`), which is a community-maintained set of guidelines that attempts to define a good set of conventions and principles.

Each rule in Rubocop may be enabled and disabled, either at a global level by configuring a `.rubocop.yml` file at the root of your project or by adding special comments to each Ruby file that exclude offenses from being counted. Let's give it a go in a new cookbook.

Running Rubocop against an Entire Repository

In this example, we're going to run Rubocop against a new repository to verify the output is as expected, with no errors.

First of all, let's create a new repository using `chef generate app`:

```
PS C:\Users\StuartPreston> chef generate app chefazure-ch06
```

This should generate an output similar to the following, and I have shortened the (lengthy) output:

```
Compiling Cookbooks...
Recipe: code_generator::app
  * directory[C:/Users/StuartPreston/chefazure-ch06] action create
    - create new directory C:/Users/StuartPreston/chefazure-ch06
  * template[C:/Users/StuartPreston/chefazure-ch06/.kitchen.yml] action create
    - create new file C:/Users/StuartPreston/chefazure-ch06/.kitchen.yml

  [... files are created here ...]
  * execute[initialize-git] action run
    - execute git init .
  * cookbook_file[C:/Users/StuartPreston/chefazure-ch06/.gitignore] action create
    - create new file C:/Users/StuartPreston/chefazure-ch06/.gitignore
    - update content in file C:/Users/StuartPreston/chefazure-ch06/.gitignore from none to
      33d469
  (diff output suppressed by config)
```

Now let's move into our repo directory:

```
PS C:\Users\StuartPreston> cd chefazure-ch06
```

and execute Rubocop with no other command-line options:

```
PS C:\Users\StuartPreston\chefazure-ch06> rubocop
```

```
Inspecting 7 files
.......

7 files inspected, no offenses detected
```

As you can see from the output we have no offenses detected. That's a good start. Let's add some code to a recipe and see if Rubocop detects anything wrong.

Detecting and Correcting Rubocop Violations

Let's open up our code editor (in my case Visual Studio Code):

```
PS C:\Users\StuartPreston\chefazure-ch06> code .
```

Now navigate to **cookbooks\chefazure-ch06\recipes** and open up the **default.rb** file. Let's add a simple log resource to our recipe as follows:

```
#
# Cookbook Name:: chefazure-ch06
# Recipe:: default
#
# Copyright (c) 2016 The Authors, All Rights Reserved.

log "Hello, World!"
```

The code should look similar to the code shown in Figure 6-1. Save the file.

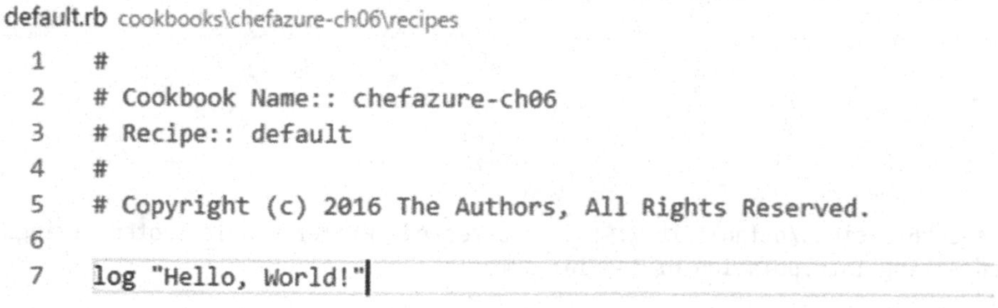

default.rb cookbooks\chefazure-ch06\recipes

```
1    #
2    # Cookbook Name:: chefazure-ch06
3    # Recipe:: default
4    #
5    # Copyright (c) 2016 The Authors, All Rights Reserved.
6
7    log "Hello, World!"
```

Figure 6-1. *Adding a log resource to the default recipe in our cookbook*

Now we're going to run Rubocop again and see what results we get:

```
PS C:\Users\StuartPreston\chefazure-ch06> rubocop
```

```
Inspecting 7 files
..C....

Offenses:

cookbooks/chefazure-ch06/recipes/default.rb:7:5: C: Prefer single-quoted strings when you
don't need string interpolation or special symbols.
log "Hello, World!"
    ^^^^^^^^^^^^^^^
cookbooks/chefazure-ch06/recipes/default.rb:7:20: C: Final newline missing.
log "Hello, World!"

7 files inspected, 2 offenses detected
```

As we can see from the output, two style offenses have been detected in the code from adding one seemingly innocuous line of code. Impressive! We can now correct them and try it again. We can make the changes manually ourselves or use the (experimental) autocorrect feature of Rubocop.

■ **Note**   Some text editors will automatically add a final newline to your file if you forget, so you may only see one offense here!

Rubocop Autocorrect

While there are some Rubocop violations that have multiple possible fixes, Rubocop does a good job of correcting code automatically by simply typing rubocop -a.

Autocorrect works best when there is only one solution to the problem; otherwise it will leave the offense alone. Let's run rubocop -a against our code and see what happens:

```
PS C:\Users\StuartPreston\chefazure-ch06> rubocop -a
```

```
Inspecting 7 files
..C....

Offenses:

cookbooks/chefazure-ch06/recipes/default.rb:7:5: C: [Corrected] Prefer single-quoted strings
when you don't need string interpolation or special symbols.
log "Hello, World!"
    ^^^^^^^^^^^^^^^
cookbooks/chefazure-ch06/recipes/default.rb:7:20: C: [Corrected] Final newline missing.
log "Hello, World!"

7 files inspected, 2 offenses detected, 2 offenses corrected
```

We can see in our example we now have corrected two offenses. This can also be seen in Figure 6-2. Our quoted string was changed to single quotes, and a new line was added at the end of the file for consistency.

default.rb cookbooks\chefazure-ch06\recipes

```
1   #
2   # Cookbook Name:: chefazure-ch06
3   # Recipe:: default
4   #
5   # Copyright (c) 2016 The Authors, All Rights Reserved.
6
7   log 'Hello, World!'
8
```

Figure 6-2. Our corrected recipe after being run through Rubocop in autocorrect mode

Suppressing Rubocop Offenses

While it would be great if we could use and enforce the default Rubocop rules for all our projects without modification, sometimes you will break so many rules that you want to defer fixing them until a later point, or perhaps you have a rule that simply doesn't make sense for your project.

If you have a legitimate reason to suppress an offense there are a few ways to accomplish this:

1. You may generate a .rubocop_todo.yml file from your failing tests, with the intent of fixing them later.

2. You may add blanket exclusions to your .rubocop.yml file.

3. You may add per-line exclusions as a comment in each file.

4. You may exclude sections of files.

5. You may exclude entire files.

Generating a todo file

A Rubocop todo file is simply a partial configuration file that can be included in your Rubocop configuration. As you gradually solve the problems you remove the line from the todo file until there's none left.

Let's change our **default.rb** file so it triggers our first warning again:

```
#
# Cookbook Name:: chefazure-ch06
# Recipe:: default
#
# Copyright (c) 2016 The Authors, All Rights Reserved.

log "Hello, World!"
```

Now let's generate a rubocop-todo.yml file by using rubocop --auto-gen-config:

```
PS C:\Users\StuartPreston\chefazure-ch06> rubocop --auto-gen-config
```

```
Inspecting 7 files
..C....

Offenses:

cookbooks/chefazure-ch06/recipes/default.rb:7:5: C: Prefer single-quoted strings when you
don't need string interpolation or special symbols.
log "Hello, World!"
    ^^^^^^^^^^^^^^^

7 files inspected, 1 offense detected
Created .rubocop_todo.yml.
Run `rubocop --config .rubocop_todo.yml`, or
add inherit_from: .rubocop_todo.yml in a .rubocop.yml file.
```

If we inspect the contents of the .rubocop_todo.yml file we can see the exclusions created for the specific 'cops' (Rubocop tests) that we are no longer interested in testing for:

```
PS C:\Users\StuartPreston\chefazure-ch06> cat .rubocop_todo.yml
```

```
# This configuration was generated by
# `rubocop --auto-gen-config`
# on 2015-11-05 16:18:50 +0000 using RuboCop version 0.34.2.
# The point is for the user to remove these configuration records
# one by one as the offenses are removed from the code base.
# Note that changes in the inspected code, or installation of new
# versions of RuboCop, may require this file to be generated again.

# Offense count: 1
# Cop supports --auto-correct.
# Configuration parameters: EnforcedStyle, SupportedStyles.
Style/StringLiterals:
  Enabled: false
```

To take on the new configuration, you can either specify rubocop -c .rubocop_todo.yml from the command line, or (the preferred approach) is to create a new file called .rubocop.yml and insert the following line:

```
inherit_from: .rubocop_todo.yml
```

Now when you execute rubocop without any parameters it will pick up the `.rubocop_todo.yml` file and suppress any defined rules there:

```
PS C:\Users\StuartPreston\chefazure-ch06> rubocop
```

```
Inspecting 7 files
.......

7 files inspected, no offenses detected
```

Adding Blanket Exclusions

As we mentioned before, the .rubocop.yml file is where we apply any configuration that is global to the whole repository. So let's replace our **.rubocop.yml** file with the contents of the **.rubocop_todo.yml** file, as it already has some rules in it:

```
PS C:\Users\StuartPreston\chefazure-ch06> cp .rubocop_todo.yml .rubocop.yml
PS C:\Users\StuartPreston\chefazure-ch06> rubocop
```

```
Inspecting 7 files
.......

7 files inspected, no offenses detected
```

Ok so what's the difference? Although the same outcome is achieved, you would place rules you wanted to suppress permanently for the whole team in the **.rubocop.yml** file and rules that you eventually want to fix in the **.rubocop_todo.yml** file.

Finally let's have a look at how to exclude cops from running on a per-line basis.

Adding Per-line Exclusions

To exclude cops from running on a per-line basis, we need to add a Ruby comment to that line.

First, let's remove our .rubocop.yml to bring back an error that needs correcting, and run Rubocop again to detect our mistake. We can use the -D parameter to see the full cop name, which we'll need to use to specify our exclusion.

```
PS C:\Users\StuartPreston\chefazure-ch06> rm .rubocop.yml
PS C:\Users\StuartPreston\chefazure-ch06> rubocop -D
```

```
Inspecting 7 files
..C....

Offenses:

cookbooks/chefazure-ch06/recipes/default.rb:7:5: C: Style/StringLiterals: Prefer single-
quoted strings when you don't need string interpolation or special symbols.
log "Hello, World!"
    ^^^^^^^^^^^^^^^

7 files inspected, 1 offense detected
```

We can take the cop name "Style/StringLiterals" and put that in a comment against our code with a rubocop:disable directive, as shown in Figure 6-3. The resulting code should look like this:

```
#
# Cookbook Name:: chefazure-ch06
# Recipe:: default
#
# Copyright (c) 2016 The Authors, All Rights Reserved.

log "Hello, World!" # rubocop:disable Style/StringLiterals
```

default.rb cookbooks\chefazure-ch06\recipes

```
1    #
2    # Cookbook Name:: chefazure-ch06
3    # Recipe:: default
4    #
5    # Copyright (c) 2016 The Authors, All Rights Reserved.
6
7    log "Hello, World!" # rubocop:disable Style/StringLiterals
8    |
```

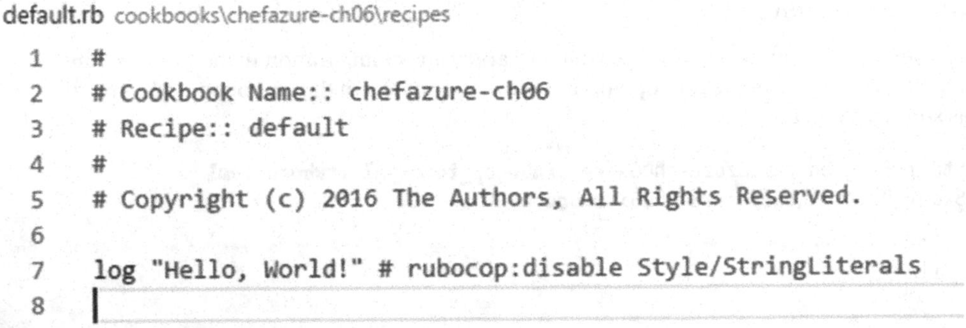

Figure 6-3. Suppressing a rubocop rule at line level

Now when you execute rubocop -D again, there should be no offenses detected:

```
PS C:\Users\StuartPreston\chefazure-ch06> rubocop -D
```

```
Inspecting 7 files
.......

7 files inspected, no offenses detected
```

Suppressing Specific Rules Per Section

A per-section Rubocop suppression is achieved by surrounding the code with a comment to disable and then enable the rule. Here's an example:

```
#
# Cookbook Name:: chefazure-ch06
# Recipe:: default
#
# Copyright (c) 2016 The Authors, All Rights Reserved.

# rubocop:disable Style/StringLiterals
log "Hello, World!"
# rubocop:enable Style/StringLiterals
```

When we run rubocop now, our section is excluded from the **listed** rules, and we get the output shown below:

```
PS C:\Users\StuartPreston\chefazure-ch06> rubocop
```

```
Inspecting 7 files
.......

7 files inspected, no offenses detected
```

Suppressing All Rules in a Section

Finally, you can override Rubocop from running any rules against a section of code by using the all directive. Here's an example:

```
#
# Cookbook Name:: chefazure-ch06
# Recipe:: default
#
# Copyright (c) 2015 The Authors, All Rights Reserved.

# rubocop:disable all
log "Hello, World!"
# rubocop:enable all
```

When we run rubocop now, **all** rules in that section are suppressed from execution:

```
PS C:\Users\StuartPreston\chefazure-ch06> rubocop
```

```
Inspecting 7 files
.......

7 files inspected, no offenses detected
```

Rubocop Options

Rubocop can be executed with a range of options; these are all documented in Table 6-1, you can also get the list by running rubocop -h:

```
PS C:\Users\StuartPreston> rubocop -h
```

Table 6-1. *Rubocop command-line options*

Command-line Argument	Description
-v/--version	Displays the current version and exits.
-V/--verbose-version	Displays the current version plus the version of Parser and Ruby.
-L/--list-target-files	List all files Rubocop will inspect.
-F/--fail-fast	Inspects in modification time order and stops after first file with offenses.
-C/--cache	Store and reuse results for faster operation.
-d/--debug	Displays some extra debug output.
-D/--display-cop-names	Displays cop names in offense messages.
-c/--config	Run with specified config file.
-f/--format	Choose a formatter.
-o/--out	Write output to a file instead of STDOUT.
-r/--require	Require Ruby file.
-R/--rails	Run extra Rails cops.
-l/--lint	Run only lint cops.
-a/--auto-correct	Autocorrect certain offenses. Note: Experimental - use with caution.
--only	Run only the specified cop(s) and/or cops in the specified departments.
--except	Run all cops enabled by configuration except the specified cop(s) and/or departments.
--auto-gen-config	Generate a configuration file acting as a TODO list.
--exclude-limit	Limit how many individual files --auto-gen-config can list in Exclude parameters, default is 15.
--show-cops	Shows available cops and their configuration.
--fail-level	Minimum severity for exit with error code. Full severity name or uppercase initial can be given. Normally, auto-corrected offenses are ignored. Use A or autocorrect if you'd like them to trigger failure.
-s/--stdin	Pipe source from STDIN. This is useful for editor integration.

That covers the basics of Rubocop. Where possible try to maintain zero violations in your project or distribute your **.rubocop.yml** files with your repo so that it is clear what is acceptable to the project to be ignored or suppressed. Let's move on to some of the other quality tools within the ChefDK.

Using FoodCritic

FoodCritic is a static code analyzer that checks for what it considers to be poor cookbook authoring practices when using the Chef language. Compiling, converging, and executing real cookbook tests take time, and tools such as FoodCritic help us 'fail fast' before any code has been executed. It can also flag problems that would cause your Chef Client run to fail.

FoodCritic Rules

There are currently 58 default FoodCritic rules that are executed against the specified cookbooks. A complete list can be generated by using the command foodcritic -l:

```
PS C:\Users\StuartPreston\chefazure-ch06> foodcritic -l
```

FC001: Use strings in preference to symbols to access node attributes
FC002: Avoid string interpolation where not required
FC003: Check whether you are running with chef server before using server-specific features
FC004: Use a service resource to start and stop services
FC005: Avoid repetition of resource declarations
FC006: Mode should be quoted or fully specified when setting file permissions
FC007: Ensure recipe dependencies are reflected in cookbook metadata
FC008: Generated cookbook metadata needs updating
FC009: Resource attribute not recognised
FC010: Invalid search syntax
FC011: Missing README in markdown format
FC012: Use Markdown for README rather than RDoc
FC013: Use file_cache_path rather than hard-coding tmp paths
FC014: Consider extracting long ruby_block to library
FC015: Consider converting definition to a LWRP
FC016: LWRP does not declare a default action
FC017: LWRP does not notify when updated
FC018: LWRP uses deprecated notification syntax
FC019: Access node attributes in a consistent manner
FC021: Resource condition in provider may not behave as expected
FC022: Resource condition within loop may not behave as expected
FC023: Prefer conditional attributes
FC024: Consider adding platform equivalents
FC025: Prefer chef_gem to compile-time gem install
FC026: Conditional execution block attribute contains only string
FC027: Resource sets internal attribute
FC028: Incorrect #platform? Usage
FC029: No leading cookbook name in recipe metadata
FC030: Cookbook contains debugger breakpoints
FC031: Cookbook without metadata file
FC032: Invalid notification timing
FC033: Missing template
FC034: Unused template variables
FC037: Invalid notification action
FC038: Invalid resource action
FC039: Node method cannot be accessed with key
FC040: Execute resource used to run git commands
FC041: Execute resource used to run curl or wget commands
FC042: Prefer include_recipe to require_recipe
FC043: Prefer new notification syntax
FC044: Avoid bare attribute keys
FC045: Consider setting cookbook name in metadata
FC046: Attribute assignment uses assign unless nil
FC047: Attribute assignment does not specify precedence

```
FC048: Prefer Mixlib::ShellOut
FC049: Role name does not match containing file name
FC050: Name includes invalid characters
FC051: Template partials loop indefinitely
FC052: Metadata uses the unimplemented "suggests" keyword
FC053: Metadata uses the unimplemented "recommends" keyword
```

Each FoodCritic rule is documented at http://foodcritic.io - for example Figure 6-4 shows the first rule that is tested against your cookbook: FC001.

FC001: Use strings in preference to symbols to access node attributes

`style` `attributes`

Use strings rather than symbols when referencing node attributes. This warning will be shown if you reference a node attribute using symbols.

Symbols in node attributes.

This example would match the FC001 rule because `node[:cookbook][:package]` accesses node attributes with symbols

```
# Don't do this
package node[:cookbook][:package] do
  action :install
end
```

Modified version

This modified example would not match the FC001 rule:

```
package node['cookbook']['package'] do
  action :install
end
```

Figure 6-4. FoodCritic rule explanation as seen at http://www.foodcritic.io/#FC001

To see FoodCritic in action, let's go back to our recipe **cookbooks/chefazure-ch06/default.rb** in our code editor and modify it as follows so that when executed it would log three messages as part of the Chef Client run:

```
#
# Cookbook Name:: chefazure-ch06
# Recipe:: default
#
# Copyright (c) 2015 The Authors, All Rights Reserved.

log 'Hello, Adam!' do
  level :info
end

log 'Hello, Alan!' do
  level :info
end

log 'Hello, Ross!' do
  level :info
end
```

Now let's see what FoodCritic identifies about our cookbook:

```
C:\Users\StuartPreston\chefazure-ch06> foodcritic cookbooks/chefazure-ch06
```

FC005: Avoid repetition of resource declarations: cookbooks/chefazure-ch06/recipes/
default.rb:7
FC011: Missing README in markdown format: cookbooks/chefazure-ch06/README.md:1

We can see that we have triggered the rule FC005: Avoid repetition of resource declarations. If we look up this rule (as seen in Figure 6-5), we can see the problem and a possible solution is presented to us.

FC005: Avoid repetition of resource declarations

`style`

When writing Chef recipes you have the full power of Ruby at your disposal. One of the cases where this is helpful is where you need to declare a large number of resources that only differ in a single attribute - the canonical example is installing a long list of packages.

Unnecessarily repetitive

This example matches the FC005 rule because all the resources of type `package` differ only in a single attribute - the name of the package to be upgraded. This rule is very simple and looks only for resources that all differ in only a single attribute. For example - if only one of the packages specified the version then this rule would not match.

Modified version

This modified example would not match the FC005 rule. It takes advantage of the fact that Chef processes recipes in two distinct phases. In the first 'compile' phase it builds the resource collection. In the second phase it configures the node against the resource collection.

Don't worry about changing your recipe if it already does what you want - the amount of Ruby syntactic sugar to apply is very much a matter of personal taste. Note that this rule also isn't clever enough yet to detect if your resources are wrapped in a control structure and not suitable for 'rolling up' into a loop.

```ruby
# You could do this
package 'erlang-base' do
  action :upgrade
end
package 'erlang-corba' do
  action :upgrade
end
package 'erlang-crypto' do
  action :upgrade
end
package 'rabbitmq-server' do
  action :upgrade
end
```

```ruby
# It's shorter to do this
%w{erlang-base erlang-corba erlang-crypto rabbitmq-server}.each do
|pkg|
  package pkg do
    action :upgrade
  end
end
```

Figure 6-5. *FoodCritic rule explanation as seen at http://foodcritic.io/#FC005*

We can now go back to our recipe and change it to match the desired style:

```ruby
#
# Cookbook Name:: chefazure-ch06
# Recipe:: default
#
# Copyright (c) 2015 The Authors, All Rights Reserved.

%w(Adam Alan Ross).each do |friend|
  log "Hello, #{friend}!" do
    level :info
  end
end
```

■ **Note**   On a Windows machine, the path to the cookbook must be passed in with forward slashes (e.g., cookbooks/chefazure-ch06) rather than backslashes (e.g., cookbooks\chefazure-ch06).

We can now retest and ensure we do not get any FC005 matches returned:

```
PS C:\Users\StuartPreston\chefazure-ch06> foodcritic cookbooks/chefazure-ch06
```

We are left with one further warning that we will suppress in the next section:

```
FC011: Missing README in markdown format: cookbooks/chefazure-ch06/README.md:1
```

Suppressing FoodCritic Messages

Rules in FoodCritic are identified by a tag, which takes the format FC + number: for example, FC001. To exclude rules with specific tags, the -t option is used with a ~ in front of the tag name. For example, if we wished to exclude the tag FC011: Missing README in markdown format we would specify the following command at the command line:

```
PS C:\Users\StuartPreston\chefazure-ch06> foodcritic cookbooks/chefazure-ch06 -t ~FC011
```

The results list should now be an empty line, indicating that no issues were found with the cookbook:

Suppressing FoodCritic Messages for an Entire cookbook

To exclude rules for all users of a repo, we can create a **.foodcritic** file at the root of the specific cookbook, containing a list of the rules we want to exclude. For example, to exclude the rule FC011: Missing README in markdown format, the file should contain a single line as follows:

```
PS C:\Users\StuartPreston\chefazure-ch06> echo "~FC011" > cookbooks/chefazure-ch06/.
foodcritic
PS C:\Users\StuartPreston\chefazure-ch06> foodcritic cookbooks/chefazure-ch06
```

Again the results returned should be an empty line, indicating no issues were found:

Further FoodCritic Options

FoodCritic has a number of additional options that can be seen by typing foodcritic -h as shown in Table 6-2.

Table 6-2. *FoodCritic command-line options*

Command-line Argument	Description
-t, --tags TAGS	Check against (or exclude ~) rules with the specified tags.
-l, --list	List all enabled rules and their descriptions.
-f, --epic-fail TAGS	Fail the build based on tags. Use 'any' to fail on all warnings.
-c, --chef-version VERSION	Only check against rules valid for this version of Chef.
-B, --cookbook-path PATH	Cookbook path(s) to check.
-C, --[no-]context	Show lines matched against rather than the default summary.
-E, --environment-path PATH	Environment path(s) to check.
-I, --include PATH	Additional rule file path(s) to load.
-G, --search-gems	Search rubygems for rule files with the path foodcritic/rules/**/*.rb
-P, --progress	Show progress of files being checked.
-R, --role-path PATH	Role path(s) to check.
-S, --search-grammar PATH	Specify grammar to use when validating search syntax.
-V, --version	Display the foodcritic version.
-X, --exclude PATH	Exclude path(s) from being linted.

Now that we've covered the basic of code linting and static analysis, we'll move on to explain how to test your recipes.

Cookbook Testing

Cookbook Testing with Chef generally falls into two areas: Unit Testing and Acceptance Testing. From a Unit Testing perspective, we're interested in testing individual units of code, independently of other circumstances in the system, such as the state of the environment. Because unit tests should not have any external dependencies such as connections to a remote system they should execute at speed.

From an Acceptance Testing perspective, we're interested in testing that once we apply our code to an environment, the described target state is reached.

The Chef ecosystem has a great Unit Testing tool called ChefSpec, which is a set of extensions on top of the popular behavior-driven development (BDD) testing framework RSpec, and a great tool for Acceptance Testing called Test Kitchen that is a complete framework that allows you to test your cookbooks against multiple platforms. Figure 6-6 differentiates the types of testing and the tools used.

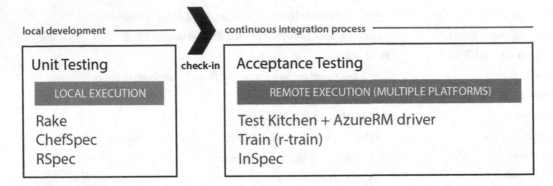

Figure 6-6. *Types of Cookbook Testing*

Using ChefSpec

ChefSpec is a framework that simulates a Chef Client run and allows you to test resources and recipes without any other external dependencies. As a result, ChefSpec tests execute very quickly. Because of this, ChefSpec tests are typically placed early in a CI system's pipeline after static analysis and are typically the first indicator of problems that may exist within a cookbook.

ChefSpec is based on a behavior-driven development (BDD) framework called RSpec that uses a natural language domain-specific language (DSL) to describe scenarios in which systems are being tested. RSpec allows a scenario to be set up, then executed with dummy parameters. The results are then compared to a predefined set of expectations. This syntax is shown in Figure 6-7 below.

Syntax

The syntax of RSpec-based tests should follow the natural language descriptions of RSpec itself. The tests themselves should create an English-like sentence: "The sum of one plus one equals two, and not three." For example:

```
describe '1 plus 1' do
  it 'equals 2' do
    a = 1
    b = 1
    sum = a + b
    expect(sum).to eq(2)
    expect(sum).not_to eq(3)
  end
end
```

where:

- `describe` creates the testing scenario: `1 plus 1`
- `it` is a block that defines a list of parameters to test, along with parameters that define the expected outcome
- `describe` and `it` should have human readable descriptions: "one plus one equals two"
- `a`, `b`, and `sum` define the testing scenario: `a` equals one, `b` equals one, the `sum` of one plus equals two
- `expect()` defines the expectation: the sum of one plus one equals two—`expect(sum).to eq(2)`—and does not equal three–`expect(sum).not_to eq(3)`
- `.to` tests the results of the test for true; `.not_to` tests the result of the test for false; a test passes when the results of the test are true

Figure 6-7. Syntax of an RSpec test (credit: https://docs.chef.io/chefspec.html)

Generating ChefSpec tests for Cookbooks

Luckily for us, cookbooks by default have a default set of ChefSpec tests created. They can be found under <cookbook>/spec/unit/recipes. Test 'specifications' by convention are named _spec.rb so that tools can find them by this pattern.

Figure 6-8 shows us the structure that is generated and a default test that has been generated.

```
EXPLORER                          default_spec.rb  cookbooks\chefazure-ch06\spec\unit\recipes

▲ WORKING FILES                    1   #
   default.rb  cookbooks\chefazure-ch0...  2   # Cookbook Name:: chefazure-ch06
▲ CHEFAZURE-CH06                   3   # Spec:: default
   ▲ cookbooks                     4   #
      ▲ chefazure-ch06             5   # Copyright (c) 2016 The Authors, All Rights Reserved.
         ▷ recipes                 6
         ▲ spec                    7   require 'spec_helper'
            ▲ unit                 8
               ▲ recipes           9   describe 'chefazure-ch06::default' do
                  default_spec.rb  10    context 'When all attributes are default, on an unspecified platform' do
         spec_helper.rb            11      let(:chef_run) do
         Berksfile                 12        runner = ChefSpec::ServerRunner.new
         chefignore                13        runner.converge(described_recipe)
         metadata.rb               14      end
      ▷ test                       15
      .gitignore                   16      it 'converges successfully' do
      .kitchen.yml                 17        expect { chef_run }.to_not raise_error
      README.md                    18      end
                                   19    end
                                   20  end
                                   21
```

Figure 6-8. *Directory structure showing the default test specification file created by chef generate app*

Executing ChefSpec Tests

ChefSpec tests are executed from the cookbook directory and not the root of the repo. So let's execute the default tests by changing directory into the cookbook directory and running rspec.

■ **Tip**   Use the -f documentation flag to get a list of the tests that are executed, also if your terminal supports it you can add the --color flag to get results in color.

```
PS C:\Users\StuartPreston\chefazure-ch06> cd cookbooks/chefazure-06
PS C:\Users\StuartPreston\chefazure-ch06\cookbooks\chefazure-ch06> rspec -f documentation
```

```
chefazure-ch06::default
  When all attributes are default, on an unspecified platform
    converges successfully

Finished in 0.71881 seconds (files took 15.13 seconds to load)
1 example, 0 failures
```

We can see from the output that we have one example, zero failures. This is the expected behavior. Let's break down the default tests to understand what it is doing a bit more.

```
#
# Cookbook Name:: chefazure-ch06
# Spec:: default
#
# Copyright (c) 2016 The Authors, All Rights Reserved.

require 'spec_helper'
```

The statement require 'spec_helper' means that this file is including some statements from the common file **spec/spec_helper.rb**. All of the spec files will require this statement at the top of the file otherwise ChefSpec will not get loaded correctly. Let's have a look at the default test:

```
describe 'chefazure-ch06::default' do
  context 'When all attributes are default, on an unspecified platform' do
    let(:chef_run) do
      runner = ChefSpec::ServerRunner.new
      runner.converge(described_recipe)
    end

    it 'converges successfully' do
      expect { chef_run }.to_not raise_error
    end
  end
end
```

Working outwards from the test:

- The test itself (it 'converges successfully') is testing that the chef_run does not raise an error when it converges.

- The **let** statement assigns variables that can be used elsewhere in the context block (in our case, **chef_run**).

- The **context** block (context 'When all attributes are default, on an unspecified platform') provides a grouping for the test, and can be used to run different tests according to the platform being tested (not used here).

- The **describe** statement (describe 'chefazure-ch06::default') is the scenario that is being tested. In this case a recipe: chefazure-ch06::default.

What we are trying to do with ChefSpec test is provide tests that cover each scenario you are writing recipes for, so that we can write the minimum recipe code that satisfies the test and eventually allows safe refactoring of the recipe code.

Imagine you have a scenario that means you want to write a recipe to ensure a specific file is deleted. Most of the tests follow the pattern of the following:

```
expect(chef_run).to <action>_<resource>('<name>')
```

We know in Chef to write this recipe we need to use the **file** resource and the **:delete** action, so our resulting test would look something like this:

```
expect(chef_run).to delete_file('c:/test.txt')
```

The resource in our recipe would look something like this:

```
file 'c:/test.txt' do
  action :delete
end
```

We can see the resource name, the name of the file and the action match those we specified in the test.

Let's try it. First of all, open up the **cookbooks/chefazure-ch06/spec/unit/recipes/default_spec.rb** in your text editor and add the following text within the context block:

```
it 'deletes the test.txt file' do
  expect(chef_run).to delete_file('c:/test.txt')
end
```

The resulting file should look as shown in Figure 6-9:

```
default_spec.rb   cookbooks\chefazure-ch06\spec\unit\recipes

1    #
2    # Cookbook Name:: chefazure-ch06
3    # Spec:: default
4    #
5    # Copyright (c) 2016 The Authors, All Rights Reserved.
6
7    require 'spec_helper'
8
9    describe 'chefazure-ch06::default' do
10     context 'When all attributes are default, on an unspecified platform' do
11       let(:chef_run) do
12         runner = ChefSpec::ServerRunner.new
13         runner.converge(described_recipe)
14       end
15
16       it 'converges successfully' do
17         expect { chef_run }.to_not raise_error
18       end
19
20       it 'deletes the test.txt file' do
21         expect(chef_run).to delete_file('c:/test.txt')
22       end
23     end
24   end
25   |
```

Figure 6-9. Adding a test to our default_spec.rb file

Now we can execute our test by running rspec with the -f documentation and --color options:

```
PS C:\Users\StuartPreston\chefazure-ch06\cookbooks\chefazure-ch06> rspec -f documentation
--color
```

After a few seconds you should see a similar test failure to below.

```
chefazure-ch06::default
  When all attributes are default, on an unspecified platform
    converges successfully
    deletes the test.txt file (FAILED - 1)

Failures:

  1) chefazure-ch06::default When all attributes are default, on an unspecified platform
deletes the test.txt file
     Failure/Error: expect(chef_run).to delete_file('c:/test.txt')
       expected "file[c:/test.txt]" with action :delete to be in Chef run. Other file
resources:

     # ./spec/unit/recipes/default_spec.rb:21:in `block (3 levels) in <top (required)>'

Finished in 1.06 seconds (files took 15.93 seconds to load)
2 examples, 1 failure

Failed examples:

rspec ./spec/unit/recipes/default_spec.rb:20 # chefazure-ch06::default When all attributes
are default, on an unspecified platform deletes the test.txt file
```

The output shows you exactly which test has failed so you can go back to it and resolve it. It is, of course, correct that this test fails - we haven't written the recipe yet! This style of test-first development is a commonly accepted practice in the development world. We first of all write our test, see it fail, write the minimum amount of code to satisfy the test, and then refactor our solution, maintaining test success all the while. Figure 6-10 shows the workflow behind this practice.

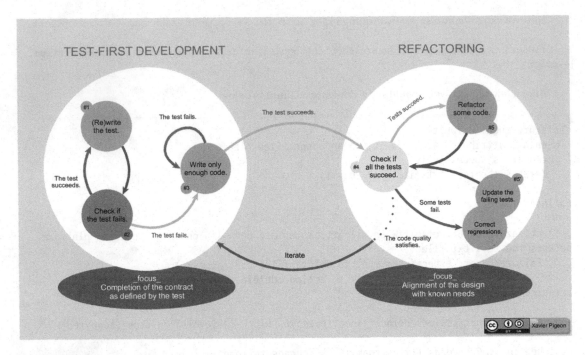

Figure 6-10. *Test-first development process (image credit: Xavier Pigeon)*

We can now add to our **default.rb** recipe to satisfy the test:

```
file 'c:/test.txt' do
  action :delete
end
```

Having done that, let's retry our test using rspec:

```
PS C:\Users\StuartPreston\chefazure-ch06\cookbooks\chefazure-ch06> rspec -f documentation
--color
```

```
chefazure-ch06::default
  When all attributes are default, on an unspecified platform
    converges successfully
    deletes the test.txt file

Finished in 1.05 seconds (files took 14.8 seconds to load)
2 examples, 0 failures
```

We have satisfied our tests and everything is 'green'.

Adding Code Coverage to Cookbook Tests

ChefSpec offers a crude code coverage mechanism to let you know which resources have been touched by your tests as a percentage.

To enable it, simply add the following line to your **spec_helper.rb** file (found in your cookbook within the **spec** folder):

```
at_exit { ChefSpec::Coverage.report! }
```

Now when you run the RSpec tests you should get a coverage report at the end:

```
PS C:\Users\StuartPreston\chefazure-ch06\cookbooks\chefazure-ch06> rspec -f documentation
--color
```

```
chefazure-ch06::default
  When all attributes are default, on an unspecified platform
    converges successfully
    deletes the test.txt file

Finished in 9.38 seconds (files took 5.04 seconds to load)
2 examples, 0 failures

ChefSpec Coverage report generated...
  Total Resources:   1
  Touched Resources: 1
  Touch Coverage:    100.0%

You are awesome and so is your test coverage! Have a fantastic day!
```

Now we have seen how to add unit tests to your cookbooks to simulate behavior, we can now take a look at the other side of testing, using Test Kitchen and InSpec to perform acceptance tests on your recipes against real servers.

Using Test Kitchen and InSpec with Azure Resource Manager

Test Kitchen (see http://kitchen.ci) is a test framework that allows you to execute code on one or more platforms in isolation, ensuring that no prior state exists. Test Kitchen is written in Ruby (so is cross-platform) and has a plug-in architecture that allows you to use it against popular cloud, virtualization, or bare metal resources. It is not directly connected with the Chef toolset, but is distributed with the ChefDK, which means it should be ready for us to use on our workstation.

Test Kitchen in the context of Chef makes it easy to add Acceptance Tests to our infrastructure code because we can spin up a brand new machine, execute our recipes, and then run tests to ensure the system is in the desired state after execution. Then the machine can either be thrown away, or optionally you can continue to work on it until you are closer to a working solution.

There are four primary stages of the Test Kitchen workflow: **create**, **converge**, **verify,** and **destroy** and these are shown in Figure 6-11.

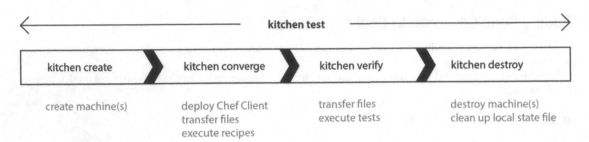

Figure 6-11. *"kitchen test" workflow*

This workflow can be used for both development purposes and also integrated within a Continuous Integration (CI) pipeline - if we complete the entire workflow and get no errors then we can continue to the next stage of our CI/CD pipeline. We'll be covering this more in chapter 8.

In this chapter we'll be using Test Kitchen with the Azure Resource Manager driver, **kitchen-azurerm** and identifying some of the commonly used configuration parameters. Let's start by getting the **kitchen-azurerm** packages installed and configured for our Azure subscription.

Installing the Azure Resource Manager Driver for Test Kitchen

I'm going to assume at this point that you have a recent ChefDK installed (if not, full details were provided in chapter 1), so from your shell we can install the kitchen driver for Azure Resource Manager (see **https://github.com/pendrica/kitchen-azurerm**) by using the chef gem install kitchen-azurerm command:

```
PS C:\Users\StuartPreston> chef gem install kitchen-azurerm
```

You should see output similar to the below if all was successful. You may see other dependencies get installed at the same time too - this is normal:

```
Successfully installed kitchen-azurerm-0.2.6
Parsing documentation for kitchen-azurerm-0.2.6
Installing ri documentation for kitchen-azurerm-0.2.6
Done installing documentation for kitchen-azurerm after 0 seconds
1 gem installed

PS C:\Users\StuartPreston>
```

We can now proceed with the rest of the configuration.

Configuring the Credentials File

In chapter 4 we set up a Service Principal and granted that Service Principal access to your Azure Subscription. We then configured your ~/**.azure/credentials** file so that it could be used for provisioning resources in Azure. We will be reusing that same mechanism here.

To recap; our credentials file should look something like this:

```
[b6e7eee9-YOUR-GUID-HERE-03ab624df016]
client_id = "48b9bba3-YOUR-GUID-HERE-90f0b68ce8ba"
client_secret = "my-top-secret-password"
tenant_id = "9c117323-YOUR-GUID-HERE-9ee430723ba3"
```

where the first line is our Subscription ID, the **client_id** is the Application ID of the Service Principal, the **client_secret** is the Shared Secret assigned to the application, and the **tenant_id** is the Tenant ID for the Subscription.

Configuring Test Kitchen within a Chef Repo

Test Kitchen is driven from a single, declarative configuration file called **.kitchen.yml** that resides in the root of your repo. A chef-generated app generated this file automatically for us at the beginning of this chapter, and Listing 6-1 shows the default **.kitchen.yml** file that you'll find in your repository.

Listing 6-1. default .kitchen.yml file

```
---
driver:
  name: vagrant

provisioner:
  name: chef_zero

# Uncomment the following verifier to leverage Inspec instead of Busser (the
# default verifier)
# verifier:
#   name: inspec

platforms:
  - name: ubuntu-14.04
  - name: centos-7.1

suites:
  - name: default
    run_list:
      - recipe[chefazure-ch06::default]
    attributes:
```

■ **Tip** If you do not have a .kitchen.yml file in your repo, one can be created automatically by typing `kitchen init` in the location you want one.

We can see our default configuration file has four mains sections:

- **Driver** - in this section we provide the name of the driver to be used. The default driver supports Vagrant, which is a tool that is typically used in concert with a local virtualization provider such as Oracle VirtualBox. In our case we will be changing this to use the Azure Resource Manager driver.

- **Provisioner** - the provisioner is used to specify what action should be taken when we 'converge' our machine. We want to use the chef_zero provisioner, which provides the capability to transfer and execute recipes from our cookbook(s) within the machine itself.

- **Platforms** - a list of platforms can be provided here. In the example we can see both Ubuntu-14.04 and CentOS 7.1 have been added. Test Kitchen builds a test matrix based on a combination of platforms and suites.

- **Suites** - a suite is where we provide a run list containing the list of Chef recipes we wish to execute in order. We can also override any attributes that are settable within those recipes.

If you execute `kitchen list` at this point, we are provided with a list of the test instances that *would* be created if we ran `kitchen create`:

```
Instance                Driver    Provisioner   Verifier   Transport   Last Action
default-ubuntu-1404     Vagrant   ChefZero      Busser     Ssh         <Not Created>
default-centos-71       Vagrant   ChefZero      Busser     Ssh         <Not Created>
```

> ■ **Note**   If you see an error message, then it is likely you do not have Vagrant installed. We do not require Vagrant for the purposes of the book; however if you are interested in running Test Kitchen locally then you can download it from `https://www.vagrantup.com/downloads.html`

We're going to edit our **.kitchen.yml** so that it uses the Azure Resource Manager (ARM) driver; so open the file in your text editor and edit it as follows:

```
---
driver:
  name: azurerm

driver_config:
  subscription_id: 'b6e7eee9-YOUR-GUID-HERE-03ab624df016'
  location: 'West Europe'
  machine_size: 'Standard_DS2'

provisioner:
  name: chef_zero
```

```
platforms:
  - name: windows2012-r2
    driver_config:
      image_urn: MicrosoftWindowsServer:WindowsServer:2012-R2-Datacenter:latest
    transport:
      name: winrm

verifier:
  name: inspec

suites:
  - name: default
    run_list:
      - recipe[chefazure-ch06::default]
    attributes:
```

We can see the driver name was changed to azurerm, and there's a driver_config section that takes a subscription_id, location, and machine_size parameters. These parameters should be self-explanatory. Something that requires more explaining is the image_urn parameter.

The **image_urn** parameter is a four-part string in the format **Publisher:Offer:Sku:Version** that uniquely identifies an image in Azure. Here are some examples:

- MicrosoftWindowsServer:WindowsServer:2012-R2-Datacenter:latest

- Canonical:UbuntuServer:14.04.3-LTS:latest

- Canonical:UbuntuServer:15.04:latest

- OpenLogic:CentOS:7.1:latest

In chapter 5 we explained how to derive these values; so if you skipped that bit, now would be a good time to go back and read it as it is a slightly awkward mechanism to discover these images.

Creating an Instance - Kitchen Create

If we have our credentials file configured correctly, a valid subscription ID in our .kitchen.yml and a valid image_urn entry, we're ready to start up a machine in Azure. To do this we use the kitchen create command. It will take a few minutes to provision.

```
PS C:\Users\StuartPreston\chefazure-ch06> kitchen create
```

```
-----> Starting Kitchen (v1.4.2)
-----> Creating <default-windows2012-r2>...
       Creating Resource Group: kitchen-default-windows2012-r2-20151107T001229
       Creating Deployment: deploy-fc2ef6c5988cb47e
       Resource Microsoft.Network/publicIPAddresses 'publicip' provisioning status is
       Running
       Resource Microsoft.Network/virtualNetworks 'vnet' provisioning status is Running
       Resource Microsoft.Storage/storageAccounts 'storagefc2ef6c5988cb47e' provisioning
       status is Running
       Resource Microsoft.Compute/virtualMachines 'vm' provisioning status is Running
       Resource Microsoft.Compute/virtualMachines 'vm' provisioning status is Running
```

```
      Resource Microsoft.Compute/virtualMachines 'vm' provisioning status is Running
[...]
      Resource Microsoft.Compute/virtualMachines 'vm' provisioning status is Running
      Resource Microsoft.Compute/virtualMachines/extensions 'vm/enableWinRM' provisioning
      status is Running
      Resource Microsoft.Compute/virtualMachines/extensions 'vm/enableWinRM' provisioning
      status is Running
      Resource Microsoft.Compute/virtualMachines/extensions 'vm/enableWinRM' provisioning
      status is Running
[...]
      Resource Microsoft.Compute/virtualMachines/extensions 'vm/enableWinRM' provisioning
      status is Running
      Resource Template deployment reached end state of 'Succeeded'.
      IP Address is: 104.40.217.123 [kitchen-c2ef6c5988cb47e.westeurope.cloudapp.azure.com]
      Finished creating <default-windows2012-r2> (9m39.36s).
-----> Kitchen is finished. (9m42.75s)
```

At the end of the creation process we have a machine running and we are presented its IP address. Test Kitchen stores this in a state file (named **.kitchen/default-windows2012-r2.yml** in our case) so that later phases can use this information to connect to the machine.

Converging an Instance - Kitchen Converge

Converging an instance simply means bringing the machine toward the desired state so that it can be ready for testing. We have specified the **chef_zero** provisioner in our configuration file (it's the default), which means that when we execute kitchen converge the following things will happen:

- The repository and any cookbooks specified as a dependency are transferred to the target machine using the specified transport (WinRM in our case).

- If not installed already, a Chef Client will be downloaded and installed on the machine.

- Chef Client will execute the specified recipes on the machine.

We already have a very basic recipe set up in our repository, which attempts to delete a file. Let's converge our machine using kitchen converge and watch the output:

```
PS C:\Users\StuartPreston\chefazure-ch06> kitchen converge
```

```
-----> Starting Kitchen (v1.4.2)
-----> Converging <default-windows2012-r2>...
      Preparing files for transfer
      Preparing dna.json
      Preparing cookbooks from project directory
      Removing non-cookbook files before transfer
      Preparing validation.pem
      Preparing client.rb
-----> Installing Chef Omnibus (install only if missing)
      Downloading package from https://opscode-omnibus-packages.s3.amazonaws.com/
windows/2008r2/i386/chef-client-12.5.1-1-x86.msi
```

```
Download complete.
Successfully verified C:\Users\azure\AppData\Local\Temp\chef-true.msi

Installing Chef Omnibus package C:\Users\azure\AppData\Local\Temp\chef-true.msi
Installation complete
Transferring files to <default-windows2012-r2>
Starting Chef Client, version 12.5.1
Creating a new client identity for default-windows2012-r2 using the validator key.
resolving cookbooks for run list: ["chefazure-ch06::default"]
Synchronizing Cookbooks:
  - chefazure-ch06 (0.1.0)
Compiling Cookbooks...
Converging 1 resources
Recipe: chefazure-ch06::default
  * file[c:/test.txt] action delete (up to date)

Running handlers:
Running handlers complete
Chef Client finished, 0/1 resources updated in 01 minutes 01 seconds
Finished converging <default-windows2012-r2> (3m12.08s).
-----> Kitchen is finished. (3m14.35s)
```

We can see that our recipe executed, and our file was found to be in the correct state (deleted), as seen by the following section:

```
Converging 1 resources
Recipe: chefazure-ch06::default
  * file[c:/test.txt] action delete (up to date)
```

No action was taken on our instance because the file did not already exist; therefore the machine was in the desired state as specified by the recipe. We can modify our recipe on our workstation and rerun kitchen converge as many times as we like.

■ **Note**   Each time you run kitchen converge with an updated recipe or suite of recipes you run the risk of changing the state of the machine to an unexpected starting position for the next run. It is always wise to destroy your machines regularly to ensure your recipes can run end to end.

Using InSpec and Kitchen Verify

InSpec is a recently released testing framework, similar to ChefSpec in that it uses BDD-like language constructs in the test specifications. However, InSpec does no simulation of the Chef Client run; instead it tests the actual running state of the machine. This makes InSpec tests a powerful tool for post-convergence automated testing, as we can use it to ensure that each action specified in our recipe has brought the machine to the correct target state. To give a couple of examples, here's an example test to verify the 'OS family' on our target machine is Windows:

```
describe os[:family] do
  it { should eq 'windows' }
end
```

Here's another test that tests whether an Apache configuration has a Listen parameter set to the value '443':

```
describe apache_conf do
  its('Listen') { should eq '443'}
end
```

A full list of Resources and Matchers are available at https://docs.chef.io/inspec_reference.html. As an example test, let's run a couple of checks on our Windows 2012 R2 machine:

- We'll check the machine has a DHCP Client service installed, enabled, and running
- We'll also check that the machine is NOT listening on TCP port 80, as we have not installed a Web Server on it.

Looking at the list of resources, we can see that there are both the **Service** resource and **Host** resources available to accomplish this task. So let's open up the file **test/integration/default/default_spec.rb** in your text editor and replace the contents with the text below:

```
describe service('Dhcp') do
  it { should be_installed }
  it { should be_enabled }
  it { should be_running }
end

describe host('localhost', port: 80, proto: 'tcp') do
  it { should_not be_reachable }
end
```

Once complete, the file should look like Figure 6-12.

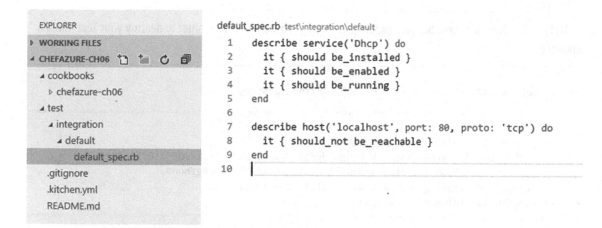

Figure 6-12. *Inspec example spec located at test/integration/default/default_spec.rb*

We can now run `kitchen verify` to get our test results.

```
PS C:\Users\StuartPreston\chefazure-ch06> kitchen verify
```

```
-----> Starting Kitchen (v1.4.2)
-----> Verifying <default-windows2012-r2>...
..."Test-NetConnection -ComputerName localhost -RemotePort 80| Select-Object -Property
ComputerName, RemoteAddress, RemotePort, SourceAddress, PingSucceeded | ConvertTo-Json"
.

Finished in 8 seconds (files took 6.57 seconds to load)
4 examples, 0 failures
```

As seen from the output, we have 0 failures. Of course this isn't a real test as if it was a real test we would now add some tests that we expect to pass (perhaps you are looking to define a Web Server on port 80, so it "should be_listening"). The beauty of using Test Kitchen for this is that it is a rapid, repeatable process.

For now, we've spent some credit running this VM with a public IP address on Azure and don't need it any longer so let's destroy it.

Destroying our Instance - Kitchen Destroy

Destroying our server is as simple as typing kitchen destroy. What is actually happening here is that we are deleting an Azure Resource Group that contains all the resources created by kitchen create. It actually takes some time to acquire locks on all the resources in Azure, so once the delete request has been accepted by Azure, the operation continues in the background, allowing you to continue to the next stage, or to start up a new instance.

■ **Note**   The author cannot be held responsible for large Azure bills if you forget to destroy your Test Kitchen instances!

```
PS C:\Users\StuartPreston\chefazure-ch06> kitchen destroy
```

-----> Starting Kitchen (v1.4.2)
-----> Destroying <default-windows2012-r2>...
       Destroying Resource Group: kitchen-default-windows2012-r2-20151107T001229
       Destroy operation accepted and will continue in the background.
       Finished destroying <default-windows2012-r2> (0m5.58s).
-----> Kitchen is finished. (0m8.95s)

Other Test Kitchen Commands

We covered the basic four stages of Test Kitchen above, but there are a couple of other commands that are useful to know about:

- You can run kitchen test in order to execute all phases of Test Kitchen in order without stopping.

- You can run kitchen diagnose --all in order to diagnose problems with configuration (note: most issues are caused by formatting issues in the .yml file.)

- Finally, instead of running through each test suite and platform sequentially, these can be executed in parallel by running kitchen <command> --concurrency <n> where n is the number of threads you wish to start.

Summary

We've now taken a very quick lap through some important quality tools that are provided with the Chef Development Kit. We are able to run linters such as Rubocop and FoodCritic against our code to address consistency and code quality issues. We can add ChefSpec unit tests to simulate the behavior of our recipes and catch unexpected behavior early in the development cycle. We can configure Test Kitchen to use Azure Resource Manager to define ephemeral (short-lived) machines that we can use for testing, and we can use a Chef Zero provisioner and InSpec tests to verify the real state of the target system after convergence.

In the next two chapters we're going to take everything we have learned from the book so far about real-world scenarios and see what a starting point for a Continuous Integration/Continuous Delivery pipeline might look like.

CHAPTER 7

■ ■ ■

Chef Concepts in the Real World

All this cookbook development is nice and simple when we're following the demos in Chef Fundamentals, or being taught the ins and outs of attributes and data bags by a trainer. But what happens in the real world? That is what this chapter seeks to answer by summarizing some of the established patterns and practices from environments of varying shapes and sizes and highlighting some common mistakes and dead-ends.

Chef is a wonderfully flexible and extensible toolset; and because of this, many people have invented their own ways of working with it that work for them. In practice, there are a few tips, patterns, and practices that make sense to adopt and I'll be presenting some of those here for consideration.

Let's consider the case of a typical company that has a single instance of Chef and needs to implement a release process across three environments: Development (Dev), Test, and Production (Prod), as depicted in Figure 7-1.

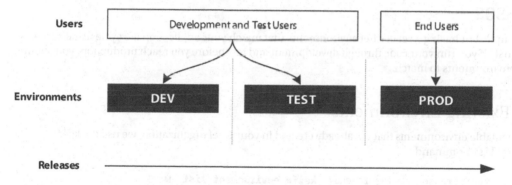

Figure 7-1. *Typical environment structure for releasing software within an organization*

Releases need to progress in a rapid but stable manner through the environments, and we need to ensure that by making changes in lower environments (Dev and Test), we don't impact any users of the Production system. Let's step through some of the aspects of Chef you may want to look at.

Avoid Using the _default Environment

All those nodes you bootstrapped when doing your Chef training probably went into the **_default** environment, didn't they? But did you know that **version constraints cannot be applied to the _default environment**? (as shown in Figure 7-2).

© Stuart Preston 2016
S. Preston, *Using Chef with Microsoft Azure*, DOI 10.1007/978-1-4842-1476-3_7

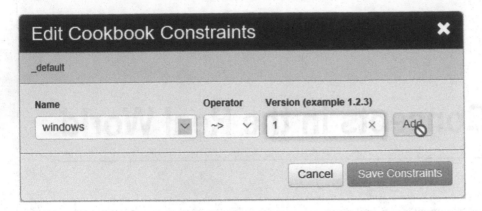

Figure 7-2. *Setting a cookbook constraint on the _default environment is not possible*

If we cannot version a cookbook, it means that every time we upload a cookbook to the Chef server, the latest version of the cookbook will always be used in the Chef run. For this reason, where possible move your nodes to a specific environment at the earliest opportunity. We'll discuss how to create Chef environments in the next section.

Use Chef Environments to Reflect Your Internal Release Processes

It sounds simple, but having a set of Chef environments that match your application life cycle usually makes the most sense. If you run your code through development and test before you reach production, you should have Chef environments to match.

Listing Existing Environments

To list the available environments that are already created in your Chef organization, we use the `knife environment list` command:

```
PS C:\Users\StuartPreston\chefazure-ch07> knife environment list -w
```

```
_default: https://api.chef.io/organizations/pendrica-chefazure/environments/_default
```

We can see in our organization that we currently have only a _default environment.

Creating New Environments

Environments are specified via an **environment.json** file that is added to your repo. The environments file is usually stored in the **environments** folder within a Chef repository; however it does not take effect when you upload a cookbook. We must use the `knife environment` command to upload a new environment definition. This process is shown in Figure 7-3.

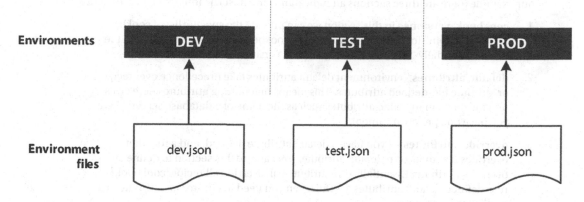

Figure 7-3. *Environment file relationship to Environments*

Environment File Contents

An environment file should be located in your repo at **/environments/<environment>.json**. Let's have a look at an example file, **test.json**:

```
{
  "chef_type": "environment",
  "name": "test",
  "json_class": "Chef::Environment",
  "description": "Test environment",
  "cookbook_versions": {
    "couchdb": "= 11.0.0",
    "my_cookbook": "= 1.2.0"
  },
  "default_attributes": {
    "apache2": {
      "listen_ports": [
        "80",
        "443"
      ]
    }
  },
  "override_attributes": {
    "apache2": {
      "min_spareservers": "5"
    }
  }
}
```

In our example there are three sections after the **name** and **description** field that are self-explanatory:

1. **cookbook_versions** - in this section we can provide the specific list of cookbook versions to "pin" for this environment. Any cookbooks that do not appear in the list are essentially "unpinned" (i.e., the latest version will always be used).

2. **default_attributes** - environment default attributes take precedence over recipe or attribute file-defined attributes. This means that putting attributes here gives us a mechanism to define attributes such as the name of a database server where you have one per environment.

3. **override_attributes** - if you have a default attribute defined, and a role that overrides it with its own default attribute, you can use this section to define an override_attribute. Essentially this attribute will override all recipe/cookbook/role-defined default attributes. Useful when you need to enforce an attribute in a particular environment.

Uploading a New Environment File

Environments can be uploaded at the command line using the command `knife environment`:

```
PS C:\Users\StuartPreston\chefazure-ch07> knife environment from file ./environments/test.json
```

```
Updated Environment test
```

Now that we've created a new environment, we need to move some Chef nodes to it. As we know, all nodes within Chef are assigned the **_default** environment if one isn't specified; this can be changed from either the server or the client, at the command line, or by modifying the client.rb file.

> ■ **Note** You may also create environments using the management portal but this is not recommended as it is a manual, non-repeatable action, and doesn't lend itself to good continuous delivery practices.

Changing the Environment for a Node

Remembering that each node that runs Chef Client uses a configuration file client.rb, we can specify the environment in the **client.rb** and this has the effect of overriding the server-assigned environment for that run (and storing that value for future runs or for searches against the Chef server). We can also use the **knife** command or the **Chef management portal** in order to achieve this. We'll use this section to go through each of the options.

Specifying the Environment for a Server in client.rb

It's relatively simple to modify your **client.rb** to specify your environment. Simply add the following line:

```
environment <environment_name>
```

for example:

```
environment prod
```

Once the file is saved, Chef Client will notify the server at the beginning of the client run that it is overriding the environment set on the server, and the server will save that environment for future runs.

■ **Tip** If you are interested in managing your Chef Client configuration, have a look at the chef-client cookbook, available on the Chef Supermarket at `https://supermarket.chef.io/cookbooks/chef-client`

Specifying the Environment for a Server Using Knife

To change the server environment from Knife, you can issue the `knife node environment_set` command from your workstation. This runs against the configured Chef server as per your knife.rb file. The command takes the node name and environment_name parameters. So next is how to set a node called **vm.chef-azure-book** to the **test** environment:

```
PS C:\Users\StuartPreston\chefazure-ch07> knife node environment_set vm.chef-azure-book test
```

```
vm.chef-azure-book:
  chef_environment: test
```

The new environment will then be used from the next Chef Client run.

Specifying the Environment for a Server Using the Chef Management Portal

When using the Chef management portal, you will find an **Environment** field on the **Nodes** tab. Simply select the node and select the new environment, as shown in Figure 7-4.

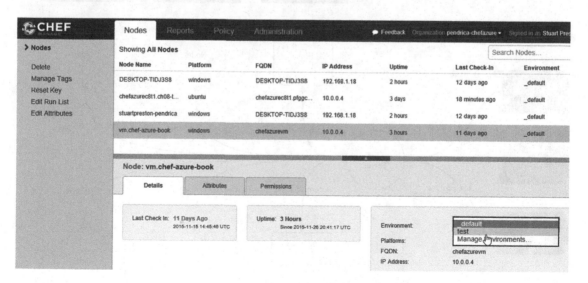

Figure 7-4. *Setting an environment using the Chef management portal*

Searching for Servers in an Existing Environment

Imagine that if you wanted a list of all servers that are in the **_default** environment, you would issue the following knife search command, which will return the **name** attribute of servers in that environment:

```
PS C:\Users\StuartPreston\chefazure-ch07> knife search "chef_environment:_default" -a name
```

```
4 items found
DESKTOP-TIDJ3S8:
  name: DESKTOP-TIDJ3S8
chefazurec8t1.ch08-test1:
  name: chefazurec8t1.ch08-test1

stuartpreston-pendrica:
  name: stuartpreston-pendrica

vm.chef-azure-book:
  name: vm.chef-azure-book
```

Controlling Releases through Environments Using the Environment and Role Patterns

Environments are a way of logically grouping servers, commonly aligned to the testing stages of an application. Releases are sent through the environments and then tested at each stage. Figure 7-5 depicts this typical set of environments.

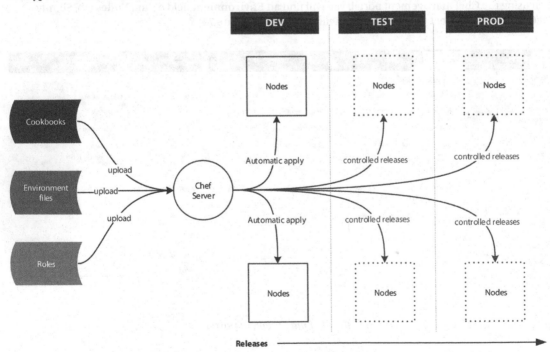

Figure 7-5. *Typical set of environments within an organization*

The environment pattern is simply a way of splitting out your environmental information from your application cookbooks, realizing that they may have a separate life cycle.

Remember that cookbooks can be versioned, and roles cannot. This means it is a bad practice to modify roles once deployed to a node, as any change to a role's run list impacts all environments simultaneously. That would not be a controlled release process! So how we get around this? By sticking to the following principles during cookbook development:

1. **No nesting of roles.** Each role should refer to one or more "capability" recipes that are provided by an application cookbook.

Example role **roles/myapp-frontend.rb**:

```
{
  "name": "myapp-frontend",
  "chef_type": "role",
  "json_class": "Chef::Role",
  "default_attributes": {
  },
  "description": "This is a single role that points to the standard-app-a frontend
capability recipe",
  "run_list": [
    "recipe[myapp_a::default]",
  ],
  "env_run_lists" : {
  }
}
```

2. Application cookbooks should include and manage the dependencies for that application (remembering that dependencies are specified in the application cookbook's **metadata.rb** file).

Example **metadata.rb**:

```
name 'myapp_a'
maintainer 'Stuart Preston'
maintainer_email 'stuart@pendrica.com'
license 'all_rights'
description 'Installs/Configures myapp_a'
long_description 'Installs/Configures chefazure-ch07'
version '0.1.0'

depends 'mysql'
depends 'rabbitmq'
```

3. Default attributes for each environment (e.g., location of database server in that environment) should be specified in the environment JSON file.

4. Default Role attributes should be avoided (as they override default environment attributes that are unlikely to be desirable).

5. Each node should be assigned the relevant roles that exist within the environment JSON file.

An overview diagram of how these principles work together is shown in Figure 7-6. If you manage to stick to these simple rules, you'll have the basis for a continuous delivery solution, with controlled releases into production. The running version in each environment is now a composite of the application cookbook version, combined with the attributes and version constraints from the environment cookbook.

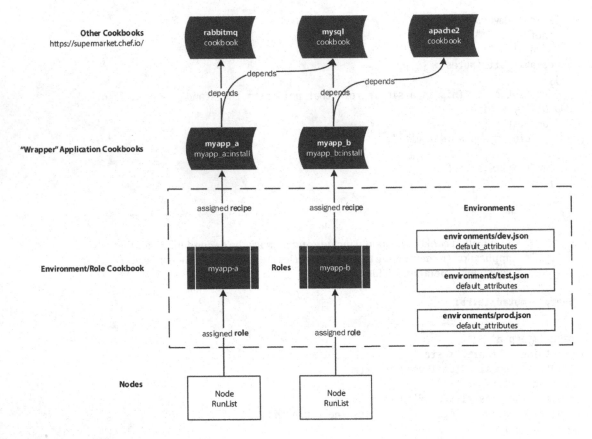

Figure 7-6. *Node/Role/Recipe relationships*

Attribute Precedence

There are 15 levels of attribute precedence that go from a default attribute in a cookbook through to a forced overridden attribute set at an environment level, as shown in Figure 7-7:

	Attribute Files	Node / Recipe	Environment	Role
default	1	2	3	4
force_default	5	6		
normal	7	8		
override	9	10	12	11
force_override	13	14		
automatic		15		

Figure 7-7. Attribute precedence in Chef. Source: `https://docs.chef.io/attributes.html`

When using the environment pattern we are generally interested in setting default attributes:

1. **Attribute files** (application cookbook) - here we are setting the default attributes for our application, generally pointing them at Dev values (just in case they are accidentally pushed to a Production environment).

2. **Environment attributes** (environment cookbook) - here we are setting the default attributes for an environment. Conveniently these override those set in an attribute file so we can use this mechanism to set environmental attributes (such as the connection string to the database in each environment).

3. **Roles** - Generally the use of role attributes is not a good practice as they override default Environment attributes. However, they can be a useful tool depending on your implementation scenario. Just remember that if you want to use Environment attributes over Role attributes in this scenario you'll have to mark the environment attribute as an **override_attribute**.

Semantic Versioning Overview

As mentioned, we typically use Semantic Versioning in order to version our cookbooks. Semantic versioning is a standard for versioning, created in the community that brings a common understanding to version numbering. Full details can be found at `http://semver.org/spec/v2.0.0.html`.

The premise of Semantic versioning is simple; given a version number **Major.Minor.Patch**, increment the following:

- **Major** version when you make incompatible API changes,
- **Minor** version when you add functionality in a backwards-compatible manner, and
- **Patch** version when you make backwards-compatible bug fixes.

Luckily, public cookbooks, environment cookbooks, and pretty much all versioning in the Chef and Ruby ecosystem follow this numbering scheme. This numbering scheme is shown in Figure 7-8.

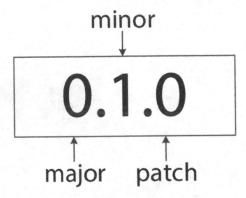

***Figure 7-8.** Semantic Versioning structure*

The semantic version numbering scheme allows us to use version constraints in our cookbook metadata. A reminder of some of the more typical constraints is shown in Table 7-1.

***Table 7-1.** Typical version contraints used in Ruby and Chef cookbooks*

Constraint	Meaning
= 0.1.0	Matches version 0.1.0
> 0.1.0	Greater than version 0.1.0
>= 1.4.5	Greater than or equal to version 1.4.5
~> 2.6	Greater than or equal to version 2.6 but less than version 3.0
~> 2.6.5	Greater than or equal to version 2.6.5 but less than version 2.7.0
< 1.1.0	Less than version 1.1.0
<= 1.4.5	Less than or equal to version 1.4.5

Summary

In this chapter, we highlighted some of the patterns and practices you should adopt when developing Chef cookbooks in the real world. Chapter 8 will take these concepts one stage further and build out a complete environment in Azure using Chef Provisioning, Jenkins, and Hosted Chef.

CHAPTER 8

■ ■ ■

Pulling It All Together: Continuous Provisioning with Chef and Azure

At this point in the book we've covered a lot of ground with both Chef and the Microsoft Azure platforms. So far we have done the following:

- Understood how to set up a development workstation for Chef

- Looked at Azure's capabilities, delved into detail on Azure Resource Manager, and used both the Azure CLI and PowerShell cmdlets to accomplish administration tasks in Azure

- Utilized the Chef VM Extensions as an efficient way of bootstrapping Chef on multiple machines

- Used Chef Provisioning to provision various types of Azure resources and scale out our architectures including both IaaS and PaaS resources

- Looked at the Chef testing landscape and the tooling that supports it, including the Test Kitchen driver for Azure Resource Manager

- Looked at Chef in the real world, including implications of environments, versioning, and runlists

It's time to pull all that together and in this advanced-level chapter we will be building a fully working, continuous provisioning pipeline, running in Azure with Chef. We'll take an incremental approach to building it so that we have something working at each stage. At the end, we'll have a framework that you can use in your own environment that allows you to add configuration management and release management on top of it.

What are we Aiming for?

To create our solution, we will need to break down our approach into four key phases, as follows:

1. Initial Chef Repository setup

2. Installing and configuring Jenkins

3. Setting up a new Chef repository in GitHub

4. Configuring the Jenkins project and building steps

Our provisioning system will work off code that is checked into source control, so we want our pipeline to have the following attributes:

- It will be triggered by commit pushes to our source control system (GitHub) for updates

- Where there is an update to a provisioning recipe, the changes will be detected and any new provisioning instructions will be executed

- If provisioning results in new servers being added, they are bootstrapped with a Chef client

- Any new servers should be assigned a role or runlist so that the first time the Chef client runs, recipes are executed on the target node

Once all this has been accomplished, we will have a working pipeline. Figure 8-1 shows the components involved. We will create a Dev environment initially and demonstrate how to add further environments that are contained within their own Azure Resource Group.

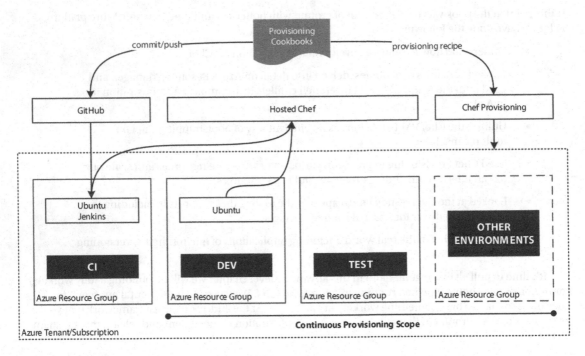

Figure 8-1. *Solution Overview*

As you can see we have a lot to do, so let's get started by setting up an application repository and get some provisioning recipes ready.

Phase 1 - Initial Chef Repository Setup

■ **Note** If you have not set up an Azure Active Directory Service Principal and configured Chef Provisioning with an Azure credentials file, head back to **Chapter 4: Authenticating to Azure Resource Manager** and complete that section first.

Initializing the Application Repository

Let's get started by creating ourselves an application repository to work in:

```
PS C:\Users\StuartPreston> chef generate app chefazure-ch08 --copyright "Stuart Preston"
--email "stuart@pendrica.com"
```

```
Compiling Cookbooks...
Recipe: code_generator::app
  * directory[C:/Users/StuartPreston/chefazure-ch08] action create
[...]
```

We'll need the keys and configuration we created in chapter 1. Assuming you extracted the starter kit into a folder ~/chef-repo, you can use the following commands:

```
PS C:\Users\StuartPreston> cd .\chefazure-ch08\
PS C:\Users\StuartPreston\chefazure-ch08> mkdir .chef
```

```
    Directory: C:\Users\StuartPreston\chefazure-ch08


Mode                LastWriteTime         Length Name
----                -------------         ------ ----
d-----        29/11/2015     16:02               chef
```

```
PS C:\Users\StuartPreston\chefazure-ch08> cd .chef
PS C:\Users\StuartPreston\chefazure-ch08\.chef> cp ~/chef-repo/.chef/*.* .
```

We can now open up our application in our preferred development environment (Visual Studio Code in my case):

```
PS C:\Users\StuartPreston\chefazure-ch08\.chef> cd ..
PS C:\Users\StuartPreston\chefazure-ch08> code .
```

We'll be using the **chefazure-ch08** cookbook within our app to house our provisioning recipes as well as all dependencies for this application. We should now have the structure as shown in Figure 8-2:

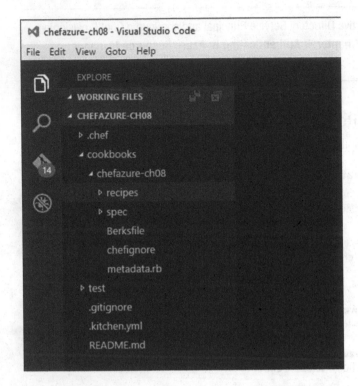

Figure 8-2. *Required initial repository structure for this chapter*

We can now move onto creating and executing the required baseline provisioning recipes.

Add Chef Provisioning Recipes

Azure Resource Groups make perfect boundaries between logical environments as they have their own storage and networking infrastructure. If we want to add another environment later, we won't affect any of the existing resources that are deployed. Figure 8-3 shows the boundaries we want to keep between logical environments.

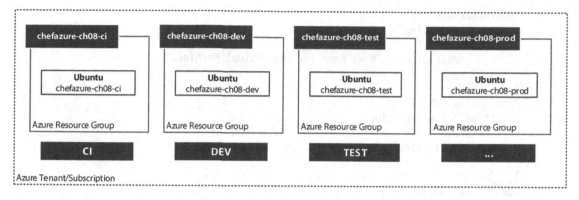

Figure 8-3. *Azure Resource Groups to be created*

When it comes to adding compute resource such as a VM inside a Resource Group, we need to use a generic Azure Resource Manager template that will allow us to create Windows and Ubuntu machines from it. The recipe associated with this template will need to refer to the Resource Group, and the template itself will need to create a Storage Account as well as a Network and IP address. Via the recipe parameters a Chef VM Extension will be added so that we don't need to bootstrap the machine manually. Here's the generic ARM template we can use, which needs to be saved inside the repository:

■ **Note** The files and source code for this chapter can be downloaded from http://bit.ly/chefazure

---

cookbooks/chefazure-ch08/files/shared/machine_deploy.json

```
{
    "$schema": "https://schema.management.azure.com/schemas/2015-01-01/deployment
    Template.json#",
    "contentVersion": "1.0.0.0",
    "parameters": {
        "location": {
            "type": "string",
            "metadata": {
                "description": "The location where the resources will be created."
            }
        },
        "vmSize": {
            "type": "string",
            "metadata": {
                "description": "The size of the VM to be created"
            }
        },
        "newStorageAccountName": {
            "type": "string",
            "metadata": {
                "description": "Unique DNS Name for the Storage Account where the Virtual
                Machine's disks will be placed."
            }
        },
```

```
    "adminUsername": {
        "type": "string",
        "metadata": {
            "description": "User name for the Virtual Machine."
        }
    },
    "adminPassword": {
        "type": "securestring",
        "metadata": {
            "description": "Password for the Virtual Machine."
        }
    },
    "dnsNameForPublicIP": {
        "type": "string",
        "metadata": {
            "description": "Unique DNS Name for the Public IP used to access the Virtual
            Machine."
        }
    },
    "imagePublisher": {
        "type": "string",
        "defaultValue": "Canonical",
        "metadata": {
            "description": "Publisher for the VM, e.g. Canonical, MicrosoftWindowsServer"
        }
    },
    "imageOffer": {
        "type": "string",
        "defaultValue": "UbuntuServer",
        "metadata": {
            "description": "Offer for the VM, e.g. UbuntuServer, WindowsServer."
        }
    },
    "imageSku": {
        "type": "string",
        "defaultValue": "14.04.3-LTS",
        "metadata": {
            "description": "Sku for the VM, e.g. 14.04.3-LTS"
        }
    },
    "imageVersion": {
        "type": "string",
        "defaultValue": "latest",
        "metadata": {
            "description": "Either a date or latest."
        }
    },
    "vmName": {
        "type": "string",
        "defaultValue": "vm",
```

```
                "metadata": {
                    "description": "The vm name created inside of the resource group."
                }
            }
        },
    "variables": {
        "location": "[parameters('location')]",
        "OSDiskName": "osdisk",
        "nicName": "nic",
        "addressPrefix": "10.0.0.0/16",
        "subnetName": "Subnet",
        "subnetPrefix": "10.0.0.0/24",
        "storageAccountType": "Standard_LRS",
        "publicIPAddressName": "publicip",
        "publicIPAddressType": "Dynamic",
        "vmStorageAccountContainerName": "vhds",
        "vmName": "[parameters('vmName')]",
        "vmSize": "[parameters('vmSize')]",
        "virtualNetworkName": "vnet",
        "vnetID": "[resourceId('Microsoft.Network/virtualNetworks',
        variables('virtualNetworkName'))]",
        "subnetRef": "[concat(variables('vnetID'),'/subnets/',variables('subnetName'))]"
    },
    "resources": [
        {
            "type": "Microsoft.Storage/storageAccounts",
            "name": "[parameters('newStorageAccountName')]",
            "apiVersion": "2015-05-01-preview",
            "location": "[variables('location')]",
            "properties": {
                "accountType": "[variables('storageAccountType')]"
            }
        },
        {
            "apiVersion": "2015-05-01-preview",
            "type": "Microsoft.Network/publicIPAddresses",
            "name": "[variables('publicIPAddressName')]",
            "location": "[variables('location')]",
            "properties": {
                "publicIPAllocationMethod": "[variables('publicIPAddressType')]",
                "dnsSettings": {
                    "domainNameLabel": "[parameters('dnsNameForPublicIP')]"
                }
            }
        },
        {
            "apiVersion": "2015-05-01-preview",
            "type": "Microsoft.Network/virtualNetworks",
            "name": "[variables('virtualNetworkName')]",
            "location": "[variables('location')]",
```

```json
            "properties": {
                "addressSpace": {
                    "addressPrefixes": [
                        "[variables('addressPrefix')]"
                    ]
                },
                "subnets": [
                    {
                        "name": "[variables('subnetName')]",
                        "properties": {
                            "addressPrefix": "[variables('subnetPrefix')]"
                        }
                    }
                ]
            }
        },
        {
            "apiVersion": "2015-05-01-preview",
            "type": "Microsoft.Network/networkInterfaces",
            "name": "[variables('nicName')]",
            "location": "[variables('location')]",
            "dependsOn": [
                "[concat('Microsoft.Network/publicIPAddresses/',
                variables('publicIPAddressName'))]",
                "[concat('Microsoft.Network/virtualNetworks/',
                variables('virtualNetworkName'))]"
            ],
            "properties": {
                "ipConfigurations": [
                    {
                        "name": "ipconfig1",
                        "properties": {
                            "privateIPAllocationMethod": "Dynamic",
                            "publicIPAddress": {
                                "id": "[resourceId('Microsoft.Network/publicIPAddresses',
                                variables('publicIPAddressName'))]"
                            },
                            "subnet": {
                                "id": "[variables('subnetRef')]"
                            }
                        }
                    }
                ]
            }
        },
        {
            "apiVersion": "2015-06-15",
            "type": "Microsoft.Compute/virtualMachines",
            "name": "[variables('vmName')]",
            "location": "[variables('location')]",
```

```
        "dependsOn": [
            "[concat('Microsoft.Storage/storageAccounts/',
            parameters('newStorageAccountName'))]",
            "[concat('Microsoft.Network/networkInterfaces/', variables('nicName'))]"
        ],
        "properties": {
            "hardwareProfile": {
                "vmSize": "[variables('vmSize')]"
            },
            "osProfile": {
                "computerName": "[variables('vmName')]",
                "adminUsername": "[parameters('adminUsername')]",
                "adminPassword": "[parameters('adminPassword')]"
            },
            "storageProfile": {
                "imageReference": {
                    "publisher": "[parameters('imagePublisher')]",
                    "offer": "[parameters('imageOffer')]",
                    "sku": "[parameters('imageSku')]",
                    "version": "[parameters('imageVersion')]"
                },
                "osDisk": {
                    "name": "osdisk",
                    "vhd": {
                        "uri": "[concat('http://',parameters('newStorageAccountName'),'.
                        blob.core.windows.net/',variables('vmStorageAccountContainer
                        Name'),'/',variables('OSDiskName'),'.vhd')]"
                    },
                    "caching": "ReadWrite",
                    "createOption": "FromImage"
                }
            },
            "networkProfile": {
                "networkInterfaces": [
                    {
                        "id": "[resourceId('Microsoft.Network/networkInterfaces',
                        variables('nicName'))]"
                    }
                ]
            },
            "diagnosticsProfile": {
                "bootDiagnostics": {
                    "enabled": "true",
                    "storageUri": "[concat('http://',parameters('newStorageAccountName'),
                    '.blob.core.windows.net')]"
                }
            }
        }
    }
  }
 ]
}
```

We need to extract the parameters from the ARM template into a recipe so that it can be provisioned. We'll do that by creating a recipe for our CI server in the same way we did in chapter 4. Remember to substitute in the correct Subscription ID in the right place:

cookbooks/chefazure-ch08/recipes/provision_jenkins.rb:

```
require 'chef/provisioning/azurerm'
with_driver 'AzureRM:b6e7eee9-YOUR-GUID-HERE-03ab624df016'

azure_resource_group 'chefazure-ch08-ci' do
  location 'West Europe'
end

azure_resource_template 'jenkins-server' do
  resource_group 'chefazure-ch08-ci'
  template_source 'cookbooks/chefazure-ch08/files/shared/machine_deploy.json'
  parameters location: 'West Europe',
            vmSize: 'Standard_D1',
            newStorageAccountName: 'chazch8ci',
            adminUsername: 'azure',
            adminPassword: 'P2ssw0rd',
            dnsNameForPublicIP: 'chefazure-ch08-ci',
            imagePublisher: 'Canonical',
            imageOffer: 'UbuntuServer',
            imageSKU: '14.04.3-LTS',
            vmName: 'chazch08jenkins'
  chef_extension client_type: 'LinuxChefClient',
            version: '1210.12',
            runlist: 'role[jenkins]'
end
```

```
PS C:\Users\StuartPreston\chefazure-ch08> knife cookbook upload chefazure-ch08
```

```
Uploading chefazure-ch08 [0.1.0]
Uploaded 1 cookbook.
```

Provisioning the CI Server

Having uploaded the cookbook and remembering that our local development workstation is connected to the same Chef organization, we can now run Chef Client on our local provisioning node and explicitly specify the **provision_jenkins** recipe for our runlist. This will provision our initial machine:

```
PS C:\Users\StuartPreston\chefazure-ch08> chef-client -r recipe[chefazure-ch08::provision_jenkins]
```

```
Starting Chef Client, version 12.5.1
[2016-01-16T00:30:37+00:00] WARN: chef-client doesn't have administrator privileges on node
DESKTOP-TIDJ3S8. This might cause unexpected resource failures.
resolving cookbooks for run list: ["chefazure-ch08::provision_jenkins"]
```

```
Synchronizing Cookbooks:
  - chefazure-ch08 (0.1.0)
Compiling Cookbooks...
Converging 2 resources
Recipe: chefazure-ch08::provision_jenkins
  * azure_resource_group[chefazure-ch08-ci] action create
    - create or update Resource Group chefazure-ch08-ci
  * azure_resource_template[jenkins-server] action deploy
    - adding a Chef VM Extension with name: [variables('vmName')] and location:
      [variables('location')]
    - Result: Accepted
    - Resource Microsoft.Network/publicIPAddresses 'publicip' provisioning status is Running
    - Resource Microsoft.Storage/storageAccounts 'chazch8ci' provisioning status is Running
    - Resource Microsoft.Network/virtualNetworks 'vnet' provisioning status is Running
    - Resource Microsoft.Network/publicIPAddresses 'publicip' provisioning status is Running
    - Resource Microsoft.Storage/storageAccounts 'chazch8ci' provisioning status is Running
    - Resource Microsoft.Network/virtualNetworks 'vnet' provisioning status is Running
    - Resource Microsoft.Storage/storageAccounts 'chazch8ci' provisioning status is Running
    - Resource Microsoft.Storage/storageAccounts 'chazch8ci' provisioning status is Running
    - Resource Microsoft.Storage/storageAccounts 'chazch8ci' provisioning status is Running
    - Resource Microsoft.Compute/virtualMachines 'chazch08jenkins' provisioning status is
      Running
    - Resource Microsoft.Compute/virtualMachines 'chazch08jenkins' provisioning status is
      Running
    - Resource Microsoft.Compute/virtualMachines 'chazch08jenkins' provisioning status is
      Running
    - Resource Microsoft.Compute/virtualMachines 'chazch08jenkins' provisioning status is
      Running
    - Resource Microsoft.Compute/virtualMachines 'chazch08jenkins' provisioning status is
      Running
[...]
    - Resource Microsoft.Compute/virtualMachines 'chazch08jenkins' provisioning status is
      Running
    - Resource Microsoft.Compute/virtualMachines/extensions 'chazch08jenkins/chefExtension'
      provisioning status is Running
    - Resource Microsoft.Compute/virtualMachines/extensions 'chazch08jenkins/chefExtension'
      provisioning status is Running
    - Resource Microsoft.Compute/virtualMachines/extensions 'chazch08jenkins/chefExtension'
      provisioning status is Running
    - Resource Microsoft.Compute/virtualMachines/extensions 'chazch08jenkins/chefExtension'
      provisioning status is Running
    - Resource Microsoft.Compute/virtualMachines/extensions 'chazch08jenkins/chefExtension'
      provisioning status is Running
    - Resource Template deployment reached end state of 'Succeeded'.
    - deploy or re-deploy Resource Manager template 'jenkins-server'

Running handlers:
Running handlers complete
Chef Client finished, 2/2 resources updated in 07 minutes 12 seconds
```

Now that our provisioning recipe has been executed locally, we can verify that the Resource Group was created successfully by visiting the Management Portal and navigating to Resource Groups, as shown in Figure 8-4:

Figure 8-4. *Management Portal showing created chefazure-ch08-ci resource group*

We can drill down further and find the VM and select Extensions to see which extensions have been installed; this is shown in Figure 8-5:

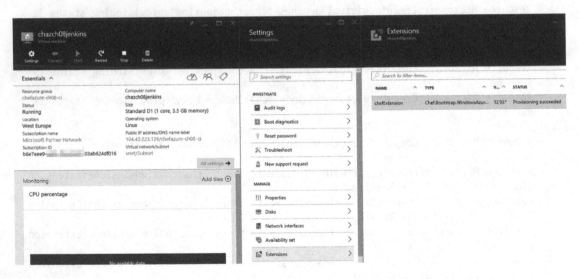

Figure 8-5. *Chef Extension in "Provisioning succeeded" status on a provisioning VM*

To check that the machine successfully registered against the Hosted Chef server, we can look on the Hosted Chef server, as shown in Figure 8-6:

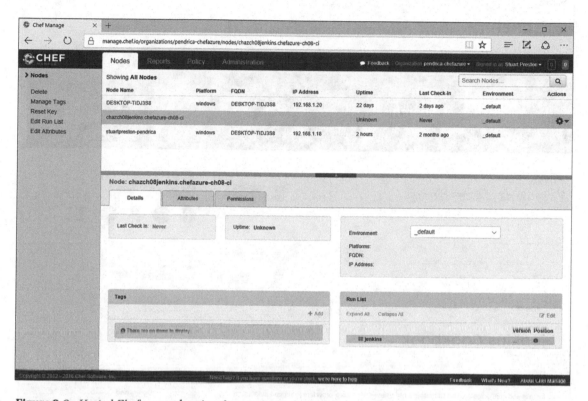

Figure 8-6. *Hosted Chef server showing the provisioned server*

While we specified the **jenkins** 'role' for this server, the role hasn't yet been uploaded to the Chef Server, so it appears in **red** for the time being.

Phase 2 - Installing and Configuring Jenkins

There are many Continuous Integration servers out there both running in a managed (hosted) way and on premises. We have chosen the popular tool Jenkins (http://jenkins-ci.org) Continuous Integration server, which has a huge list of plug-ins and support for all the popular source control systems.

There is also a publicly available cookbook on the Supermarket for installing and configuring it, which we will use. The cookbook is available at https://supermarket.chef.io/cookbooks/jenkins (as shown in Figure 8-7) and is maintained by the team at Chef, like many other high-profile cookbooks.

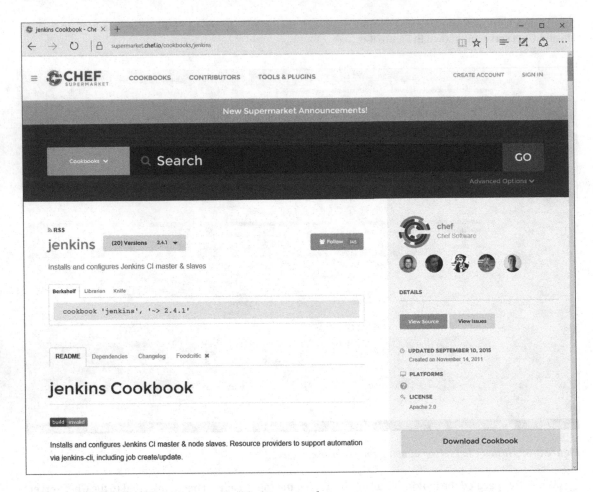

Figure 8-7. Jenkins cookbook page on the Chef Supermarket

By clicking on the **Dependencies tab**, we can see the dependent cookbooks for the Jenkins cookbook, as shown in Figure 8-8.

README	**Dependencies**	Changelog	Foodcritic ✖

Dependent cookbooks

yum ~> 3.0
runit ~> 1.5
apt ~> 2.0

Figure 8-8. Dependencies for the Jenkins cookbook

Using Berkshelf to Retrieve Public Cookbooks

Managing dependencies can get tricky over time - the more cookbooks you include, the more dependencies get included. Downloading cookbooks is a fairly simple task but when we need to upload them to our server it's a pain to work out a list of all the dependencies to upload, not to mention the cookbooks themselves clutter your repo. To avoid this pain, we can use **Berkshelf**, a dependency manager. Berkshelf takes the heavy lifting out of managing community cookbooks. It downloads the cookbooks to a location outside your repo on your local disk, ready for upload to the Chef server. Newer versions of dependencies can be downloaded by the tool automatically and it is also supported by most of the testing tools out there, including RSpec and Test Kitchen. We'll use Berkshelf to work with the Jenkins cookbook.

■ **Note** More information about Berkshelf can be found at `http://berkshelf.com`

First, we need to update our **Berksfile** (a file where you list the dependencies and their sources) so that it knows we have a dependency on the **jenkins** cookbook. The Berksfile lives in the cookbook folder, rather than the root of the repo. Let's edit our Berksfile and add the dependency to the Jenkins cookbook as follows (additions in **bold**):

cookbooks/chefazure-ch08/Berksfile:

```
source 'https://supermarket.chef.io'

metadata

cookbook 'jenkins'
```

To download the cookbook and all dependencies to your local workstation, we can run the `berks install` command:

■ **Note** `berks install` should be executed from the cookbook folder rather than the root of the repo

---

```
PS C:\Users\StuartPreston\chefazure-ch08> cd cookbooks\chefazure-ch08
PS C:\Users\StuartPreston\chefazure-ch08\cookbooks\chefazure-ch08> berks install
```

```
Resolving cookbook dependencies...
Fetching 'chefazure-ch08' from source at .
Fetching cookbook index from https://supermarket.chef.io...
Installing apt (2.9.2)
Installing jenkins (2.4.1)
Using chefazure-ch08 (0.1.0) from source at .
Installing packagecloud (0.1.1)
Installing runit (1.7.6)
Installing yum (3.9.0)
```

Where did the cookbooks install to? Dependency cookbooks are kept outside of our repo in the ~/.berkshelf/cookbooks folder:

```
PS C:\Users\StuartPreston\chefazure-ch08\cookbooks\chefazure-ch08> ls ~/.berkshelf/cookbooks


    Directory: C:\Users\StuartPreston\.berkshelf\cookbooks


Mode                LastWriteTime     Length Name
----                -------------     ------ ----
d-----        16/01/2016     06:21            apt-2.9.2
d-----        16/01/2016     06:21            jenkins-2.4.1
d-----        16/01/2016     06:21            packagecloud-0.1.1
d-----        16/01/2016     06:21            runit-1.7.6
d-----        16/01/2016     06:21            yum-3.9.0
```

Creating a Recipe to Install Jenkins

Now that we have successfully added a dependency on the Jenkins cookbook, we need to create a recipe within our cookbook that includes the Jenkins cookbook and any additional configuration we wish to perform.

To start, create a new file **cookbooks/chefazure-ch08/recipes/install_jenkins.rb** and add the following content to it, to simply include the master recipe from the jenkins cookbook:

cookbooks/chefazure-ch08/recipes/install_jenkins.rb:

```
include_recipe 'jenkins::master'
```

We also need to add a dependency on the Jenkins cookbook to our metadata file in the cookbook folder. After modification the file should look like the following:

cookbooks/chefazure-ch08/metadata.rb:

```
name 'chefazure-ch08'
maintainer 'Stuart Preston'
maintainer_email 'stuart@pendrica.com'
license 'all_rights'
description 'Installs/Configures chefazure-ch08'
long_description 'Installs/Configures chefazure-ch08'
version '0.1.1'

depends 'jenkins'
```

Uploading the Cookbook and Dependencies

The neat thing about Berkshelf is that the **cookbooks** folder in our repo is not littered with cookbooks that we need to keep up to date, and the berks upload command lets us upload all of our dependent cookbooks to the server in one go. Let's do that, remembering that we run the command from the cookbook folder:

```
PS C:\Users\StuartPreston\chefazure-ch08\cookbooks\chefazure-ch08> berks install
PS C:\Users\StuartPreston\chefazure-ch08\cookbooks\chefazure-ch08> berks upload
```

```
Uploaded apt (2.9.2) to: 'https://api.chef.io:443/organizations/pendrica-chefazure'
Uploaded chefazure-ch08 (0.1.0) to: 'https://api.chef.io:443/organizations/pendrica-chefazure'
Uploaded jenkins (2.4.1) to: 'https://api.chef.io:443/organizations/pendrica-chefazure'
Uploaded packagecloud (0.1.1) to: 'https://api.chef.io:443/organizations/pendrica-chefazure'
Uploaded runit (1.7.6) to: 'https://api.chef.io:443/organizations/pendrica-chefazure'
Uploaded yum (3.9.0) to: 'https://api.chef.io:443/organizations/pendrica-chefazure'
```

Preparing and Uploading Role Definitions

Remember that Roles consist of attributes (if appropriate) and a run list? We're going to create the **jenkins** role we referred to earlier in the chapter and set its runlist to the recipe we just created. That way when we next run the Chef client on the Jenkins server, the recipe should be executed.

Create a new file (and roles folder) **roles/jenkins.json**

roles/jenkins.json:

```
{
  "name": "jenkins",
  "chef_type": "role",
  "json_class": "Chef::Role",
  "default_attributes": {
  },
  "description": "jenkins role",
  "run_list": [
    "recipe[chefazure-ch08::install_jenkins]"
  ],
  "env_run_lists" : {
  }
}
```

Now we can upload our Jenkins role to the Chef server so it is ready for use:

```
PS C:\Users\StuartPreston\chefazure-ch08> knife role from file roles/jenkins.json
```

```
Updated Role jenkins!
```

If we refresh the Hosted Chef page in our browser, we will see that the runlist for our chczch08jenkins node now expands correctly, as shown in Figure 8-9:

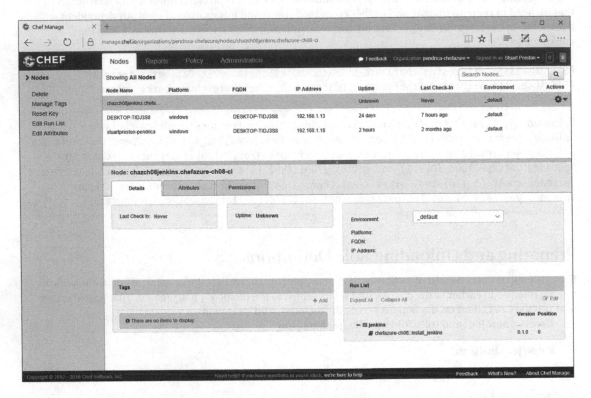

Figure 8-9. *Hosted Chef showing expanded Runlist for our Jenkins server*

Configuring the Jenkins Server

Let's run the Chef Client manually on the server so that it picks up our latest changes. To find out what hostname or IP address to connect to, we can have a look in the publicIP resource for our VM in the Azure Management Portal, as shown in Figure 8-10:

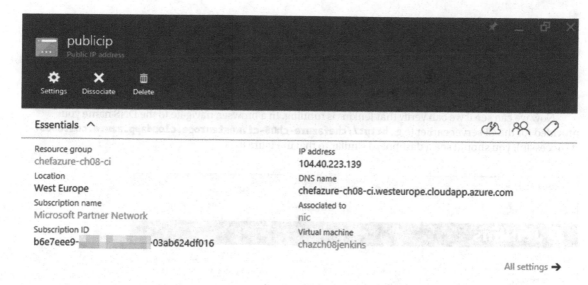

Figure 8-10. *Azure Management Portal showing the full DNS name of our CI server*

The DNS name should take the form **<dnsNameForPublicIP>.<location>.cloudapp.azure.com** where:

- **dnsNameForPublicIP** was specified in the parameters of the provisioning recipe

- **location** is the short name for the datacenter location, e.g. "westeurope"

Using an SSH client, connect to the server and run sudo chef-client:

azure@chefazurech08ci:~$ **sudo chef-client**

(note the below output has been abbreviated)

```
Starting Chef Client, version 12.6.0
resolving cookbooks for run list: ["chefazure-ch08::jenkins_ci_install"]
Synchronizing Cookbooks:
  - chefazure-ch08 (0.1.0)
  - jenkins (2.4.1)
  - apt (2.9.2)
  - runit (1.7.6)
  - packagecloud (0.1.1)
  - yum (3.9.0)
Compiling Cookbooks...
Converging 15 resources

[...]

  * apt_package[jenkins] action install
  * service[jenkins] action restart
    - restart service service[jenkins]
  * service[jenkins] action enable (up to date)
  * service[jenkins] action start (up to date)
```

```
Running handlers:
  - AzureExtension::ReportHandler
Running handlers complete

Chef Client finished, 15/15 resources updated in 58 seconds
```

Now we can see if we can verify that Jenkins is running. In a browser, navigate to the DNS name you provided for the CI server earlier (e.g., **http://chefazure-ch08-ci.westeurope.cloudapp.azure.com:8080**). If successful, you should see a dashboard similar to that in Figure 8-11.

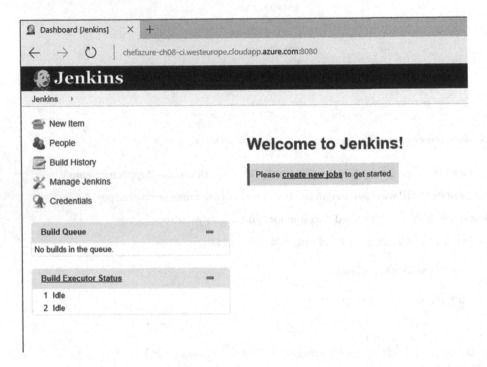

Figure 8-11. *Jenkins Dashboard*

Adding Plug-ins to Jenkins

To start with, we will probably want to use Git, and the popular GitHub and Build Pipeline plug-ins in our Jenkins implementation, and these can be configured from a recipe by adding the content below (in bold) to **cookbooks\chefazure-ch08\recipes\install_jenkins.rb:**

```
include_recipe 'jenkins::master'

package 'git' do
  action :install
end
```

```
jenkins_plugin 'github' do
  action :install
  notifies :restart, 'service[jenkins]', :delayed
end

jenkins_plugin 'build-pipeline-plugin' do
  action :install
  notifies :restart, 'service[jenkins]', :delayed
end
```

As we are now using Berkshelf to manage our uploads, we need to bump the version of our cookbook to version 0.1.1 in **cookbooks\chefazure-ch08\metadata.rb** (this is because the previous version is locked by Berkshelf, and besides - it is a good practice to get into the habit of incrementing the version number when changes come through the system). The resulting **metadata.rb** file should look similar to the one below:

cookbooks\chefazure-ch08\metadata.rb:

```
name 'chefazure-ch08'
maintainer 'Stuart Preston'
maintainer_email 'stuart@pendrica.com'
license 'all_rights'
description 'Installs/Configures chefazure-ch08'
long_description 'Installs/Configures chefazure-ch08'
version '0.1.1'

depends 'jenkins'
```

Now we need to notify Berkshelf of our new version (berks update), and upload it to the server (berks upload):

```
PS C:\Users\StuartPreston\chefazure-ch08\cookbooks\chefazure-ch08> berks update
```

```
Resolving cookbook dependencies...
Fetching 'chefazure-ch08' from source at .
Fetching cookbook index from https://supermarket.chef.io...
Using apt (2.9.2)
Using chefazure-ch08 (0.1.1) from source at .
Using jenkins (2.4.1)
Using runit (1.7.6)
Using yum (3.9.0)
Using packagecloud (0.1.1)
```

```
C:\Users\StuartPreston\chefazure-ch08\cookbooks\chefazure-ch08> berks upload
```

```
Skipping apt (2.9.2) (frozen)
Uploaded chefazure-ch08 (0.1.1) to: 'https://api.chef.io:443/organizations/pendrica-chefazure'
Skipping jenkins (2.4.1) (frozen)
Skipping packagecloud (0.1.1) (frozen)
Skipping runit (1.7.6) (frozen)
Skipping yum (3.9.0) (frozen)
```

We can now execute Chef Client again on our Jenkins server, where we can see at the end of the run, we successfully invoke a restart on the Jenkins service:

azure@chazch08jenkins:~$ **sudo chef-client**

```
Starting Chef Client, version 12.6.0
resolving cookbooks for run list: ["chefazure-ch08::install_jenkins"]
Synchronizing Cookbooks:
  - jenkins (2.4.1)
  - apt (2.9.2)
  - runit (1.7.6)
  - packagecloud (0.1.1)
  - yum (3.9.0)
  - chefazure-ch08 (0.1.1)
Compiling Cookbooks...
Converging 18 resources
Recipe: jenkins::_master_package

[...]

  * service[jenkins] action restart
    - restart service service[jenkins]

Running handlers:
  - AzureExtension::ReportHandler
Running handlers complete

Chef Client finished, 17/39 resources updated in 01 minutes 58 seconds
```

Verifying Jenkins Plug-in Installation

To verify that the plug-ins were installed we can navigate to **Manage Jenkins ➤ Manage Plugins** and click on the **Installed** tab in the browser dashboard; we should see two plug-ins installed as shown in Figure 8-12.

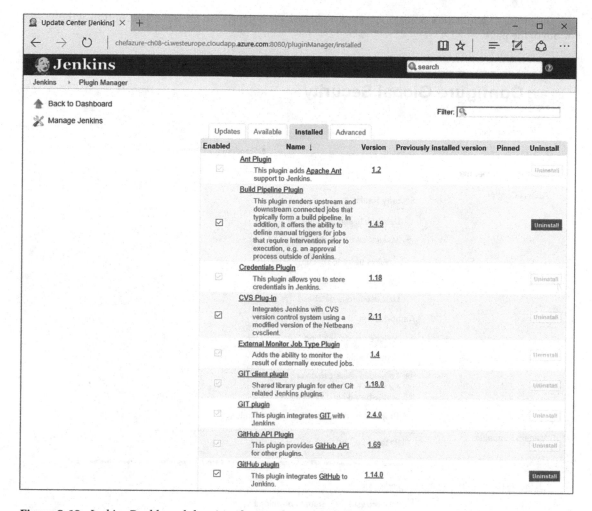

Figure 8-12. *Jenkins Dashboard showing plug-ins that are installed*

Now that we have our plug-ins installed we can start working with the Jenkins server itself to define jobs relevant to our pipeline.

Securing Access to Jenkins

Before we start configuring Jenkins jobs that potentially contain sensitive data, we should lock down access to the system and create our first account:

- From the Jenkins dashboard, select **Manage Jenkins**, then **Configure Global Security.**
- Click **Enable Security**. The page will expand to offer a choice of access control.
- Select **Jenkins' own user database.**
- Uncheck **Allow users to sign up.**
- Select **Logged-in users can do anything.**

The options should look similar to Figure 8-13 below. Do not forget to press the **Save** button at the bottom of the page.

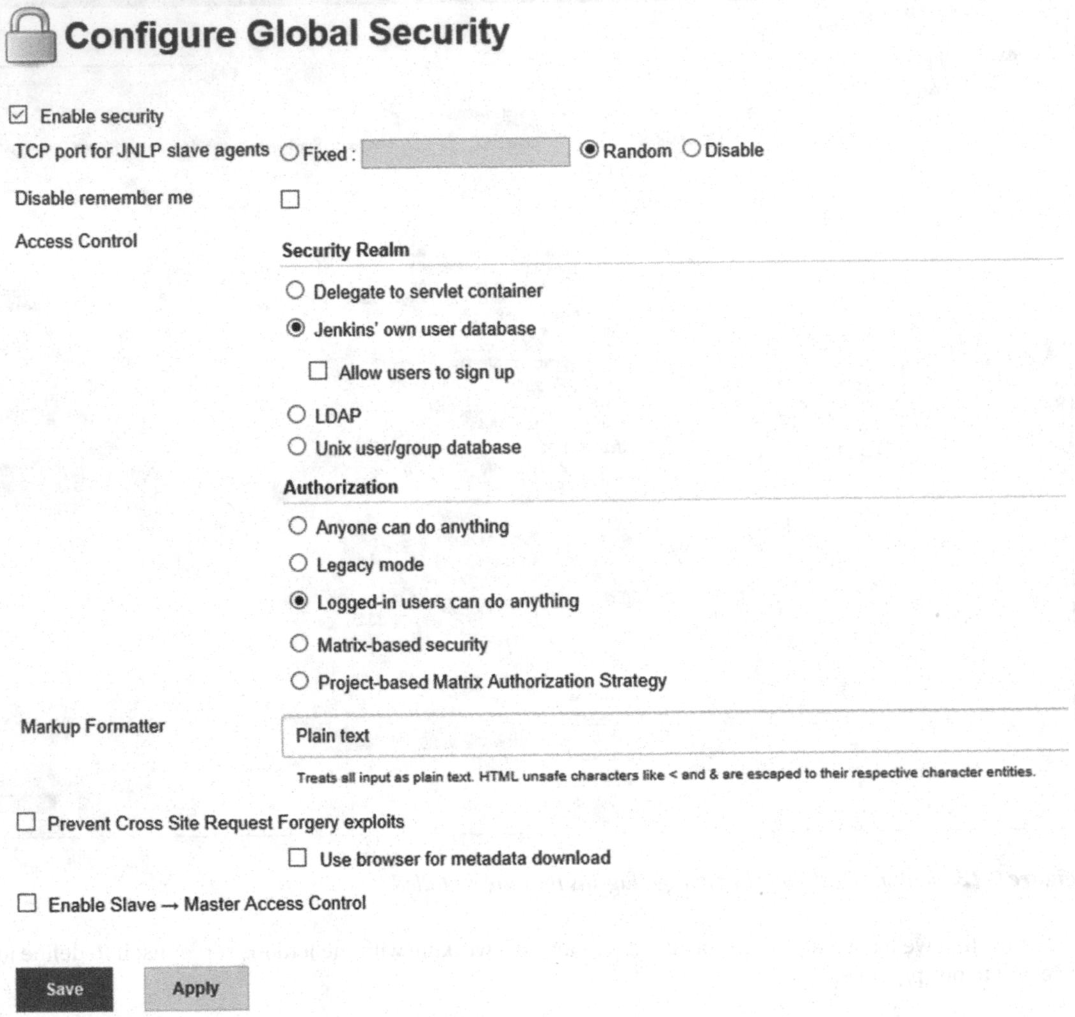

🔒 Configure Global Security

☑ Enable security

TCP port for JNLP slave agents   ○ Fixed : [＿＿＿＿＿＿]   ⦿ Random   ○ Disable

Disable remember me   ☐

Access Control

Security Realm

    ○ Delegate to servlet container

    ⦿ Jenkins' own user database

       ☐ Allow users to sign up

    ○ LDAP

    ○ Unix user/group database

Authorization

    ○ Anyone can do anything

    ○ Legacy mode

    ⦿ Logged-in users can do anything

    ○ Matrix-based security

    ○ Project-based Matrix Authorization Strategy

Markup Formatter

| Plain text |

Treats all input as plain text. HTML unsafe characters like < and & are escaped to their respective character entities.

☐ Prevent Cross Site Request Forgery exploits

       ☐ Use browser for metadata download

☐ Enable Slave → Master Access Control

[Save]   [Apply]

Figure 8-13. *Configure Global Security option in Jenkins*

On pressing **Save**, you will be prompted to create the first account as shown in Figure 8-14:

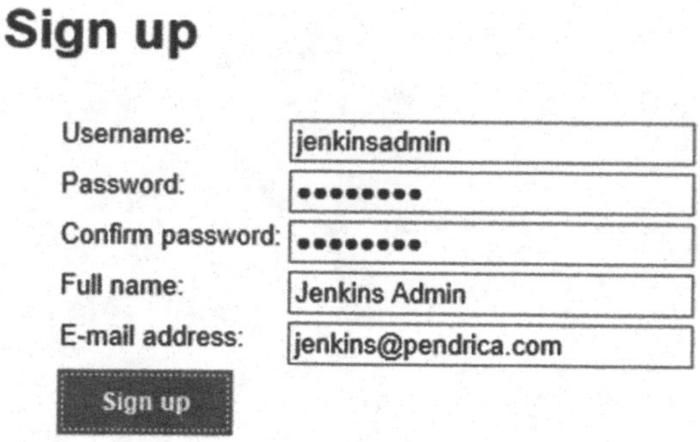

Sign up

Username:	jenkinsadmin
Password:	••••••••
Confirm password:	••••••••
Full name:	Jenkins Admin
E-mail address:	jenkins@pendrica.com

Sign up

Figure 8-14. *"First Account" Sign-up page shown in Jenkins*

You will now be logged in automatically.

Adding Chef Dependencies to Jenkins

We need to install some Ruby Gems on our Jenkins server, and to do so we can edit the install_jenkins.rb and use the gem_package resource to add our new dependencies.

cookbooks\chefazure-ch08\recipes\install_jenkins.rb:

```
include_recipe 'jenkins::master'

package 'git' do
  action :install
end

jenkins_plugin 'github' do
  action :install
  notifies :restart, 'service[jenkins]', :delayed
end

jenkins_plugin 'build-pipeline-plugin' do
  action :install
  notifies :restart, 'service[jenkins]', :delayed
end

package 'build-essential' do
  action :install
end

gem_package 'chef-provisioning' do
  action :install
end
```

197

```ruby
gem_package 'chef-provisioning-azurerm' do
  action :install
end

gem_package 'rspec' do
  action :install
end

gem_package 'rake' do
  action :install
end

gem_package 'rubocop' do
  action :install
end
```

As we have made a change we need to increment our version number, update the Berkshelf dependencies, and upload the new cookbook to the Chef server:

cookbooks\chefazure-ch08\metadata.rb:

```ruby
name 'chefazure-ch08'
maintainer 'Stuart Preston'
maintainer_email 'stuart@pendrica.com'
license 'all_rights'
description 'Installs/Configures chefazure-ch08'
long_description 'Installs/Configures chefazure-ch08'
version '0.1.2'

depends 'jenkins'
```

Now we need to notify Berkshelf of our new version (berks update), and upload it to the server (berks upload):

```
PS C:\Users\StuartPreston\chefazure-ch08\cookbooks\chefazure-ch08> berks update
```

```
Resolving cookbook dependencies...
Fetching 'chefazure-ch08' from source at .
Fetching cookbook index from https://supermarket.chef.io...
Using apt (2.9.2)
Using chefazure-ch08 (0.1.2) from source at .
Using jenkins (2.4.1)
Using runit (1.7.6)
Using yum (3.9.0)
Using packagecloud (0.1.1)
```

```
PS C:\Users\StuartPreston\chefazure-ch08\cookbooks\chefazure-ch08> berks upload
```

```
Skipping apt (2.9.2) (frozen)
Uploaded chefazure-ch08 (0.1.2) to: 'https://api.chef.io:443/organizations/pendrica-chefazure'
Skipping jenkins (2.4.1) (frozen)
Skipping packagecloud (0.1.1) (frozen)
Skipping runit (1.7.6) (frozen)
Skipping yum (3.9.0) (frozen)
```

We can now execute Chef Client again on our Jenkins server, where we can see at the end of the run, we successfully invoke a restart on the Jenkins service:

```
azure@chazch08jenkins:~$ sudo chef-client
```

```
Starting Chef Client, version 12.6.0
resolving cookbooks for run list: ["chefazure-ch08::install_jenkins"]
Synchronizing Cookbooks:
  - chefazure-ch08 (0.1.2)
  - jenkins (2.4.1)
  - apt (2.9.2)
  - runit (1.7.6)
  - yum (3.9.0)
  - packagecloud (0.1.1)
Compiling Cookbooks...
Converging 24 resources
[...]
Running handlers:
  - AzureExtension::ReportHandler
Running handlers complete

Chef Client finished, 7/33 resources updated in 58 seconds
```

Phase 3 - Setting Up a New Chef Repository in GitHub

For our scenario, we want our Jenkins jobs to be triggered by changes to the master branch in our repo. So we need a hosted Git repository for this.

You may already have your own hosted Git solution, such as Visual Studio Team Services (formerly Visual Studio Online), GitLab, or Atlassian Stash/Bitbucket and a similar procedure will apply to those. The basic steps to upload your repository are as follows.

- Log in to GitHub at **https://github.com** and create an account if necessary.

- Click on the plus sign and create a **New repository** (example values are shown in Figure 8-15).

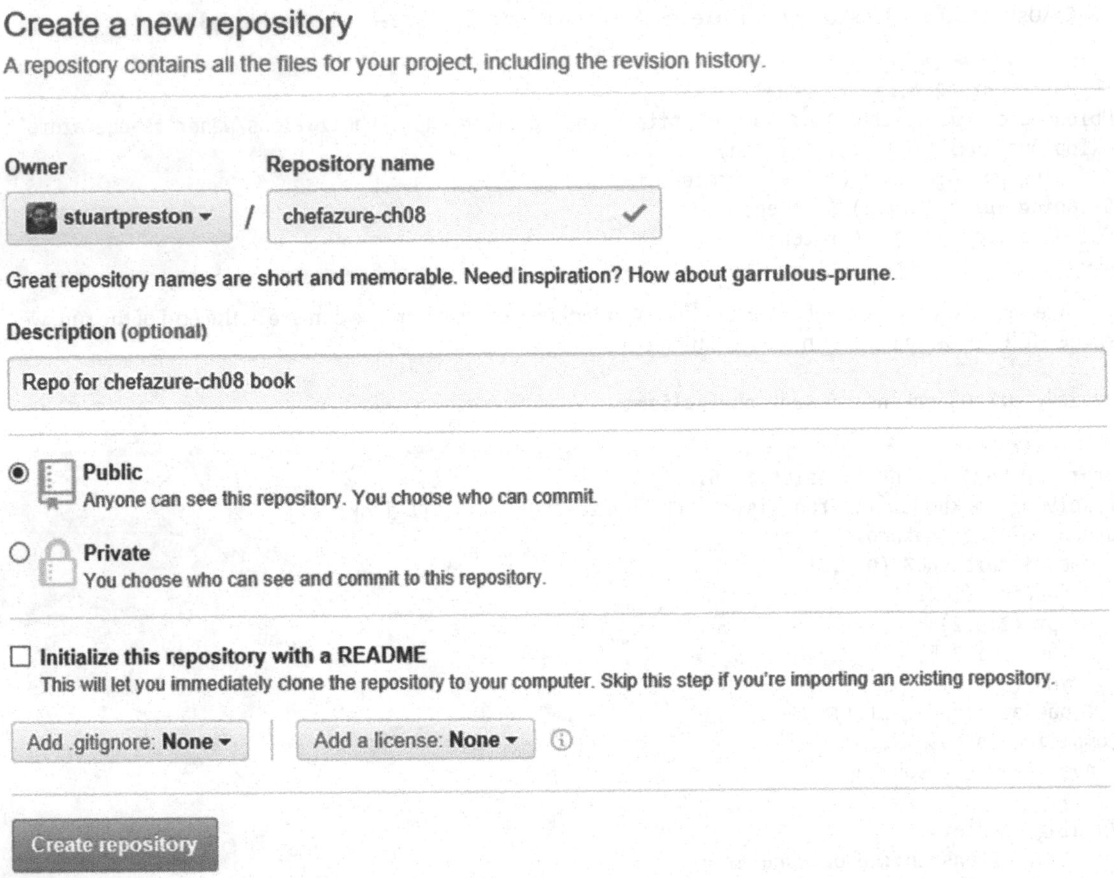

Create a new repository

A repository contains all the files for your project, including the revision history.

Owner   **Repository name**

[🖼 stuartpreston ▾] / [chefazure-ch08   ✓]

Great repository names are short and memorable. Need inspiration? How about **garrulous-prune**.

Description (optional)

[Repo for chefazure-ch08 book]

◉ 📖 **Public**
     Anyone can see this repository. You choose who can commit.

○ 🔒 **Private**
     You choose who can see and commit to this repository.

☐ **Initialize this repository with a README**
     This will let you immediately clone the repository to your computer. Skip this step if you're importing an existing repository.

[Add .gitignore: **None** ▾]   [Add a license: **None** ▾]   ⓘ

[Create repository]

Figure 8-15. *GitHub Create repository screen*

- Press the **Create repository** button.
- Now that we have a new blank repository on GitHub, we can set this as the 'remote' for our local repository and push to it. We will need to commit our changes first.

Configuring a .gitignore File to Exclude Sensitive Information

As we do not want to share our keys with the world, we need to add the following line to our Git ignore file so that they won't get included when we commit changes. Note the .gitignore file is in the root of our repo:

```
.gitignore:
.vagrant
Berksfile.lock
*~
*#
.#*
\#*#
.*.sw[a-z]
*.un~
```

```
# Bundler
Gemfile.lock
bin/*
.bundle/*

.kitchen/
.kitchen.local.yml

.chef/
```

After saving the file, we can stage our changes for git, and then commit them:

```
PS C:\Users\StuartPreston\chefazure-ch08> git add .
PS C:\Users\StuartPreston\chefazure-ch08> git commit -m 'initial commit'
```

```
[master (root-commit) 979f481] initial commit
 15 files changed, 490 insertions(+)
 create mode 100644 .gitignore
 create mode 100644 .kitchen.yml
 create mode 100644 README.md
 create mode 100644 cookbooks/chefazure-ch08/Berksfile
 create mode 100644 cookbooks/chefazure-ch08/chefignore
 create mode 100644 cookbooks/chefazure-ch08/files/shared/machine_deploy.json
 create mode 100644 cookbooks/chefazure-ch08/metadata.rb
 create mode 100644 cookbooks/chefazure-ch08/recipes/default.rb
 create mode 100644 cookbooks/chefazure-ch08/recipes/install_jenkins.rb
 create mode 100644 cookbooks/chefazure-ch08/recipes/provision_jenkins.rb
 create mode 100644 cookbooks/chefazure-ch08/roles/jenkins.json
 create mode 100644 cookbooks/chefazure-ch08/spec/spec_helper.rb
 create mode 100644 cookbooks/chefazure-ch08/spec/unit/recipes/default_spec.rb
 create mode 100644 test/integration/default/serverspec/default_spec.rb
 create mode 100644 test/integration/helpers/serverspec/spec_helper.rb
```

Connecting a Local Git Repo to the Remote

We can now connect our local repository with the remote by using the git remote add command and specifying the URI of the GitHub repo:

```
PS C:\Users\StuartPreston\chefazure-ch08> git remote add origin https://github.com/
stuartpreston/chefazure-ch08.git
PS C:\Users\StuartPreston\chefazure-ch08> git push -u origin master
```

```
Username for 'https://github.com': stuartpreston
Password for 'https://stuartpreston@github.com':
Counting objects: 32, done.
Delta compression using up to 4 threads.
Compressing objects: 100% (20/20), done.
Writing objects: 100% (32/32), 5.53 KiB | 0 bytes/s, done.
```

```
Total 32 (delta 0), reused 0 (delta 0)
To https://github.com/stuartpreston/chefazure-ch08.git
 * [new branch]      master -> master
Branch master set up to track remote branch master from origin.
```

We now have our changes committed and pushed to our remote Git repository in GitHub.

Phase 4 - Configuring the Jenkins Project

In Jenkins, a job is a container for the build process including all build steps. We're going to create and configure a job, using the following steps:

- From the home page, press **create new jobs**.

- You are taken to a page to enter the **item name** and the **type** of project. We'll use "Provisioning" as the item name and a **Freestyle** project as shown in Figure 8-16.

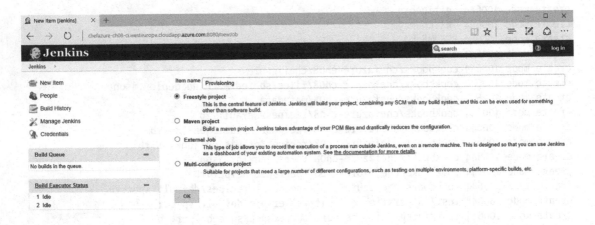

Figure 8-16. *Jenkins Create Job/Project creation page*

We are then taken to the project creation page as shown in Figure 8-17.

Adding a New Project

There are a multitude of settings that we could set; however the key ones for us relate to how we access source control. We can then add a few Build Steps that execute in order based on a trigger. To add a new project, the options we need to set or select are the following:

- **Project name:** Provisioning

- **GitHub project:** (selected)

  - Project url: **https://github.com/stuartpreston/chefazure-ch08**

  - (advanced) Display name: chefazure-ch08

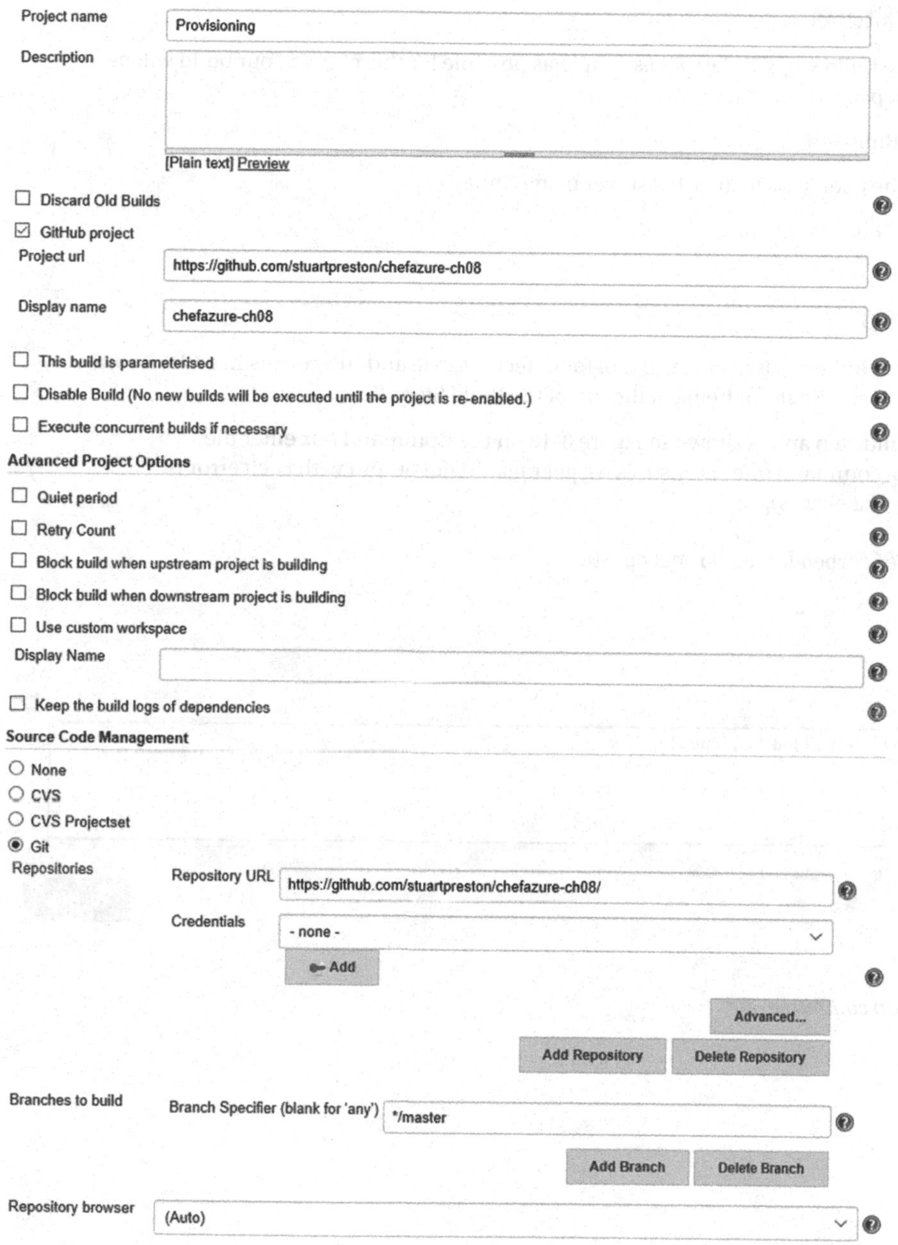

Project name   Provisioning

Description

                    [Plain text] Preview

☐ Discard Old Builds   ❷
☑ GitHub project
Project url   https://github.com/stuartpreston/chefazure-ch08   ❷

Display name   chefazure-ch08   ❷

☐ This build is parameterised   ❷
☐ Disable Build (No new builds will be executed until the project is re-enabled.)   ❷
☐ Execute concurrent builds if necessary   ❷

Advanced Project Options

☐ Quiet period   ❷
☐ Retry Count   ❷
☐ Block build when upstream project is building   ❷
☐ Block build when downstream project is building   ❷
☐ Use custom workspace   ❷
Display Name   ❷

☐ Keep the build logs of dependencies   ❷

Source Code Management

○ None
○ CVS
○ CVS Projectset
◉ Git
Repositories

            Repository URL   https://github.com/stuartpreston/chefazure-ch08/   ❷

            Credentials   - none -   ∨

                              ⌸ Add   ❷

                                                              Advanced...

                                        Add Repository   Delete Repository

Branches to build

            Branch Specifier (blank for 'any')   */master   ❷

                                        Add Branch   Delete Branch

Repository browser   (Auto)   ∨   ❷

Figure 8-17. *Jenkins Job creation screen*

Adding Build Steps

Now we can add some build steps. To keep it as simple as possible for this chapter, our build will be comprised of three steps.

- Execute Rubocop
- Upload the cookbook to the Chef server using Knife
- Execute Chef Provisioning

Execute Rubocop

As we saw in chapter 6, Rubocop is a powerful tool for detecting style and ruby errors in code. It runs very quickly, so it is a prime candidate for being at the top of the Build Steps list:

- Add a Build step and as shown in Figure 8-18; in the Command box enter the following command (the -D ensures we get meaningful output with each error or warning that occurs):

```
/opt/chef/embedded/bin/rubocop -D
```

Build

▥ **Execute shell**   ❷

Command `/opt/chef/embedded/bin/rubocop -D`

See the list of available environment variables

Delete

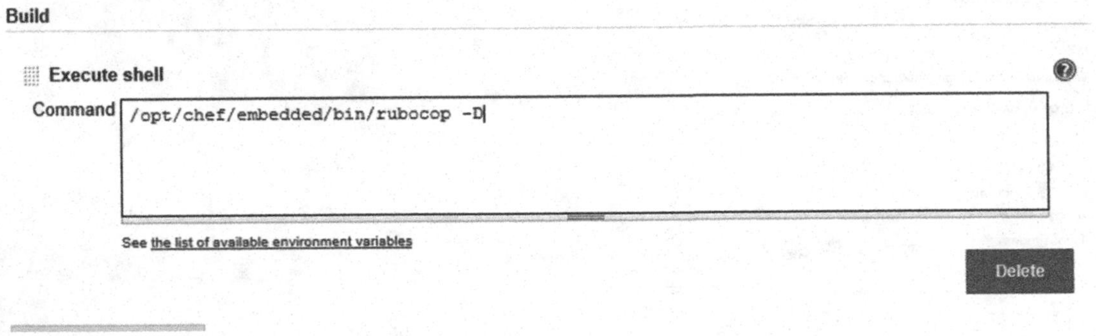

***Figure 8-18.** Rubocop command*

Press **Save** and run the build, by clicking the **Build Now** link on the Jenkins dashboard for the Provisioning project, as shown in Figure 8-19:

Figure 8-19. *Jenkins dashboard*

While the build is running, you can visit the **Console Output** screen as shown in Figure 8-20 to see any output that was written to the console (STDOUT) during the run. If you miss it, don't worry - the output will be saved for inspection later (you can view it by navigating to any build and pressing **Console Output**).

● Console Output

```
Started by user anonymous
Building in workspace /var/lib/jenkins/jobs/Provisioning/workspace
Cloning the remote Git repository
Cloning repository https://github.com/stuartpreston/chefazure-ch08/
 > git init /var/lib/jenkins/jobs/Provisioning/workspace # timeout=10
Fetching upstream changes from https://github.com/stuartpreston/chefazure-ch08/
 > git --version # timeout=10
 > git -c core.askpass=true fetch --tags --progress https://github.com/stuartpreston/chefazure-ch08/
+refs/heads/*:refs/remotes/origin/*
 > git config remote.origin.url https://github.com/stuartpreston/chefazure-ch08/ # timeout=10
 > git config --add remote.origin.fetch +refs/heads/*:refs/remotes/origin/* # timeout=10
 > git config remote.origin.url https://github.com/stuartpreston/chefazure-ch08/ # timeout=10
Fetching upstream changes from https://github.com/stuartpreston/chefazure-ch08/
 > git -c core.askpass=true fetch --tags --progress https://github.com/stuartpreston/chefazure-ch08/
+refs/heads/*:refs/remotes/origin/*
 > git rev-parse refs/remotes/origin/master^{commit} # timeout=10
 > git rev-parse refs/remotes/origin/origin/master^{commit} # timeout=10
Checking out Revision 979f48128dfe4a0e5ea3beff9ae7ec31fafa522d (refs/remotes/origin/master)
 > git config core.sparsecheckout # timeout=10
 > git checkout -f 979f48128dfe4a0e5ea3beff9ae7ec31fafa522d
First time build. Skipping changelog.
[workspace] $ /bin/sh -xe /tmp/hudson1147570158868479540.sh
+ /opt/chef/embedded/bin/rubocop -D
Inspecting 9 files
.........

9 files inspected, no offenses detected
Finished: SUCCESS
```

Figure 8-20. *Console Output from Jenkins build process*

By inspecting the console output, we can see that Rubocop executed, checked the files in our workspace (corresponding to our Chef repo). and hopefully there are no offenses. If there are, then the build will fail and you will need to correct these errors before moving on.

Upload the Cookbook to the Chef Server Using Knife

When the Rubocop step is successful we want to upload the **chefazure-ch08** cookbook to the server to make our provisioning recipes available. We can accomplish this using the knife cookbook tool running locally on the Jenkins server.

Before we do that, we need to make our **knife** configuration (i.e., the content of the ~/chef-repo/.chef folder, excluding the validation key) available to Jenkins. I find the simplest way to accomplish the required result is to manually copy the files from your machine into the home directory using SCP, SFTP or your preferred tool and then copy them as root (using sudo) into /etc/chef:

```
azure@chazch08jenkins:$ cd /etc/chef
azure@chazch08jenkins:/etc/chef$ sudo cp /home/azure/stuartpreston-pendrica.pem .
azure@chazch08jenkins:/etc/chef$ sudo cp /home/azure/knife.rb .
```

Once the Knife configuration is available on the server, we can add another Build Step to our Jenkins job of type **Execute Shell**. The format the command takes is as follows:

```
/opt/chef/embedded/bin/knife cookbook upload <cookbook_name> -c /etc/chef/knife.rb -o
./cookbooks --force
```

Where:

- **<cookbook_name>** is the name of the cookbook we wish to upload

- **-c /etc/chef/knife.rb** is the path to our Knife configuration file

- **-o ./cookbooks** is an override to the location of cookbooks that will point to our cookbooks folder during a build

- **--force** is used to overwrite any existing cookbook on the server with the same version

The build step is shown in Figure 8-21 below:

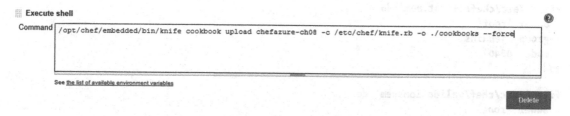

Figure 8-21. *Command line for uploading the cookbook using Knife*

We can trigger a new build manually by pressing **Save** and pressing the **Build Now** button. We should see the output as seen in Figure 8-22.

Figure 8-22. *Knife command running via Jenkins*

In the output from this build we can see Rubocop inspecting nine files, followed by Knife uploading the cookbook to the server.

Configuring Jenkins for Chef Provisioning

Before we can execute our first Chef Provisioning recipe via Jenkins, we need to make some modifications to the configuration of the Jenkins server. This is because the keys that the Chef client will need to read are not available to the Chef client when it is executed from Jenkins. We'll need to change the permissions on the **client.pem** and **validation.pem** files. Additionally, we will need a separate **client.rb** file to use for provisioning purposes. The reason for that is that the client.rb that is installed on the machine through the Azure VM Extension is incompatible with being run as the Jenkins user.

So we'll need to make some changes as follows - first we need to *append* two file resources and a template resource to our **install_jenkins** recipe:

cookbooks/chefazure-ch08/recipes/install_jenkins.rb

```
file '/etc/chef/client.pem' do
  owner 'root'
  group 'jenkins'
  mode '0640'
end

file '/etc/chef/validation.pem' do
  owner 'root'
  group 'jenkins'
  mode '0640'
end

template '/etc/chef/client-provisioning.rb' do
  source 'client-provisioning.erb'
  owner 'root'
  group 'jenkins'
  mode '0640'
end
```

We need to create the .erb template that is referred to in the **install_jenkins** recipe. We put this template in the templates folder. As you can see from the recipe, at the end we'll expect all three files to be created with permissions that allow read access to members of the Jenkins group on the server.

cookbooks/chefazure-ch08/templates/client-provisioning.erb:

```
node_name "<%= Chef::Config[:node_name] %>"
chef_server_url "<%= Chef::Config[:chef_server_url] %>"
validation_client_name "<%= Chef::Config[:validation_client_name] %>"
client_key "<%= Chef::Config[:client_key] %>"
validation_key "<%= Chef::Config[:validation_key] %>"
file_cache_path "/var/lib/jenkins/.chef"
log_location "/dev/stdout"
log_level :info
```

We will also need to update our metadata.rb again with a new version:

metadata.rb:

```
name 'chefazure-ch08'
maintainer 'Stuart Preston'
maintainer_email 'stuart@pendrica.com'
```

```
license 'all_rights'
description 'Installs/Configures chefazure-ch08'
long_description 'Installs/Configures chefazure-ch08'
version '0.1.3'

depends 'jenkins'
```

Once this has been saved, we need to perform a berks update and berks upload to the Chef server:

```
PS C:\Users\StuartPreston\chefazure-ch08\cookbooks\chefazure-ch08> berks update
```

```
Fetching 'chefazure-ch08' from source at .
Fetching cookbook index from https://supermarket.chef.io...
Using apt (2.9.2)
Using chefazure-ch08 (0.1.3) from source at .
Using jenkins (2.4.1)
Using packagecloud (0.1.1)
Using runit (1.7.6)
Using yum (3.9.0)
```

```
PS C:\Users\StuartPreston\chefazure-ch08\cookbooks\chefazure-ch08> berks upload
```

```
Skipping apt (2.9.2) (frozen)
Uploaded chefazure-ch08 (0.1.3) to: 'https://api.chef.io:443/organizations/pendrica-
hcfazure'
Skipping jenkins (2.4.1) (frozen)
Skipping packagecloud (0.1.1) (frozen)
Skipping runit (1.7.6) (frozen)
Skipping yum (3.9.0) (frozen)
```

Back on our Jenkins server, we can rerun Chef client again (or wait 30 minutes for the changes to take effect from the scheduled Chef client):

```
azure@chazch08jenkins:/etc/chef$ sudo chef-client
```

```
Starting Chef Client, version 12.6.0
resolving cookbooks for run list: ["chefazure-ch08::install_jenkins"]
Synchronizing Cookbooks:
  - runit (1.7.6)
  - apt (2.9.2)
  - jenkins (2.4.1)
  - packagecloud (0.1.1)
  - yum (3.9.0)
  - chefazure-ch08 (0.1.3)
Compiling Cookbooks...
Converging 26 resources
[...]
```

```
Recipe: chefazure-ch08::install_jenkins
  * jenkins_plugin[build-pipeline-plugin] action install (up to date)
  * apt_package[build-essential] action install (up to date)
  * gem_package[chef-provisioning] action install (up to date)
  * gem_package[chef-provisioning-azurerm] action install (up to date)
  * gem_package[rspec] action install (up to date)
  * gem_package[rake] action install (up to date)
  * gem_package[rubocop] action install (up to date)
  * file[/etc/chef/client.pem] action create
    - change mode from '0700' to '0640'
  * file[/etc/chef/validation.pem] action create
    - change mode from '0700' to '0640'
  * file[/etc/chef/client.pem] action create (up to date)
  * file[/etc/chef/validation.pem] action create (up to date)
  * template[/etc/chef/client-provisioning.rb] action create
    - create new file /etc/chef/client-provisioning.rb
    - update content in file /etc/chef/client-provisioning.rb from none to 3e6261
    --- /etc/chef/client-provisioning.rb        2016-01-16 22:53:17.255588400 +0000
    +++ /etc/chef/.client-provisioning.rb20160116-14225-7a41z9  2016-01-16
         22:53:17.255588400 +0000
    @@ -1 +1,8 @@
    +node_name "chazch08jenkins.chefazure-ch08-ci"
    +chef_server_url https://api.chef.io/organizations/pendrica-chefazure
    +validation_client_name "pendrica-chefazure-validator"
    +client_key "/etc/chef/client.pem"
    +validation_key "/etc/chef/validation.pem"
    +file_cache_path "/var/lib/jenkins/.chef"
    +log_location "/dev/stdout"
    +log_level :info
    - change mode from '' to '0640'
    - change owner from '' to 'root'
    - change group from '' to 'jenkins'

Running handlers:
  - AzureExtension::ReportHandler
Running handlers complete

Chef Client finished, 1/36 resources updated in 19 seconds
```

Execute a Chef Provisioning Recipe

We're nearly complete on our Jenkins job creation - we need to add our final build step, which is to execute Chef Provisioning. Chef Provisioning typically executes inside a normal Chef client, but in our case we are using a special Chef client configuration that is separate from the one for the Jenkins server itself. That way we can continue to service Jenkins, while sending Provisioning recipes through the Chef Provisioning configuration.

To accomplish this, we need to add another Build Step to our Jenkins job of type **Execute Shell**. The format the command takes is as follows:

```
/opt/chef/embedded/bin/chef-client -c /etc/chef/client-provisioning.rb -o recipe[chefazure-
ch08::default]
```

Where:

- **-c /etc/chef/client-provisioning.rb** points to our custom configuration file for Chef Provisioning

- **-o recipe[chefazure-ch08::default]** is a run list override - we only want to run the provisioning recipes that are included by the default recipe in our cookbook

The build step is shown in Figure 8-23 below:

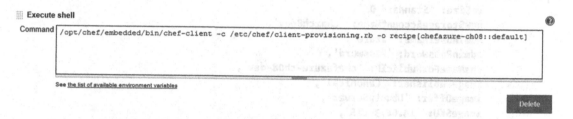

Figure 8-23. Command line for executing our custom Chef Client install

Authenticating to Microsoft Azure from Jenkins

To set up authentication from Jenkins to Azure, we need to copy the credentials file we created in chapter 4. The Jenkins home directory is typically **/var/lib/jenkins** but this may vary in your environment.

If you are logged in as the **azure** user, you may find it easier to su to the **jenkins** user to avoid permissions problems as follows:

```
azure@chazch08jenkins: $ sudo su jenkins
jenkins@chazch08jenkins:~$ mkdir ~/.azure
jenkins@chazch08jenkins:~$ vi ~/.azure/credentials
```

The credentials file should look similar to the following:

/var/lib/jenkins/.azure/credentials:

```
[b6e7eee9-YOUR-GUID-HERE-03ab624df016]          <- Subscription ID
tenant_id = "9c117323-YOUR-GUID-HERE-9ee430723ba3"    <- Tenant ID
client_id = "02a2ba0d-YOUR-GUID-HERE-0e7cd312d62b"    <- Application ID
client_secret = "my-top-secret-password"        <- Application Password
```

At this point we should have a fully working configuration so let's test it by adding our first provisioning recipe to our Chef repo, uploading it to GitHub, and then we can execute our job in Jenkins.

Our "dev" environment comprises a single-machine Ubuntu server and assigned to the Apache role. It is mostly a replica of the Jenkins machine, and it reuses the same ARM template. We'll add the usual Chef VM Extension to it so that it registers with a Chef Server. Ignore the fact that we don't have an Apache role on our Chef server yet - it can be added later. We are solely interested in the provisioning aspects at this stage.

Let's add a **provision_dev** recipe to our cookbook:

cookbooks/chefazure-ch08/recipes/provision_dev.rb

```
require 'chef/provisioning/azurerm'
with_driver 'AzureRM:b6e7eee9-YOUR-GUID-HERE-03ab624df016'

azure_resource_group 'chefazure-ch08-dev' do
  location 'West Europe'
end

azure_resource_template 'chefazure-ch08-dev' do
  resource_group 'chefazure-ch08-dev'
  template_source 'cookbooks/chefazure-ch08/files/shared/machine_deploy.json'
  parameters location: 'West Europe',
             vmSize: 'Standard_D1',
             newStorageAccountName: 'chazch8dev',
             adminUsername: 'azure',
             adminPassword: 'P2ssw0rd',
             dnsNameForPublicIP: 'chefazure-ch08-dev',
             imagePublisher: 'Canonical',
             imageOffer: 'UbuntuServer',
             imageSKU: '14.04.3-LTS',
             vmName: 'chazch08dev'
  chef_extension client_type: 'LinuxChefClient',
             version: '1210.12',
             runlist: 'role[apache]'
end
```

We need to add **provision_dev** recipe as an include to our default recipe, as our Jenkins job specifies that the default recipe from our cookbook is executed:

cookbooks/chefazure-ch08/recipes/default.rb

```
include_recipe 'chefazure-ch08::provision_dev'
```

Again as we've updated the cookbook we should also update our metadata to reflect the new version:

metadata.rb:

```
name 'chefazure-ch08'
maintainer 'Stuart Preston'
maintainer_email 'stuart@pendrica.com'
license 'all_rights'
description 'Installs/Configures chefazure-ch08'
long_description 'Installs/Configures chefazure-ch08'
version '0.1.4'

depends 'jenkins'
```

Pushing the changes to GitHub is as simple as adding the files, committing the change locally, and pushing to master in your repo:

```
PS C:\Users\StuartPreston\chefazure-ch08> git add .
PS C:\Users\StuartPreston\chefazure-ch08> git commit -m 'adding dev server'
```

```
[master d9bdba3] adding dev server
 1 file changed, 18 insertions(+)
```

```
PS C:\Users\StuartPreston\chefazure-ch08> git push origin master
```

```
Username for 'https://github.com': stuartpreston
Password for 'https://stuartpreston@github.com':
Counting objects: 6, done.
Delta compression using up to 4 threads.
Compressing objects: 100% (5/5), done.
Writing objects: 100% (6/6), 856 bytes | 0 bytes/s, done.
Total 6 (delta 3), reused 0 (delta 0)
To https://github.com/stuartpreston/chefazure-ch08.git
   31d3664..d9bdba3  master -> master
```

After triggering another build via the Build Now button you should see lines similar to the following in your **Console Output** log:

```
[2016-01-16T22:56:55+00:00] INFO: chef-provisioning-azurerm 0.3.2
[2016-01-16T22:56:55+00:00] INFO: chef-provisioning 1.5.1
[2016-01-16T22:56:55+00:00] INFO: Processing azure_resource_group[chefazure-ch08-dev]
action create (chefazure-ch08::provision_dev line 4)
[2016-01-16T22:56:56+00:00] INFO: Processing azure_resource_template[chefazure-ch08-dev]
action deploy (chefazure-ch08::provision_dev line 8)
[2016-01-16T22:58:40+00:00] WARN: Skipping final node save because override_runlist was given
[2016-01-16T22:58:40+00:00] INFO: Chef Run complete in 107.734846 seconds
[2016-01-16T22:58:40+00:00] INFO: Skipping removal of unused files from the cache
[2016-01-16T22:58:40+00:00] INFO: Running report handlers
[2016-01-16T22:58:40+00:00] INFO: Report handlers complete
[2016-01-16T22:58:40+00:00] INFO: Sending resource update report (run-id: 894abd54-bd28-
4836-bb19-b2961c6c9bc4)
Finished: SUCCESS
```

Verifying the Chef Provisioning run

To verify that the Chef run was successful, other than monitoring the output of the Jenkins job, we can look at the Azure management portal to verify the current provisioning state. We should see the Resource Group and Resources that we specified in our recipe visible in the portal, as shown in Figure 8-24.

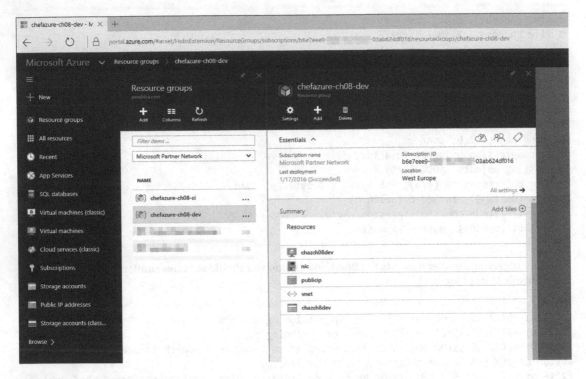

Figure 8-24. *Azure Management Portal showing a Resource Group and Resources*

We can also look in Hosted Chef to verify that there is a new Node created for the Dev environment as shown in Figure 8-25.

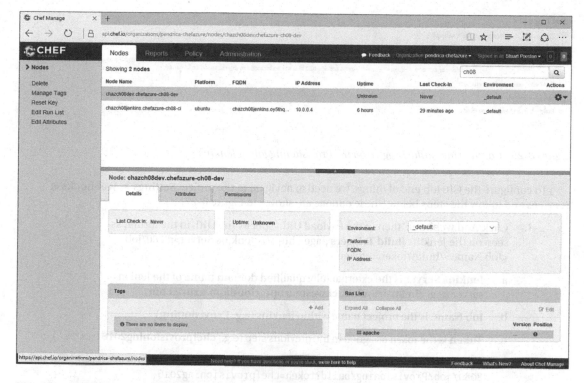

Figure 8-25. *Chef Manage (Hosted Chef) showing a registered Node*

Now that we have a fully working end-to-end provisioning process that is driven from source control, we can configure GitHub to send a notification to Jenkins on each build for a fully hands-off provisioning solution.

Triggering a Jenkins Build from GitHub

We can use GitHub's Webhook system to add a Webhook that notifies our Jenkins server whenever code is pushed to GitHub. For this to happen, your Jenkins server must have an external (public) IP address like the one described in this chapter. Otherwise, to receive events such as this, you will have to configure your Jenkins server to poll GitHub.

To configure GitHub to send notifications we need to visit our job definition in Jenkins again and navigate to **Build Triggers** as follows:

1. **Trigger builds remotely** should be ticked (selected).

2. An **authentication token** needs to be specified. This can be any random selection of characters. Don't make the token the same as any of your passwords - the default Jenkins configuration runs unencrypted on port 8080.

Once configured, your **Build Triggers** definition should look similar to that in Figure 8-26. Save the definition.

Build Triggers

☑ Trigger builds remotely (e.g., from scripts)

Authentication Token

| chefprovisioning2016 |

Use the following URL to trigger build remotely: JENKINS_URL/job/Provisioning/build?token=TOKEN_NAME or /buildWithParameters?token=TOKEN_NAME
Optionally append &cause=Cause+Text to provide text that will be included in the recorded build cause.

☐ Build after other projects are built

☐ Build periodically

☑ Build when a change is pushed to GitHub

☐ Poll SCM

Figure 8-26. *Configuring Build Triggers on the Provisioning job in Jenkins*

To configure the GitHub end of things, we need to navigate to the project **Settings ➤ Webhooks & Services** and follow the steps below (these options are shown in Figure 8-27):

1. Click 'Add webhook' then in the Payload URL, specify the URL in the format as seen on the Jenkins **Build Triggers** page - http://<Jenkins Server>:8080/job/<Job Name>/build?token=<token>

   a. **Jenkins Server** is the external fully qualified domain name of the Jenkins server (e.g. **chefazure-ch08-ci.westeurope.cloudapp.azure.com**)

   b. **Job Name** is the project name within Jenkins (e.g. **Provisioning**)

   c. **Token** is the token assigned in the previous step (e.g., **chefprovisioning2016**)

   Example URL: `http://chefazure-ch08-ci.westeurope.cloudapp.azure.com:8080/job/Provisioning/build?token=chefprovisioning2016`

2. Ensure the **Just the push event** option is selected.

3. Press **Add Webhook**.

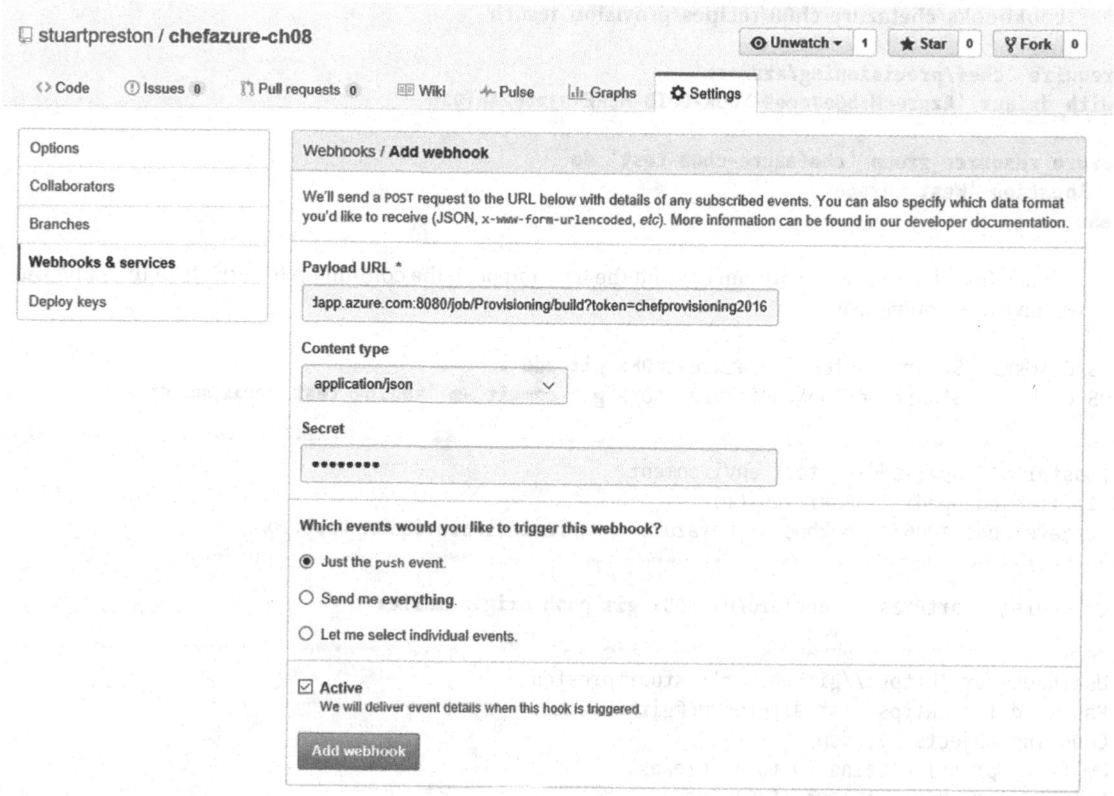

Figure 8-27. *Github webhook configuration*

To test the trigger, we can simply browse directly to the URL in a browser and confirm that it triggers a job within Jenkins.

That's it - we have now configured the Webhook, so let's start making use of it by pushing two simple changes through the system that exercise all the points of the system from trigger to provisioned resources.

Adding and Destroying a Test Environment

We're going to create a **provision_test** recipe with an Azure Resource Group resource specified within it, include it from the default recipe, push our changes, then show how resources are deleted. Let's create and update some files, starting with our default recipe that needs to be updated to add the provision_test recipe (additions shown in **bold**). Remember to leave a single blank line at the end of each file to avoid an avoidable Rubocop failure!

cookbooks/chefazure-ch08/recipes/default.rb

```
include_recipe 'chefazure-ch08::provision_dev'
include_recipe 'chefazure-ch08::provision_test'
```

217

cookbooks/chefazure-ch08/recipes/provision_test.rb

```
require 'chef/provisioning/azurerm'
with_driver 'AzureRM:b6e7eee9-YOUR-GUID-HERE-03ab624df016'

azure_resource_group 'chefazure-ch08-test' do
  location 'West Europe'
end
```

Once those files are saved, we can commit the files and push the commit up to GitHub, in the same way as we have done previously:

```
PS C:\Users\StuartPreston\chefazure-ch08> git add .
PS C:\Users\StuartPreston\chefazure-ch08> git commit -m 'adding test environment'
```

```
[master d387a94] adding test environment
 2 files changed, 7 insertions(+)
 create mode 100644 cookbooks/chefazure-ch08/recipes/provision_test.rb
```

```
C:\Users\StuartPreston\chefazure-ch08> git push origin master
```

```
Username for 'https://github.com': stuartpreston
Password for 'https://stuartpreston@github.com':
Counting objects: 7, done.
Delta compression using up to 4 threads.
Compressing objects: 100% (6/6), done.
Writing objects: 100% (7/7), 747 bytes | 0 bytes/s, done.
Total 7 (delta 3), reused 0 (delta 0)
To https://github.com/stuartpreston/chefazure-ch08.git
   2e2f109..d387a94  master -> master
```

If we look at the Jenkins server, it should now be executing a job, triggered from a GitHub Webhook. If you look at the list of Resource Groups within the Azure Management Portal once the job has completed, there should be a **chefazure-ch08-test** Resource Group created. If so, we have successfully configured everything needed for a basic continuous provisioning pipeline.

As our final piece of this chapter, let's destroy the test environment we just created. Be careful not to describe this as a rollback. It isn't - all we are doing is specifying a new target state for our test environment (destroy).

To make the changes, we simply need to add a :destroy action to our Resource Group:

cookbooks/chefazure-ch08/recipes/provision_test.rb

```
require 'chef/provisioning/azurerm'
with_driver 'AzureRM:b6e7eee9-YOUR-GUID-HERE-03ab624df016'

azure_resource_group 'chefazure-ch08-test' do
  location 'West Europe'
  action :destroy
end
```

We can push our change to GitHub again:

```
PS C:\Users\StuartPreston\chefazure-ch08> git add .
PS C:\Users\StuartPreston\chefazure-ch08> git commit -m 'destroying test environment'
```

```
[master 63b30ab] destroying test environment
 1 file changed, 1 insertion(+)
```

```
PS C:\Users\StuartPreston\chefazure-ch08> git push origin master
```

```
Username for 'https://github.com': stuartpreston
Password for 'https://stuartpreston@github.com':
Counting objects: 6, done.
Delta compression using up to 4 threads.
Compressing objects: 100% (5/5), done.
Writing objects: 100% (6/6), 491 bytes | 0 bytes/s, done.
Total 6 (delta 4), reused 0 (delta 0)
To https://github.com/stuartpreston/chefazure-ch08.git
   d387a94..63b30ab  master -> master
```

After witnessing that a new job is created for this push, we should see the Azure Resource Group deleted from our subscription.

Summary

By using a combination of Chef, Chef Provisioning, Azure, Chef VM Extensions, GitHub, and Jenkins we are able to implement the beginnings of a sophisticated continuous provisioning pipeline. We understood the following:

- How to provision, configure, and maintain a Jenkins server for continuous provisioning using the Chef VM Extensions

- How to configure the Chef VM Extension for use with Chef Provisioning

- How to add quality gates such as Rubocop linting to the build pipeline

- How to use Berkshelf to manage dependencies for an application

- How to trigger a Jenkins job from GitHub for a completely hands-off solution driven by changes to the Chef repository

This is just a starting point of the journey with continuous provisioning and provides a framework on which to add quality, configuration management, and release management to your project.

APPENDIX A

■ ■ ■

Further Resources

We have reached the last chapter in this book, and by now you should have a good idea at what is possible when using the combination of Chef and Azure. This appendix includes some additional information and resources that didn't really fit anywhere else in the book.

Chef Server on the Azure Marketplace

For the demos and examples in this book we used the hosted Chef service at http://manage.chef.io however what if you wanted to host your own Chef server in Azure that isn't shared with anyone else and is situated in your region? Well, the fastest way to achieve this is to use the images that have been uploaded to the Azure Marketplace, as shown in Figure A-1.

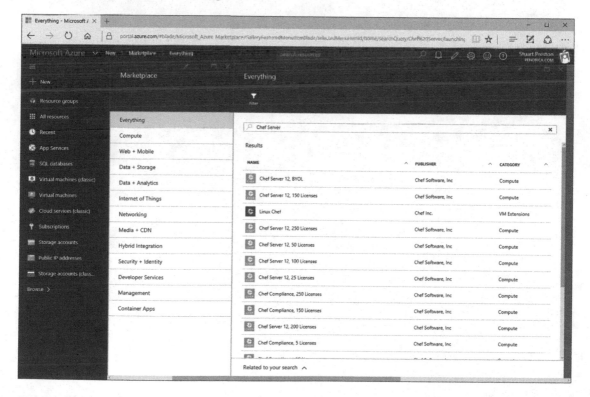

Figure A-1. *Chef Server images on the Azure Marketplace*

© Stuart Preston 2016
S. Preston, *Using Chef with Microsoft Azure*, DOI 10.1007/978-1-4842-1476-3

The server is preconfigured with Chef server, the Chef management console, Chef reporting, and Chef Analytics. This configuration is free from a Chef licensing perspective to use for deployments under 25 nodes. You will only be charged for the relevant compute, network, and storage usage costs.

■ **Note** Use of the Chef Server image is free from a Chef licensing perspective for up to 25 nodes, and there are options to purchase 25–250 node licensed versions of Chef Server in the Azure Marketplace.

Full installation instructions can be found online at `https://docs.chef.io/azure_portal.html #azure-marketplace` where you will be guided through the installation and client set-up requirements.

Azure Weekly Newsletter

Keeping up to date with the latest developments in the Azure ecosystem has always been a challenge, especially with the pace of releases from Microsoft and the various teams that work on the product. Fortunately, help is at hand in the shape of a weekly newsletter (as shown in Figure A-2) curated by the people at Endjin, a Microsoft Gold Partner based in the United Kingdom.

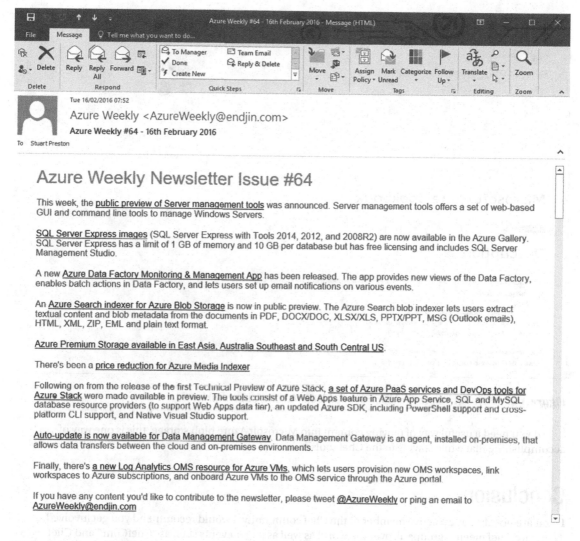

Figure A-2. *Azure Weekly Newsletter*

You can register for the newsletter and view historic content by visiting http://azureweekly.info

Microsoft Azure Cookbook

You'll have noticed that the topics in this book generally use Chef for provisioning resources in Azure rather than the operational side of things (e.g., uploading a key to the Key Vault, or uploading content to a storage account). The **microsoft_azure** cookbook, available on the Chef Supermarket at https://supermarket.chef.io/cookbooks/microsoft_azure (as shown in Figure A-3) aims to provide resources as well as providers to manage these Azure components.

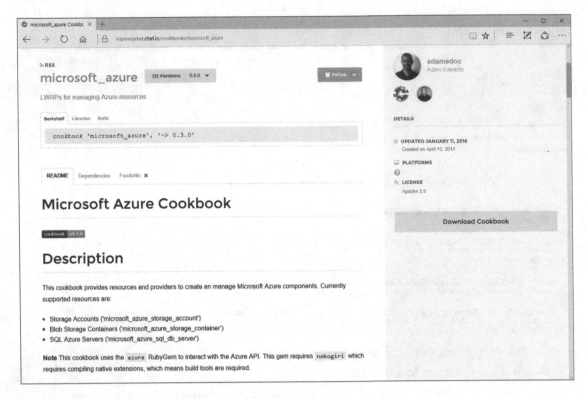

Figure A-3. Microsoft_Azure cookbook available on the Chef Supermarket

If you need a useful way of moving content into Microsoft Azure blob storage, this is one way of accomplishing that while staying in the Chef toolset.

Conclusion

If you are not already an active member of the Chef community, I would recommend you get involved. There are Chef meetup groups all over the world as well as larger events such as "ChefConf" and Chef Community Summits that are held in both the USA and Europe. Whether you are new to Chef or an expert in your domain, sharing your experiences with other Chefs is one of the easiest and best ways to contribute. You can also draw on the shared expertise of tens of thousands of Chefs all over the world to help you solve your problems and offer advice. I look forward to seeing your contributions toward making the Chef and Microsoft ecosystem an even better place!

Index

© Stuart Preston 2016
S. Preston, *Using Chef with Microsoft Azure*, DOI 10.1007/978-1-4842-1476-3

Get the eBook for only $5!

Why limit yourself?

Now you can take the weightless companion with you wherever you go and access your content on your PC, phone, tablet, or reader.

Since you've purchased this print book, we're happy to offer you the eBook in all 3 formats for just $5.

Convenient and fully searchable, the PDF version enables you to easily find and copy code—or perform examples by quickly toggling between instructions and applications. The MOBI format is ideal for your Kindle, while the ePUB can be utilized on a variety of mobile devices.

To learn more, go to www.apress.com/companion or contact support@apress.com.